Communication in U.S. Elections

New Agendas

Edited by
Roderick P. Hart and Daron R. Shaw

ROWMAN & LITTLEFIELD PUBLISHERS, INC.
Lanham • *Boulder* • *New York* • *Oxford*

ROWMAN & LITTLEFIELD PUBLISHERS, INC.

Published in the United States of America
by Rowman & Littlefield Publishers, Inc.
4720 Boston Way, Lanham, Maryland 20706
www.rowmanlittlefield.com

12 Hid's Copse Road
Cumnor Hill, Oxford OX2 9JJ, England

An earlier version of figure 9.5 appeared in Nicholas A. Valentino, "Crime News and the
Priming of Racial Attitudes during Evaluations of the President," *Public Opinion Quarterly*
63:3 (Fall 1999): p. 312. Reprinted by permission of the University of Chicago Press.

British Library Cataloguing in Publication Information Available

Library of Congress Cataloging-in-Publication Data

Communication in U.S. elections : new agendas / edited by Roderick P. Hart and Daron R. Shaw
    p. cm.
    Includes bibliographical references and index.
    ISBN 0-7425-0068-3 (cloth : alk paper) — ISBN 0-7425-0069-1 (pbk. : alk. paper)
    1. Political campaigns—United States. 2. Advertising, Political—United States. 3.
Communication in politics—United States. I. Hart, Roderick P. II. Shaw, Daron, 1966-

JK1976 .C58 2001
324.7'0973—dc21

00-0689

Printed in the United States of America

♾™ The paper used in this publication meets the minimum requirements of
American National Standard for Information Sciences—Permanence of Paper
for Printed Library Materials, ANSI/NISO Z39.48-1992.

In memory of
Annette Greenfield Strauss
Public servant, philanthropist, humanitarian

Contents

Preface

This volume is one of two books (the other is *Politics, Discourse, and American Society*) emerging from a unique scholarly conference held at the University of Texas at Austin in the spring of 2000. The conference was special in several ways. For one thing, it was the first major event sponsored by the Annette Strauss Institute for Civic Participation, a research and outreach center on campus devoted to understanding, and improving, civic engagement in the United States. The institute is named after the former mayor of Dallas, who had an extraordinary ability to get different people to work together for the benefit of the community. The legend of Annette Strauss went well beyond the confines of Dallas, Texas. By the time of her death in December of 1998, Strauss had received virtually every civic award given in that city as well as many of those bestowed at the state and national levels.

In a real sense, the story of Annette Strauss is the story of the institute itself. In an era in which voter turnout rates are dropping, and dropping persistently, we as a society must find creative ways of reversing that trend. In an era burgeoning with exciting new modes of communication—cable television and the Internet, for example—we must find ways of using those technologies to bring people together and make civic dialogue once more a reality. The challenge of the institute is thus to blend one of the oldest human instincts—the need for community—with new ways of helping people help one another. Rarely have science and society had as much in common.

It was in this spirit that twenty-two young scholars were brought to campus for a conference called "New Agendas in Political Communication." The idea of the conference was to assemble a diverse group of scholars broadly interested in political communication, persons who were at the early stages of their careers but who had already demonstrated considerable scholarly potential. The plan was to capture the energy and imagination of some of tomorrow's best scholars in two disciplines—communication and political science—and to listen to them as they set out new research agendas. In addition, an effort was made to ensure that roughly half of these scholars were social scientists (such as those in the current volume), while the other half took a cultural or humanistic approach. In short, we wanted to produce as much cross-pollination as possible so that no new idea would go unheard or untested.

This book is the result of our labors. In each case, the authors have done exactly what was asked of them: (1) stake out a broad area of investigation demanding new (or renewed) scholarly attention; (2) present original research findings showing how their work furthers that agenda; and (3) suggest the most important questions the sub-area should address in the future. This volume examines campaign communication in the United States through new eyes and it provides new answers. It acknowledges that certain traditional, sometimes endemic, forces drive modern elections, but it also shows that new phenomena—political interest groups, mass media hegemonies, popular culture, party determinacies, and the Internet—are shaping those elections in powerful and unpredictable ways. It is far too early to tell where such forces are taking us, but the authors in this volume surely help guide the way.

Naturally, these authors are not the only young scholars working on such matters. Indeed, research in political communication has never been a more active or productive endeavor. But because financial resources for the New Agendas conference were limited, we were unable to invite a suitably international group of scholars. We have tried to turn that liability into an asset here by focusing on U.S. campaigns especially, teasing out those subtle features that seem to make American elections American. No doubt, future research will track these phenomena in cross-national contexts.

This book, and the New Agendas conference itself, could not have been produced without the exceptional contributions of several exceptional individuals. I begin by thanking, first, Annette Strauss's family, whose vision, concern, and generosity of spirit have been a personal inspiration to me, as well as a reflection of those same qualities embodied in Mrs. Strauss herself. I hasten to thank my co-editors—Daron Shaw for this volume and Bat Sparrow for *Politics, Discourse, and American Politics*—for their vision and hard work throughout this project. It is gratifying to have colleagues, and friends, of such depth and character.

The New Agendas conference would not have gone as smoothly without the personal ministrations of Bill Jennings, a smart and resourceful doctoral student for whom no task is too large and for whom my expressions of gratitude are eternally insufficient. The editors are also grateful to Rowman & Littlefield Publishers, especially to Jennifer Knerr and Brenda Hadenfeldt, who immediately saw the wisdom of bringing together twenty-two bright young scholars and who went out of their way to help make that happen.

Thanks are also due to Professor Jim Fishkin, chair of the University of Texas Department of Government, who spoke at the conference banquet, and to his departmental colleagues—Melissa Collie, Bob Luskin, Brian Roberts, and Jeff Tulis—who read papers in their areas of expertise and who served as discussants. We also appreciate those in the College of Communication who performed similar functions—Max McCombs, America Rodriguez, and Chuck Whitney. And we appreciate the graduate students who chaired the sessions and helped in other important ways: Courtney Dillard, Nancy Jennings, Spiro Kiousis, Kevin Kuswa, Anna Law, Zizi Papacharissi, Kanan Sawyer, and Scott Truelove. As always, the staff assistance provided by Deanna Matthews and Margaret Surratt was extraordinary.

Finally, we want to thank three individuals who have become unparalleled friends of the Strauss Institute. Dr. Sheldon Ekland-Olson, provost of the University, Dr. Richard Lariviere, dean of the College of Liberal Arts, and Dr. Ellen Wartella, dean of the College of Communication, have supported us from the beginning, providing financial support to get us started and believing all the while in our work. These three individuals give new meaning to the phrase enlightened leadership.

Communication in U.S. Elections is neither the first word nor the last word on its subject, but it is an earnest attempt to identify what needs to be learned about campaigns and to report on some promising research programs designed to get the answers. The scholars whose work is presented here are just beginning to ask their questions and get their answers. They have more to learn and, happily, they have the energy and intelligence to learn it. For all of these reasons, it has been a personal pleasure to learn from their New Agendas.

Roderick P. Hart

1

Communicating and Electing

Daron R. Shaw

In July 2000, I sat in on an afternoon session of a rolling two-day meeting of George W. Bush's "E-Campaign" team. Many things were heating up in Austin at the time, not the least of which was the campaign. The Bush team was three weeks away from launching its revamped Web site. In five weeks they would go to Philadelphia for the GOP convention, during which time the E-Plan would have to be articulated to Republican officials and sympathetic members of the high-tech community.

The meeting's previous conversations had ranged over a number of topics. How should the campaign use the Web site to coordinate the activities of state and county campaign officials? How could the campaign use the thousands of email addresses they had already gathered to disseminate information? How might they acquire and use additional addresses? What could be done to facilitate better communication with the so-called second-tier press writing for political Web sites? How could the campaign respond to rumors about Bush that spread like a virus through email?

Amid all these questions, a single exchange caught my attention. Price Roe, a razor-sharp twenty-two-year-old, was making the case that the new Web site ought to drop cookies on all visitors. Cookies are electronic fingerprints that allow the proprietors of a site to track subsequent Web-surfing patterns of site visitors. The Bush site had not used cookies before that point. E-Campaign Chair Bill Rice expressed concern that if this were divulged during the fall, it could embarrass the campaign. Roe persisted, somewhat incredulous that any site interested in amassing information about its customer base would not drop cookies. Roe pointed out that no one with an ounce of understanding of the Web would be surprised that the campaign's site was like every other site. Rice argued that the issue wasn't whether media reports on "privacy questions" surrounding Bush's site were justified. The issue, rather, was whether they would cost the campaign a valuable news cycle that would otherwise focus on Bush's message.

In the end, the campaign decided to use cookies, although the site offered prominent privacy statements, did not seek to use its information to identify individuals, and used an "opt-in" gateway before getting any information from the cookie. The decision was made somewhat easier by virtue of the fact that the competition was already doing just that. Al Gore's site included a warning that they would drop cookies at some later time during the campaign. The Bush decision was also influenced by the fact that any privacy issues regarding the Web site were likely to be pointed out soon after the launch. Sure enough, the Reuters news service ran a story questioning privacy guarantees of visitors to the Bush site. The story hit the wires only four hours after the revamped site was unveiled.

I saw the 1992 presidential campaign up close, and these two days eight years later were astonishing to me. The Web and email were in their infancy in 1992. Even at that time, email was greatly enhancing the ability of top-level campaign officials to communicate with one another, but there was little effort to cultivate lists of email addresses or to explore the viral possibilities of message dissemination. As for the Internet, having a Web site was considered cutting edge. Actually maintaining it and incorporating it into a broader communicative strategy was a pipe dream. Figuring I could milk stories from the 1992 race until at least 2004, I was taken aback by how soon my understanding of modern campaign communication had become obsolete. By the standards of 1992, the 2000 campaign was a whole new ballgame.

For students of political communication, the New Agendas conference in Austin presented both challenges and opportunities. The challenges were obvious. In the broadest sense, what is the received wisdom on politics and the media? Are theories of political communication dynamic enough to explain how voters and campaigns interact in contemporary elections? How can these theories be adapted to new developments, new techniques?

And while computers are now a big part of the campaign story, our challenges in the area of political communication are not confined merely to the rise of the personal computer. One also finds the proliferation of cable television and cable networks, as well as the continued penetration of telephones. Perhaps more importantly, there have been parallel changes in how Americans think and act toward each other and toward politics. Robert Putnam's influential book *Bowling Alone* (2000) describes the breakdown of community and group activity that defined American social life a half century ago. Putnam cites the rise of television as the main culprit, but he assiduously and empirically documents how atomistic Americans have become in addition. The ascendance of a culture in which communication is more passive, isolated, and dispersed cannot help but affect politics. Yet we have only be-gun to consider how these changes affect us as citizens and as voters.

The opportunities evident at the New Agenda conference are only slightly less apparent. Where and how voters get their information have always been interesting to people who write and think about politics. Election dynamics are becoming a particularly trenchant subject, as democratization continues throughout Eastern Europe and the Americas. Political communication scholars in the United States are thus in the spotlight as an international au-dience looks for insights garnered about modern, media-driven campaigns. The United States is not an old nation in most ways, but when it comes to electronic campaigning it is positively ancient.

While some in the field of political science contend that the United States is still an exceptional case, I believe it is increasingly likely that American campaigns will become the template for democratic elections throughout the world. Prominent examples of this influence abound. Look at the gleeful symbiosis, for example, between the Clintonites and Tony Blair's Labor cam-paigns in Great Britain. Or consider the more personal, but nonetheless sig-nificant, role James Carville played in Ehud Barak's bid to unseat Benjamin Netanyahu in Israel in 1999. Or more generally, what about the plethora of American consultants in the recent Russian and Mexican elections? In my view, these are harbingers of campaigns to come. Scholars in the United States, then, have a special opportunity, and a special obligation, to get the story of political communication right because what began here is moving elsewhere rapidly.

This book takes aim at these challenges and opportunities. Its chapters contain the thoughts and preliminary research of a handful of talented young scholars. While more established researchers continue to offer insight and context as the nation barrels down the information superhighway, it is the young guard of academia who will assess the great leap forward these mar-vels of communication present.

Before turning to their work, some context is useful. In particular, the re-mainder of this chapter delineates a bit of what we know about political campaign communication, discusses some of the recent changes in the area, presents five research nodes that structure this volume, and then considers the common themes and further issues apparent in some of the empirical chapters.

WHAT WE KNOW ABOUT CAMPAIGN COMMUNICATION

The Old Classics

The traditional starting point for almost any treatment of American politi-cal communication is the groundbreaking research of Paul Lazarsfeld and his

Columbia University colleagues in the 1940s. The story is, by now, old hat: Interviews with real voters during the election campaigns of 1944 and 1948 contradicted the presumption that Americans were attentive to and informed about politics. The result was a shift in scholars' notions of the public opinion paradigm. Rather than the image of informed, attentive voters conjured up by the writings of Alexis de Tocqueville and the watercolors of Norman Rockwell, the data told us that voters were largely unengaged and uninformed, didn't think or talk much about politics and, when they did, they were passive participants in community-wide information networks dominated by a handful of elites.

This sociological model of voting was challenged by the social psychologists of the Michigan school a few years later. Pointing out that there was little psychological explanation for the reality described by the Columbia scholars, the Michigan researchers used national survey data to develop a model of voting driven by party identification. Again, voters were found to be inattentive and unknowledgeable. In the seminal book *The American Voter* (Campbell et al. 1960), the focus shifted from group-based models of communication to individual-level explanations of information acquisition and processing. Most notably, the social psychologists argued that voters develop attachments to one or the other political party early in life and rely on this predisposition to structure political reality and serve as a perceptual screen. The "funnel of causality" became the ultimate expression of both arguments.

For both the Columbia and Michigan schools, political communication was thought to have the potential to persuade and mobilize voters. This simple fact has often been overlooked or ignored by subsequent scholarship. It is true that Lazarsfeld and his colleagues were a bit vague in specifying the dynamic driving group elites and attentive opinion leaders to acquire information. There is, however, nothing deterministic in their account of information flow during the 1948 election. In *Voting* (Campbell et al. 1960), groups were found to have often preferred one party to the other, but these tendencies were erratic. Furthermore, contrary and persuasive information was found to work its way into the communities and to affect the ultimate distribution of the vote.

In fact, there are several specific and pointed examples in *Voting* of the authors' belief that political communication matters. For example, in their discussion of political effects, Berelson et al. (1954) wrote, "It seems clear that an impending defeat for the Democratic Party was staved off by a refocusing of attention on the socio-economic concerns which had originally played such a large role in building that party's majority in the 1930s" (270). In detailing the susceptibility of voters to political information, they argued, "The individual voter may not have a great deal of detailed information, but he has picked up the crucial general information as part of the social learning itself.

. . . He cannot live in an American community without knowing broadly where political parties stand" (320).

For the Michigan scholars, party identification was viewed as a powerful but not omnipotent explanatory variable. In fact, the authors of *The American Voter* explicitly acknowledged that factors besides party identification influenced the electoral decision. Campbell et al. tell us that even though "the distribution of party identification in that year favored Democrats by about 3 to 2. . . . We know that the actual components of the 1952 vote were more pro-Republican than pro-Democrat" (529). Indeed, since *The American Voter* drew on data from the 1950s—during which the minority party won both presidential elections—it is not too surprising that the potential for persuasion was acknowledged. Consider too the funnel of causality. At the top of the funnel is party identification, which acts as a perceptual screen, limiting the volume and content of information available to a given voter, but the inputs to the funnel are powerfully driven by political contexts. In short, elections and campaigns matter.

This line of reasoning is expanded by one of the principal figures of the Michigan school, Philip Converse. In "The Nature of Belief Systems in Mass Publics" (1964), Converse presented evidence that voters' opinions are inconsistent (across time and issue domains), and that they have low levels of ideological clarity. For our purposes, it is this second argument that merits closer attention. Converse observed that voters rarely used ideological language ("liberal" or "conservative") to describe their politics. They are more apt to refer to party identification or "the nature of the times" when rationalizing their preferences. In other words, opinions and preferences are greatly influenced by economic and social conditions, as well as (presumably) the manner in which the candidates and the media frame those conditions.

The New Classics

Even though the Columbia and Michigan scholarship leave room for campaign and election effects, the prominence of more predictable variables in their analyses leads to many questions. Most of these questions have centered on whether and how voters use information provided by campaigns. In *The Responsible Electorate*, V. O. Key (1966) contended that voters (in his famous phrase) "are not fools" and that campaign communication can matter. He suggested that while voters are not especially well informed about issue or policy particulars, they managed to use the campaign to get a broad sense of how things are going. This sense allowed voters to act as "rational gods" of reward and punishment.

Fiorina expanded Key's conception of voter rationality in *Retrospective Voting in American National Elections* (1981). Fiorina argued that simple retrospective evaluations about the condition of the country were critical for voters' preferences in a given election. More importantly, he detailed the interactive and dynamic relationship between these evaluations and more durable attitudes (such as party identification). Fiorina was also much less sanguine than Key about the notion that these individual-level processes facilitated aggregate-level democratic accountability. Fiorina posited that parties have weakened and that institutions have changed such that the system's ability to foster accountability is very much in doubt.

Popkin elaborated on Fiorina's premise in *The Reasoning Voter* (1991). Going further than either Fiorina or Key, Popkin argued that voters not only use summary judgments about the condition of the country to decide their ballot but they also use pieces of seemingly innocuous information to engage in "gut-level" reasoning. Political communication, therefore, matters— even when it is something as seemingly trivial as Dan Quayle misspelling "potato" or Gerald Ford trying to eat an unshucked tamale. Much of Popkin's conceptualization drew on the pathbreaking work on "heuristics" and "cues" done by psycholinguists such as Daniel Kahneman and Amos Tversky in the 1970s.

The role of information and rationality is not the only controversial aspect to the established understanding of political communication. Social psychologists Nie, Verba, and Petrocik also focused their attention on the role of political context. In *The Changing American Voter* (1976), they presented data on the heightened issue awareness among voters in the 1960s and early 1970s, a time when politics "mattered." On a different front, Achen (1975) offered a powerful broadside against *The American Voter*, emphasizing changes in survey research methodology made since the early 1960s. Neither Achen nor Nie et al. claimed that the Michigan school precludes the possibility of persuasive communicative effects.

Other scholars looked to fashion a more sophisticated understanding of how political communication operates. Some focused on how the news media affect elections and voters. McCombs and Shaw (1972), for example, offered a theory of agenda setting, arguing that the media influence not what voters think, but what they think about. McCombs later expanded his theoretical construct to encompass "second-level" agenda setting, in which *candidates* were also linked to issue agendas. Iyengar and Kinder (1987) delineated the phenomenon of "priming," by which the media provided the context and criteria that voters then used to evaluate issues and candidates. In his more recent research, Iyengar (1991) contended that the media further influenced voters and politics through their "framing" of issues. He added, however, that the media often wasted their potential influence by using narrow, "episodic" frames as opposed to broader, "thematic" frames.

A smattering of content analytic studies show that the news media's professional dynamics can have somewhat perverse effects on elections and voting. For example, several studies find that the media emphasize the strategies and poll standings of the candidates—the "horse race" (Capella and Jamieson 1997; Just et al. 1996; Kerbel 1995; Lichter and Noyes 1995; Patterson 1993; Robinson and Sheehan 1983; Sabato 1991). Many of these same studies argued that the media favor negative stories—scandals, gaffes, and other manifestations of "gotcha" journalism (Capella and Jamieson 1997; Just et al. 1996; Kerbel 1995; Lichter and Noyes 1995; Patterson 1993; Robinson and Sheehan 1983; Sabato 1991). Both of these trends are presumed to have deleterious effects on voters' attitudes toward the political system.

Others scholars focused on how voters process information presented by the news media and the candidates. Memory-based processing, for example, assumes that voters' minds are like storage bins, with voters searching these bins for relevant considerations when they respond to a pollster or cast a vote. Zaller (1992) largely relied on a memory-based understanding of information processing in his analysis of public opinion dynamics. He wrote:

> The effect of persuasive communication depends on the other ideas already present in a person's mind and on the opposing ideas to which the individual may be concurrently exposed. This makes resistance to a political campaign, where a campaign normally consists of a dominant campaign (or message) and a countervalent campaign, a rather complicated phenomenon. If a person has a large internal mass of stored information, or exposure to countervalent information sources, no simple piece of information from a dominant campaign is likely to have much effect. But if a person has little prior information and little access to alternative communication flows, information reaching him from a dominant campaign will have a large effect. (266)

In other words, Zaller argued that the nature of the elite debate and the sophistication of recipients mitigate the effects of political communication. Most notably, Zaller said that mildly sophisticated voters are the most likely to move in response to political messages. Highly sophisticated voters, in contrast, are less susceptible because they are more likely to be partisan and selective about the information they choose to accept. Low-sophistication voters are also less susceptible because they are unlikely to be exposed to the message in the first place. Shifts in opinion among these groups therefore occur only when (1) there is a breakdown in the consensus among party elites so that highly sophisticated voters receive contradictory messages, or (2) the political debate becomes sufficiently intense to reach middle- or even low-sophistication voters.

In an important challenge to the standard conception of information processing, Milton Lodge (1995a) championed the idea that voters process political information "on-line." That is, when voters access and accept new information, they use it to update their prior perception or opinion on an issue or candidate. This new "prior" then becomes the baseline against which all subsequent information acts. This process borrows from Bayesian inference and has sparked a debate about the extent to which voters engage in on-line versus memory-based processing. The debate rages on, although recent experimental studies suggest that voters use different strategies for different contexts.

Recent studies have also examined the role of informational ambiguity in elections. Put another way, we know a good deal about how candidates communicate their issue positions, but little about how positional clarity affects opinions and votes. Several major analyses have considered ambiguity in the past few years, most notably Alvarez's *Issues and Information in Presidential Elections* (1997), which summarized much of the existing literature and then made the case for the strong influence of ambiguity on preference consistency, volatility, and extremity.

Similarly, Bartels addressed ambiguity in three separate works. In *Presidential Primaries* (1988), Bartels identified three effects of uncertainty. First, he argued that knowledge is a necessary condition for supporting a candidate—voters don't support someone if they don't know anything about him or her. Second, even if voters know a little bit about a candidate, Bartels said that they prefer known quantities to less well-known quantities. Third, he contended that the levels of information available to the public influence the process of evaluation. If voters know a good deal about the candidates, their appraisals tend to be more substantive. Bartels also pointed out that learning does occur during primary campaigns. Ironically, however, he observed that information is *least* available when it would be most valuable: when a "momentum" candidate suddenly breaks through. Bartels tells us that horse-race information fills this vacuum and is thus a critical part of the momentum process.

In addition to his famous study of primaries, Bartels (1986, 1996) also examined the effects of information and ambiguity on general election voters. In his 1996 article, he estimated what their preferences would look like under conditions of full information. In doing so, Bartels offered a different take on the James Fishkin–led (1995) debate about the effects of political deliberation. Bartels is something of a moderate in this controversy, though. He found that information *does* change the structure of elections and opinionation, although not as much as one might think.

A final area of recent research deals with the general topic of campaign effects. Gelman and King (1993) have become a touchstone for this literature with their analysis of movement in the preelection candidate preference polls. After considering a number of explanations for this movement, they concluded that presidential campaigns affect elections by activating the latent preferences of voters. These latent preferences, they argued, are a function of the state of the economy and general approval of incumbent performance. Holbrook (1996) identified significant effects associated with certain presidential campaign events, but concluded that these tend to "matter" only in close elections. Other scholars, most notably Finkel (1993), are even more skeptical about presidential campaign effects. Studies of congressional campaigns, on the other hand, tend to presume such effects: Most detail the importance of money, which can be taken as a surrogate for campaigning. The debate about campaign effects remains, however. The only point of unanimity across these works is that we have a long way to go before we can operationalize and estimate the import of campaigning in a comprehensive and meaningful way.

In sum, the seminal works of the 1940s, 1950s, and 1960s told us that the electorate was not sufficiently attentive to politics to be greatly moved by communication. These works did not, however, suggest that any movement was impossible or that campaigns did not influence elections. The research of the 1970s, 1980s, and 1990s focuses on reestimating campaign and media effects, looking to specify conditional or interactive relationships, and expanding our conception of how people use and acquire political information.

CHANGES IN POLITICAL COMMUNICATION

But if we are making progress toward a more subtle and nuanced understanding of how citizens acquire and use political information, are we also keeping up with changes that might alter these relationships? Absent a crystal ball, we can only guess. It seems, however, that technology is moving faster than our ability to react to it.

A first step toward figuring how far we are behind the curve is to be a bit more precise about how political communication has changed since, say, 1990. A simple way of structuring such a discussion is to think in terms of outlets, access, and receptivity. "Outlet" refers to various media and other sources of political information. The questions here are fairly obvious. Is television still dominant or has the Internet become a viable challenger? How has cable television altered the volume and pattern of news consumption? And what of newspapers, magazines, and radio?

The proliferation of political information outlets is undeniable. In 1992, CNN was the only cable news network. In 2000, one found CNN, CNN Headline News, CNBC, C-SPAN, MSNBC, and FOX News. In 1992, the only TV magazines were *60 Minutes* and *20/20*. In 2000, *20/20* ran twice a week and *60 Minutes* spawned *60 Minutes II*. There is also *48 Hours,* which ran more than once a week. Throw in the stalwart *Nightline* and the comedic *Politically Incorrect*, and one is confronted with a smorgasbord of offerings.

On-line, there has been an enormous expansion in the number and variety of political Web sites. In chapter 11 of this book, Robert Klotz estimates that approximately 70 percent of the candidates now running for federal office have Web sites. The Republican and Democratic national, senate, and congressional parties all have Web sites, as does a vast majority of state parties. All major news services—ABC, CBS, CNN, NBC, Fox, Reuters, AP, and Bloomberg—offer political Web sites as well. So do the *New York Times*, the *Los Angeles Times*, the *Washington Post, USA Today*, and a host of other elite and regional newspapers. There are also dozens of nonpartisan or independent web sites, such as Project Vote Smart and Open Secrets (both of which provide campaign finance information), the Polling Report, Gallup, and the Roper Center (which offer polling data), as well as government sites, such as the Federal Election Commission.

In contrast, radio, newspapers, and magazines have been relatively quiet over the past decade. Even here, though, we have seen the emergence of Dr. Laura Schlesinger as a force in talk radio and John Kennedy Jr.'s founding of the pop-politics magazine *George*. Furthermore, the emergence of Rush Limbaugh's syndicated talk show and the national newspaper *USA Today* in the late 1980s have had a lingering impact on the style and substance of political information.

The broad point to be made here is almost self-evident: There are many more outlets for political information today than in 1990. There is also much more competition for voters' attention, as "niche" entertainment has been raised to an art form by the Internet and cable/satellite television.

This point leads to the second subject in our brief overview of changes in political communication: "Access"—the public's willingness to seek out political information. Put plainly, are Americans taking advantage of the dizzying array of cable news outlets and political news web sites? Or are higher levels of mistrust and cynicism causing voters to tune out?

Several articles of faith dominate our present understanding of how (and how often) the public acquires political information. We assume that the acquisition of political information is limited and that it tends to occur late in the general election campaign cycle. When it does occur, television is still assumed to be the 800-pound gorilla of dissemination. There is, however, more diversity within television news. Moreover, the "new media" are mounting challenges, as millions of Americans either are on-line or soon will be. In addition, newspapers, magazines, and radio are becoming less important. Are the old articles of faith still valid?

The truth is that we really do not know. Surely there have been stunning changes in how we communicate over the past decade, but the particulars of these changes have not been particularly well delineated by political communication scholars. Let us see what progress can be made with a few basic facts.

According to a January 2000 national survey conducted by the Pew Research Center, 62 percent the American people say they watch television on a given day; 52 percent go on-line, access the Internet, or use email; 47 percent read a newspaper; and 44 percent listen to radio. In other words, television is still the dominant venue for accessing information, but the PC has passed all other outlets.

Furthermore, the gap between TV and the PC is closing fast. The Pew data estimate that 68 percent of Americans use a computer on a daily basis today. The 52 percent who go on-line daily represent a twenty-point jump over the 32 percent who did so in 1995. Conversely, traditional television outlets are not being accessed as often as they were only seven years earlier. Regular consumption of local television news was down from 77 percent in 1993 to 56 percent in 2000. Similarly, regular viewership of nightly network news is down from 60 percent to 31 percent. Viewership of TV magazine shows declined from 52 percent to 30 percent.

The Pew survey also shows that even cable television audiences have been of uneven size since the mid-1990s. For example, CNN's regular viewership went from 35 percent in 1993 to 21 percent in 2000. C-Span dipped from 11 percent to 4 percent in 1998, bouncing back up to 11 percent in 2000. Fox News and CNBC have stabilized at 17 percent and 13 percent, respectively.

In short, the sheer volume and diversity of entry points make it difficult to track absolute levels of voter access. Put another way, it is difficult to estimate the extent to which Americans acquire political information given the multitude of outlets and the treacherous problems associated with recall measures of usage. It is probably the case that information is being accessed more than ever before. It is also likely that systematic biases affect who is accessing this information.

The third subject worthy of consideration is "receptivity"—the public's willingness to update their beliefs and opinions based on information they receive. People must have access to political information for it to have an effect. Merely encountering information is no guarantee, however, that a voter will find it credible and alter his or her opinion accordingly.

If access is a slippery concept to quantify, receptivity is even more so. What data we have suggest contrary trends. On the one hand, greater numbers of independents and weakening partisanship (Wattenberg 1990, 1991) indicate higher receptivity. The logic here is simple: People who strongly identify with Democrats or Republicans are suspicious of information coming from "the other side." It stands to reason that fewer strong identifiers make for less aggregate resistance to information from the outside.

On the other hand, greater levels of mistrust and cynicism indicate lower receptivity. If voters believe that government and politics are corrupt and/or incompetent, they are prone to disbelieve information originating from these sources. The data here are becoming convincing. Capella and Jamieson (1997) documents decreased levels of trust and increased cynicism over the 1990s, attributing both to the media's coverage of politics and campaigns. Hetherington (1998, 1999) demonstrates the public's growing mistrust of government and he shows how this can affect broader political attitudes and behaviors.

The core problem, then, is that we have not identified a measure or specified a model of receptivity. This leads to speculative theorizing, which, in turn, produces the aforementioned interesting (but contradictory) hypotheses. This confusion distinguishes receptivity from outlets and access, both of which are presumed to have increased since 1990. Conversely, these three subjects are linked together by the fact that they have all clearly changed over this interval. The scope, magnitude, and consequences of change are, however, far less clear.

THINKING ABOUT NEW AGENDAS

Given the recent changes in political communication, the authors in this volume pursue two tasks. First, they attempt to identify subject areas that are vital to students of politics and to citizens of a democracy, especially where there is a relative paucity of theoretical insight and empirical research at the current time. Second, they attempt to use existing theory and knowledge to understand problems of political communication likely to affect us at the dawn of a new millennium. The chapters in this book can be grouped into five broad nodes.

Informing the Modern Electorate

The two chapters in this section tackle the role of information and political discussion in the most recent election campaigns. In chapter 2, Dietram Scheufele harkens back to the themes of the Columbia school in his examination of how political talk affects voters. Scheufele does so by integrating a theoretical and empirical understanding of interpersonal communication with the well-trodden framework of media effects. In particular, he argues that interpersonal communication after exposure to media coverage both mobilizes *and* polarizes the electorate. In so doing, Scheufele touches not only on the classic arguments of Berelson et al. but also on the recent research on TV advertising effects by Ansolabehere and Iyengar (1996) and Finkel and Geer (1998).

In chapter 3, Scott Althaus expands on the influential recent work of Delli Carpini and Keeter (1996) and Bartels (1996) by considering how congressional election outcomes across the 1990s might have differed if the electorate had been "fully informed." In this way, Althaus joins a burgeoning and important debate on deliberation and its effects (see Fishkin 1995). Althaus's analysis differs from previous studies (most notably Bartels's) by imputing informed preferences for nonvoters as well as voters. Althaus corroborates recent findings that candidate preferences are influenced by information, although he also shows that a variety of political factors condition the nature and magnitude of these influences.

Media Frames in Contemporary Campaigns

Chapters by Dhavan Shah and Adam Simon extend and reconsider (respectively) the literature on framing effects in election campaigns. In chapter 4, Shah pushes the framing paradigm in a new direction: How do certain kinds of news media frames affect voters' information processing, preferences, and behavior? More specifically, do media frames emphasizing "values" or "rights" or "morals" lead to the employment of compensatory (versus noncompensatory) decisions? Using a pilot survey, he finds that value frames strongly influence issue interpretations but that they tend to have a weaker influence on turnout and voting. Shah also questions the normative bias against "rights talk" implicit in other preliminary analyses.

Simon's chapter 5 asks a question that unnerves professors who teach the introductory course on political communication each semester: What do we mean by "framing"? Simon correctly points to the different conceptions floating about the field, organizing these distinct perspectives in interesting and novel ways. More importantly, he offers an innovative "rational choice" perspective on framing and priming that sheds light on important differences between those phenomena. Simon also proposes using computer-based analysis to examine speech and media texts in order to assess frames that may strongly affect public policy formation that cannot be easily described via traditional content analysis.

Interpersonal Judgments and Electoral Outcomes

At the heart of political communication is the way voters see candidates and their government. One of the fundamental assumptions of much recent research is that U.S. voters have changed since the 1950s. Although this may be true in many ways (declining party identification, less social connection, etc.), we do not have clear ideas about how these changes have affected the way voters come to view candidates or public policy initiatives.

In chapter 6, Lynn Vavreck looks at campaign effects in the 2000 New Hampshire Republican primary and contends that it is time to exploit the "true" lessons of the minimal effects of media research to better understand election campaigns. In doing so, she focuses on the McCain–Bush battle in New Hampshire and examines what happens when voters are personally connected during the campaign. Vavreck, like Scheufele in chapter 2, proposes reassessing these interpersonal contacts to craft a more accurate picture of why people vote as they do. Relying on surveys of New Hampshire voters, Vavreck finds ample evidence that contact with candidates has had strong and predictable effects on personal impressions and vote choice.

Marc Hetherington continues his impressive recent work on the role of political trust in recent elections in chapter 7. Hetherington makes a forceful case that voters are less trusting of government today than in previous years. He proceeds by arguing that this is neither an odd nor a disconnected finding. Instead, he argues, trust has a strong and direct influence on political attitudes and orientations. Voters' lack of trust constrains the range of issue positions and behaviors on the public agenda and, along with a cynical media, it makes people feel ineffectual as voters. Clearly, these are dangerous effects.

U.S. Campaigns and Group Identities

This section is comprised of two chapters that consider the role that group thinking plays in American elections. Throughout this volume, we have concentrated on U.S. elections because phenomena long observed here are beginning to appear in cross-national contests. In this section, however, we are dealing with phenomena that may well be country-specific. The United States, that is, has long been a haven for an infinite variety of subgroups and they have been the nation's glory as well as its most vexing problem.

Political parties are one such subgroup. In chapter 8, Sharon Jarvis provides an empirical examination of how party images have been projected between 1948 and 1996. Using a database of campaign speeches, political ads, campaign debates, and news media coverage, Jarvis employs a content analytic scheme to "measure the rhetorical and political nuances of party tokens in political discourse." She finds that elites have used party descriptors in much the same way over the past fifty years, contrary to what "party decline" scholars might assume. Parties are presented rather positively and in hierarchical—rather than egalitarian—terms as an inevitable part of the electoral system. Parties, in short, continue to have a kind of rhetorical vitality.

Chapter 9 continues our resurrection of the Columbia scholarship, with Nicholas Valentino introducing striking experimental evidence in his exploration of how group identities are primed by the media and candidates. Specifically, he focuses on how news media reports on crime can prime racial considerations of broader political issues. He also demonstrates that the power of sociological identities is not dead. In fact, media priming may have supplemented (replaced?) the kind of interpersonal communication initially documented by Berelson et al. and reconsidered earlier in this volume by Scheufele. Americans, it seems, often cannot see past the groups of which they are a part.

New Modes of Campaign Influence

What will the future bring to U.S. political campaigns? More specifically, what new sorts of communication approaches will be developed in the years ahead to meet the unprecedented complexities of governing one of the largest nations on earth?

Take the U.S. Congress, for example. Although we have numerous studies of how the president and the White House attempt to shape media coverage and influence public opinion, Daniel Lipinski offers one of the first comparable studies of the Congress in chapter 10. In particular, he focuses on how party leaders communicated their positions on the issue of tax cuts during the 1999 session. He finds that parties sought to influence the language and activities of individual members, both on the floor of the U.S. House of Representatives and also in their home districts. Even the casual observer of politics cannot help but notice the similarity in phrasing employed by members of the same party on the issues of the day. Lipinski gives us insight into how and why these "talking points" were developed.

Another new development in contemporary political life is the candidate web site. In chapter 11, Robert Klotz provides some of the first empirical data collected on this front. More importantly, he asks fundamental questions about the new medium: Is the information it provides novel or does the Web repeat what can be found elsewhere? Does information presented on the Web take advantage of the interactive possibilities presented by this new technology? Klotz examines Senate candidate Web sites across the 1996 and 1998 election cycles and offers some intriguing preliminary findings. He finds, for example, that Web information is not always novel but that it tends to be more detailed and more positive than information culled from other sources. Second, he finds that the Web was not a high priority for campaigns during those years, perhaps because both the possibilities and dangers of this new technology were regarded in equal measure by the campaigns.

Finally, in chapter 12, Glenn Richardson proposes a fresh way of understanding political advertising. Rather than focusing on "positive" or "negative" or "comparison" spots, Richardson looks at advertising in a broader culture context. He argues that political ads rely heavily on popular culture to connect with voters on a more emotional level than is typically acknowledged. He conducts several case studies and finds evidence of at least four types of genre-specific negative ads. Moreover, Richardson claims that the audiovisual and narrative elements of an ad can evoke emotional responses that overwhelm the ad's more substantive message.

LOOKING AHEAD

The goal of this volume, to borrow from the jargon of the MBA schools, is to "think outside the box." The New Agendas conference challenged a new generation of scholars to contemplate the dizzying array of developments we have witnessed over the past decade in political campaigns and to offer fresh perspectives about them. While we are excited by the chapters they have contributed, there is still much work to be done. Most obviously, one need only review the research presented here to see that as many questions as answers have been raised. Maybe more to the point, there are several problems with contemporary political communication research. Four problems seem especially vexing:

1. We need to clarify the critical concepts of "framing" and "priming." One cannot help but be struck by the lack of unanimity Simon describes in chapter 5, but the problem with these constructs is evident in many of the other chapters as well.
2. There has been little attempt to distinguish treatment of the press as a *medium* vs. the press as an *agent*. When we study candidates, for example, we often assume that the media are predictable, if not passive, purveyors of information. In these cases, we presume that the action is with the politicians. When studying the media, however, scholars often talk about how the media "set" the agenda, paying heed to professional norms and biases. Well, which is it?
3. When estimating the effects of campaign communication, we seldom consider the *durability* of those effects. It is true that political psychologists have looked at the atrophy of considerations—largely in an attempt to shed light on the Bayesian properties of information processing—but more often scholars note an instantaneous influence on the campaign and then move on. The question of durability is important, however, especially in the study of elections, where short-term effects may not affect the ultimate forum of interest: election day voting.
4. Similarly, the functional form of communication effects is often ignored. As the field becomes more methodologically sophisticated, we need to test and estimate nonlinear relationships. Campaigns, after all, are *systems* of people, groups, ideas, technologies, events, and chance occurrences. We need to find a way of measuring these constantly interweaving, systemic effects.

While many of the challenges facing studies of political communication are evident in this volume, there are also some impressive unifying elements here. First, many of the authors have a clear desire to dust off some of the classic theories of political communication and apply them to contemporary contexts. Scheufele, Vavreck, and Valentino all go "back to the future" in this sense. For example, after years of scholarly obsession with mass communication, a keen interest in interpersonal communication is obvious in the work presented here.

Second, one finds in this volume a consistent effort to pursue more inventive research designs. Valentino gives us a glimpse of how carefully conceived experimental studies can help us isolate the effects of subtle changes in communicative presentation and content. Too, Jarvis uses a computer program to analyze the speech and rhetorical content of several different forms of political communication in her examination of how parties are "constructed." Although Simon's proposal is even more ambitious, he relies on the same core belief in the need to better utilize the vast potential of computer technologies to facilitate higher level analyses of the form, content, and construction of political communication.

In addition, one finds a common bond of statistical sophistication here. For example, Hetherington and (especially) Althaus rely on the conventional survey approach to explore their topics, but they go beyond the cookie-cutter approach in specifying and estimating their models. While these approaches have been used elsewhere previously, they have only recently been brought to the study of political communication and that is a welcome addition indeed.

Third, there is a movement towards unifying theories across fields. Simon uses the formal theoretical framework of economics to offer a unified conception of framing and priming. Richardson merges traditional political science with communication theories of "genre" to investigate political ads. Vavreck, Valentino, and Scheufele mix sociology and politics in their efforts to detail how people acquire political information. This cross-pollination occurs within fields, as well. Shah, for instance, borrows from political psychology and public law in his treatment of "rights talk."

In the end, our hope is that the analyses and thoughts presented here convey some of the conveners' own enthusiasm and optimism, for it is clearly an exciting time to study political communication. The potential for understanding our complex democracy has never been greater. At the same time, the work in this volume also reflects some of our worries. We are concerned, for example, about voters' abilities to keep up with the enormous changes in communication technology and wonder how these changes will affect the quality and intensity of their political interactions with one another. As citizens of a democracy, we worry too about declining levels of political interest and trust, and wonder whether the mass media are a potential solution to this problem or a cause of it. It does little good, after all, to have a powerful microphone if no one wants to hear what you have to say, or if the microphone you are using systematically undermines your ability to say it. It would be hubris to think that the studies in this volume will solve such broad-based and endemic problems, but it is not foolish to hope that the work presented here will stimulate both students and researchers to take on such challenges and to find new ways of tapping the opportunities presented in an age dominated by myriad forms of political communication.

2

Democracy for Some? How Political Talk Informs and Polarizes the Electorate

Dietram A. Scheufele

Interpersonal discussion of politics is at the core of much scholarly debate about democratic citizenship (for an overview, see Schudson 1998). More recent research, however, suggests that the influence of such discussions is far more complex than previously assumed (Eliasoph 1998; Eveland and Scheufele forthcoming; Scheufele, Moy, and Friedland 1999). These researchers have suggested that the impact of media content on citizens' understanding of politics and, ultimately, on their participation behavior might be strengthened or weakened by a number of other variables, including political discussions with others. Interpersonal discussion of politics, in other words, moderates the influence of the mass media on their audiences. While public affairs media can clearly increase understanding of politics, this influence differs depending on the degree to which individuals talk about politics with other people. Specifically, we can assume that talking about certain issues with other citizens is a necessary condition for fully understanding those issues, for tying them to other, preexisting knowledge, and consequently, for meaningfully participating in political life. The complex interaction between interpersonal discussion and media use on political participation has been labeled the "differential gains model."

At first glance, the differential gains model may be reminiscent of the Columbia School's idea of a two-step flow of communication (see, for example, Lazarsfeld, Berelson, and Gaudet 1948). Lazarsfeld and his colleagues assumed that the influence of the mass media on audiences was not direct. Rather, they reasoned, opinion leaders play a key role in conveying information from the news media to broader cross sections of society and, ultimately, to the person on the street.

But the differential gains model and the idea of a two-step flow of information differ at both a methodological and a conceptual level. First, the two models differ with respect to the role that interpersonal discussion plays as part of the media use–participation relationship. This difference boils down to a methodological distinction between mediated and moderated relationships. The two-step flow model assumes that interpersonal discussion *mediates* the effects that mass media use has on audiences. Interpersonal discussion, in other words, accounts for the relationship between media use and audience effects. The differential gains model, in contrast, assumes that the relationship between media use and political behavior is *moderated* by interpersonal discussion of politics. To put it differently, the relationship between news consumption and political participation depends on the value of a third variable (Marsh 1982), such as interpersonal discussion of politics.

Second, the two-step flow model and the differential gains model differ at a more conceptual level. The two-step flow model of communication focuses on a social phenomenon, that is, the persuasive impact of mass media in particular communities. The differential gains model is more concerned with *individuals'* information processing. Do people use the mass media and interpersonal discussion to filter out specific types of content from the daily flow of information they receive through the mass media?

Of course, a differential gains model—if it holds empirically—has immense implications for democratic systems. In this chapter, I first examine interpersonal discussion and its impact on participatory behavior from a normative angle. In other words, what is the role that mass and interpersonal communication should play in democratic societies? What are the implications of these more normative questions for theorizing about various forms of communication? The model is then translated into testable theoretical statements. National survey data, collected as part of Verba, Schlozman, Brady, and Nie's Civic Participation Study (1995), provide preliminary insights into the moderating role of interpersonal discussion and its effects on different types of political participation. Given the conceptual character of this research, however, these data do not afford a formal test of the model but merely illustrate a theoretical argument. Finally, I discuss possible explanations for the processes described in the model and what they may mean for society at large.

MEDIA USE, POLITICAL PARTICIPATION, AND INTERPERSONAL COMMUNICATION

Most current research on participation is based on a very fundamental assumption: Citizens' engagement in democratic processes is a necessary condition for a healthy, functioning democracy. Of course, Berelson, Lazarsfeld, and McPhee (1954) are probably correct in their observation that getting all citizens to participate in politics is both unrealistic and undesirable from a normative standpoint. There is likely a trade-off between getting a maximum number of people involved in politics and—at the same time—maintaining high levels of information among those who do participate. Regardless of this trade-off, however, relatively stable levels of participation are necessary to ensure a functioning democracy that relies on a system of representation and, therefore, on an informed electorate.

Mass Media and Participation

Based on this assumption, the constant decrease in levels of political participation found recently is somewhat disconcerting. Dennis (1991, 23), for example, argues that "since 1960 there has been a substantial erosion in American electoral participation." Even if there has been no actual decline in political participation, it is not as high as could be expected based on increasing levels of formal education over the previous decades.

Increasing levels of participation could also have been expected based on an increasingly rich information environment, including recent technological advances in electronic communications. By creating an interactive information environment, Abramson, Arterton, and Orren (1988) argue, the electronic media seemed capable at one time of turning disparate groups or communities into an "electronic commonwealth." The emerging information environment is "so rich that the costs of learning about politics would be reduced significantly for most citizens" (Delli Carpini and Keeter 1996, 112). Consequently, levels of current-events knowledge and political participation should be far higher than they are.

Nie, Junn, and Stehlik-Barry (1996) have attempted to explain this seemingly paradoxical pattern by examining the relative effect of education on political participation. "While absolute educational attainment has an important impact on levels of political engagement, increases in education over time do not lead to commensurate increases in engagement. This is true because the educational environment is also becoming more competitive, thus requiring more and more education to yield the same amount of political engagement" (Nie et al. 1996, 142).

Based on their theorizing, we can predict that the effort individuals put into political participation will vary depending on their relative educational attainment. More specifically, political participation should be a function of a person's educational attainment relative to "the education of others with whom they compete" (Nie et al. 1996, 142).

Similar to previous research, of course, Nie et al.'s theorizing is based on the assumption that education is the central driving force behind political participation. Their analyses, however, suggest that the impact of educational attainment might be increasingly replaced by intervening variables. Specifically, they found the impact of education on voting to be heavily dependent on such variables as family income, organizational membership, or occupational status. Similar patterns resulted when political activities like working on political campaigns, serving on governmental boards, and contacting officials were examined.

This raises the question: are changes in these mediating factors responsible for the decreasing impact of educational attainment on political participation? Figure 2.1 shows levels of campaign participation in presidential election years between 1960 and 1996.[1] This participation index is measured using three items: having talked with people to influence their vote, attending political meetings, and working for a party or candidate.[2] In addition, figure 2.1 includes predicted levels of political participation, given the development of sociodemographic and media use variables.[3]

It is clear from these graphs that—given levels of education among the American people—participation could have been expected to rise substantially between 1960 and 1996. If other demographic variables like age, gender, and income are controlled in addition to education, the curve of predicted participation flattens somewhat. If media use is entered into the equation with all other variables (including education), predicted political participation declines relatively early in the time series, but in a more dramatic fashion after 1984. This raises the question of what it is about the mass media that causes such effects.

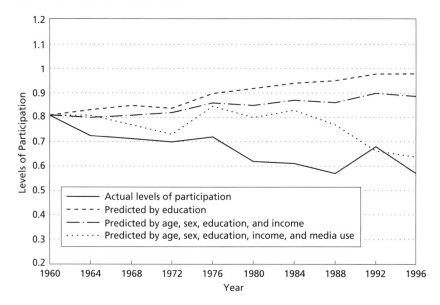

Figure 2.1.   Levels of Participation over Time (Actual vs. Predicted)

A first explanation for declining levels of political participation can be found in the decline of public trust over time (see for example, Capella and Jamieson 1997; Thomas 1998), a decline that largely parallels the trends in political participation. Since 1964, the National Election Survey has included a question measuring people's trust in the government doing "what is right." Over time, a sharp decrease can be observed in the percentage of people who trust the government "just about always" or "most of the time" between 1964 and 1980 and, after a short period of recovery, after 1984 (Hetherington 1999; see also Hetherington 1998). Moy and Pfau (2000) have summarized these trends and conducted a comprehensive study of how different coverage in different media can contribute to a decline in public trust and, ultimately, in political participation.

A second and somewhat related explanation is offered by Robert Putnam (1995, 1996) who targeted television as the main culprit in declining levels of political participation. According to Putnam, television has privatized our leisure time, and it is the only activity that inhibits participation outside the home. Results from a representative survey of 416 adults in Madison, Wisconsin, however, directly contradict Putnam's theorizing. Moy, Scheufele, and Holbert (1999) found the time individuals spent watching television to be negatively related to levels of civic engagement. This relationship, however, was not mediated by the perceptions of time pressures. Rather than time spent with a medium, Moy et al. (1999) found the *type* of media content that respondents were exposed to predicted levels of civic engagement.

While declining levels of trust and free time are potentially important variables, my research focuses on a third explanation—the role the mass media play (or do not play) in promoting citizen participation. Political information is more widely available than ever before—in newspapers, on countless television channels, and for many, the Internet. Why then does media use not translate into an *increase* in political participation? The answer to this question is multifaceted. First, the number of political issues that citizens have to keep up with every day with has been increasing exponentially over previous decades (Delli Carpini and Keeter 1996). In addition, some have argued that the mass media provide less and less mobilizing information (Lemert 1981), that is, information about where and how to participate in a community. Third, in addition to the *content* of news coverage, the *nature* of coverage has changed. Sound bites—at least during election campaigns—are getting shorter and shorter, and coverage of everyday issues is getting longer and more complex. Barnhurst and Mutz have labeled this phenomenon "the new long journalism" (1997, 52).

The Role of Interpersonal Communication

Recently, however, research has suggested that a more careful focus on interpersonal communication among citizens might explain some of the variations in participatory behavior (McLeod, Scheufele, and Moy 1999). Specifically, Eveland and Scheufele (forthcoming) suggest that citizens' understanding of politics depends on an *interaction* between mass and interpersonal communications. That is, people who engage in interpersonal discussion with others about what they have read or heard on television will have disproportionately higher levels of understanding than people who seldom talk to others about politics.

This argument is consistent with some of Eliasoph's (1998) more ethnographic research. Her findings indicate that the impact of media content on understanding politics and, ultimately, on participation might indeed be contingent upon discussing politics with others: "Talking through vague political ideas, playing with their ideas in the light of day" (Eliasoph 1998, 231) is a necessary condition for citizens to understand political processes, reconcile potentially inconsistent points of view, and engage in meaningful political activity.

Interpersonal discussion, however, is not the only potential source of influence. Rather, making sense of mediated political information is likely to be a function of two related factors: *inter*personal reflection and *intra*personal reflection. These two dimensions of news processing are based on Kosicki and McLeod's (1990) concept of information processing. Three dimensions of news processing have been identified by them: *active processors* refers to individuals who seek out additional sources based on the assumption that mass-mediated information in general is incomplete, slanted, or in other ways colored by the intentions of the communicator. *Reflective integrators* ponder or think about information they gather from mass media, or they talk to others about what they have learned in order to fully understand it. Finally, *selective scanners* use the mass media only to seek information relevant to them and then skim over or ignore irrelevant or uninteresting content.

Of particular interest for our purposes is the dimension of reflective integration. Kosicki and McLeod (1990, 78) argue that reflective integration includes "pondering and thinking about the issue *and* talking about it with friends" [emphasis added]. That is, "[It] represents the postexposure salience of information . . . and is the subject of interpersonal discussion. The key, however, is the incorporation of new information into the person's existing cognitive framework for understanding the subject" (Kosicki and McLeod 1990, 75).

Consequently, Kosicki and McLeod's (1990) operationalization of reflective integration included items tapping the degree to which individuals thought about news stories as well as the frequency with which they talked to others to see what they thought.

Using a subset of the items by Kosicki and McLeod (1990), Eveland (1997) examined the concept of reflective integration in a number of data sets over time, assessing the internal consistency and stability of the survey items as well as the construct validity of the scales formed from these items. Based on these tests, he modified the conceptual definitions of reflective integration to exclude the interpersonal aspect of the concept. Consequently, Eveland's (1997) operational definitions included only items measuring individual information processing, pondering, and trying to make sense of incoming information.

Rather than being completely *intra*personal, as Eveland (1997) argues, however, reflection also has an *inter*personal component that includes interactions with others. That is, people make sense of the information they gather from the mass media by talking to others about these issues, discussing their pros and cons, and weighing various alternatives to come to a conclusion.

Given these conceptual definitions, I put forth a definition of reflection that includes an *interpersonal* as well as an *intrapersonal* dimension. Both types of reflection need to be tested. Interpersonal reflection is based on the assumption that the impact of mediated information on a person's engagement with politics should be highest if that person is exposed to relevant information in the mass media and—at the same time—talked about it to other people, learned about other interpretations, and ultimately developed a better understanding of the problem and possible ways of solving it. Intrapersonal reflection, on the other hand, refers to the interaction of reflective thinking and media use. Only if respondents ponder information they obtained from the mass media and try to integrate it into their existing cognitive frameworks will they be able to understand political issues and then translate that understanding into political action. Reflective thinking or media use alone should produce weaker effects. If a person avoids media use or eschews intrapersonal or interpersonal reflection, the effects should be minimal.

THE DIFFERENTIAL GAINS MODEL

Although the purpose of this chapter is mostly theoretical, I provide at least an initial test of the key elements underlying the differential gains model. In order to keep the analytical details in this chapter to a minimum, I refer to data that have been explained in greater detail elsewhere (Scheufele 1999b). More specifically, I use data from the 1990 American Citizen Participation Study, a national survey of political and nonpolitical civic participation with 2,517 face-to-face interviews. The fieldwork was conducted by the National Opinion Research Center.[4] Since the Citizen Participation Study does not include any measures of how citizens process the news—that is, how they ponder what they have heard or reflect upon certain issues—that restricts this empirical overview to interpersonal reflection, as described earlier.

Previous research has consistently shown that hard-news media use affects political participation (for an overview, see McLeod et al. 1999). These effects, however, can be separated into significantly different effects for respondents with different levels of intrapersonal and interpersonal reflection. Respondents who talk to others more frequently, or who reflect more upon what they have read or seen in the mass media, are more likely to develop a more thorough understanding of politics, and consequently more likely to participate. In other words, the effects of different types of media content on participation differ in strength, depending on respondents' levels of interpersonal or intrapersonal reflection.[5] Thus, the influence of hard-news media use on political participation is not equally strong for all citizens. Rather, it appears to most influence those who also talk about politics with other people.

This is not to say that hard-news media use has no effect on participation for more reticent people. As figure 2.2 shows, there is a significant main effect of newspaper hard-news use on political participation after controls were established for demographic variables and political interest. This effect, however, is substantially stronger for people who talk to others more frequently than for those who do not.

For *television* hard-news use, the difference is less pronounced but still significant. As figure 2.3 shows, the influence of television hard-news use on political participation is generally weaker than that of newspaper hard-news use, a finding that is consistent with previous research (see for example, McLeod et al. 1999). Regardless of this weak effect for television, however, interpersonal discussion does make a difference. It increases the likelihood

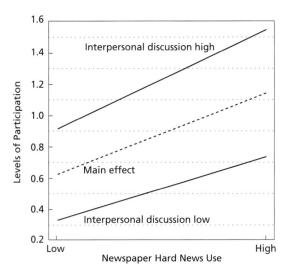

Figure 2.2.   The Influence of Interpersonal Reflection on Political Participation (adapted from Scheufele, 1999)

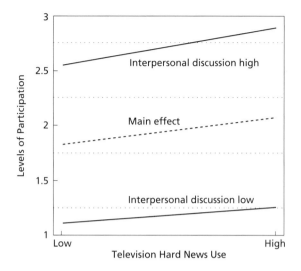

Figure 2.3.   The Influence of Intrapersonal Reflection on Political Participation (adapted from Scheufele, 1999)

of participating in politics among those viewers who talk to others more frequently about politics in comparison to those who do not.[6]

HOW TALK MOBILIZES PARTICIPATION

The purpose of this chapter is to outline a new way of thinking about the relationships among media use, interpersonal discussion, and political behavior. From the results presented here, it is clear that the notion of simple, linear links existing among these variables is simplistic. While both hard-news media use and interpersonal discussion of politics do have significant effects on people's participation, these effects vary considerably depending on the other variables. In other words, political discussion both mobilizes and polarizes the electorate. As we have seen, interpersonal discussion increases the effects of mass media use on participation for those who talk to others more frequently, thus effectively widening the gap between themselves and those who do not. Even though the mass media mobilize people, they do so in a polarized fashion, one that favors those who discuss what they read or who think more about it.

Interpersonal Discussion and Reflection as Processing Tools

How does talking about politics (or pondering it) help citizens extract certain information from the mass media and thereby influence their willingness to participate in politics? Or, to put it more pessimistically, why is it so hard for citizens to distill relevant pieces of information from the large flow of messages they are exposed to on a daily basis? At least three explanations are possible.

The first explanation has to do with the content the mass media provide, or do not provide, that enables citizens to participate meaningfully. Lemert (1981) has called this type of information "mobilizing information"—for example, how to get a permit for holding a rally, information on where to vote, or simply information about public meetings. Lemert (1981) argues that the proportion of mobilizing information in today's news coverage is significantly lower than it used to be, making it increasingly harder for citizens to identify outlets for participation. Interpersonal discussion of politics might help overcome this shortcoming in media content and help citizens figure out ways to participate. Political discussion, in other words, might well be a process of sharing experiences, applying mass-mediated information to the real world, and figuring out ways of translating media content into practical modes of participation.

In addition to content, however, trends in how the news media cover politics could provide a second explanation for the importance of interpersonal and intrapersonal reflection. More specifically, Barnhurst and Mutz (1997) have identified a trend in the presentation style of local newspapers in the United States that they call the "new long journalism." Their analysis of newspaper coverage over the course of one hundred years showed that coverage has become longer, more analytical, and increasingly more complex. This has implications for its appeal to readers. The length and complexity of news reports make it hard for audiences to extract mobilizing information and, above all, Barnhurst and Mutz (1997, 51) conclude, "the recent stories are fiercely dull."

In addition to being less appealing to readers, however, the new long journalism exposes a third explanation for why reflection is important for helping readers extract relevant information from newspapers: The new long journalism might discourage readers from discussing what they have read with other people or thinking about it in greater detail. Barnhurst and Mutz (1997) mention in passing that newspaper users no longer read entire narratives—mostly because these narratives are no longer available—but rather scan information and only retain bits and pieces of knowledge. This supposition is consistent with the distinction that Kosicki and McLeod (1990) made between what they called "selective scanners," that is, people who only attend to news content that interests them directly, and people who process news content more carefully and try to integrate it into what they already know. If Barnhurst and Mutz's (1997) assumption holds true, of course, the implications would be exactly what the differential gains model predicts: People who process news content more carefully—either by talking it over with others or thinking more about it—will also extract more mobilizing information as well. And—given Barnhurst and Mutz's (1997) trend data—the gap between those who do reflect on politics and those who do not might widen even more in the future.

NEWS AND PARTICIPATION: WHAT CAN BE DONE?

The notion of differential gains from mass media is not new; the idea, however, that interpersonal and interpersonal reflection can significantly affect political participation is somewhat novel. The theoretical model developed here reinforces Tocqueville's (1835/1984) notion that political talk *is* the soul of democracy. In other words, interpersonal *and* intrapersonal reflection play a role in the reception and processing of political news when it comes to translating mass-mediated messages into meaningful individual action. Consequently, people who consume a great deal of hard news are significantly more likely to engage in various forms of political action if they talk through these issues with others or compare them to what they already know.

It is obvious that a situation in which media coverage of politics—for whatever reason—cannot reach vast segments of the electorate is undesirable. But how can this situation be remedied? One can approach possible solutions with two types of actors in mind: the media and the audience. If media content seems to be the major reason for the differential gains phenomenon, potential solutions have to focus on journalists and their professional practices. If the audience is the main problem, we need to seek solutions in the areas of public education and political socialization.

The Internet

New forms of mass communication—such as Internet news sites—are a first potential solution to the problem of the unavailability of mobilizing information. Why can Internet news sites provide greater amounts of mobilizing information than traditional media? The answer is that the Internet is essentially unlimited by space or time constraints, constraints that impinge heavily on traditional media like newspapers and television. After telling a story about a successful demonstration, for example, an article on the web could link the user to other articles about how to get permits for marches or about locations of future demonstrations. Also, additional mobilizing information could be provided by links to sites outside the news organization's own domain. As Althaus and Tewskbury (2000, 26) write, "The Internet has an almost limitless capacity to store and transmit information. Even when traditional news services move on-line, they often supplement their normal fare with additional news and features."

Of course, it would be naive to assume that just because information is available people will use it. In other words, if Internet news outlets provide news in a format similar to newspapers—that is, in a lengthy, analytical, in-depth fashion—the additional information they provide will likely remain unused. Human beings, we are told, are "cognitive misers" or at least "satis-ficers" (Fiske and Taylor 1991), persons who use only information that is accessible to them with minimal effort and who seek out only as much information as they think is necessary to make a decision.

It is unlikely, however, that the Internet will move toward this longer, more analytical type of coverage. Barnhurst and Mutz (1997) argue that newspapers are steadily moving toward a new long journalism because they can no longer cover the news first. This role has been taken over by radio, television, and most recently, the Internet. Newspapers have therefore started to cover existing issues in greater depth than other news media. The Internet—by providing a constant stream of up-to-date information—is likely not to follow that pattern of coverage.

Public Forums

Even though the Internet might make mobilizing information more accessible to citizens, however, the fact remains that some respondents are more likely than others to engage in political discussions or reflect upon the issues. Recently, there have been efforts to engage broader cross sections of the population in deliberative forums to increase levels of interpersonal discussion (and also intrapersonal reflection) of issues. One attempt to organize such forums has attracted considerable amounts of attention, mostly due to its wide-ranging claims: James Fishkin's idea of deliberative polls (Fishkin 1991, 1995). For a deliberative poll, respondents of a traditional, representative face-to-face survey are invited to attend a forum on political issues. During the time between the initial interview and the forum, "those who agree to attend are provided with carefully balanced briefing materials, which outline the issues, provide purely factual background, and describe some of the major policy proposals mooted by politicians and the press" (Luskin and Fishkin 1998, 3). At the forum itself, participants engage in two types of interpersonal discussion. First, in randomly assigned groups of fifteen to twenty participants and a moderator, they discuss a number of preselected political issues. Second, they participate in sessions where they question policymakers, political candidates, and political experts about their views and stances on various issues. In short, these deliberative meetings attempt to increase both intrapersonal reflection (through briefing materials and instructions to prepare for the discussion) and interpersonal reflection (through facilitated discussions with other citizens and also with lawmakers and experts).

Deliberative polls have been criticized for a number of reasons (for an overview, see Merkle 1996). For the purposes of this research, of course, the question that is most relevant is whether these forums can help increase discussion and reflection among wide cross sections of the populace. Based on the experiences with deliberative polling, however, this goal may be too optimistic. Of the initial sample of 869 respondents in Fishkin's (1995) research, only 300 took up the invitation to participate in the deliberative meetings. More importantly, however, those who did participate were significantly more interested in politics (and also reported higher levels of interpersonal discussion in the initial interviews) than nonattendees (Merkle 1996). This raises the question of the degree to which these forums increase levels of reflection or if they merely attract people who talk more about the issues in the first place.

Family Communication Patterns

The most promising solution lies in habitual changes due to adolescent socialization. Socialization process refers to how individuals learn at an early age to both interpersonally and intrapersonally reflect upon mediated information and translate it into meaningful political participation.

As far as intrapersonal reflection is concerned, recent research indicates that children who grow up in a household where parents regularly read (or even subscribe) to a newspaper are far more likely as adults to read a daily newspaper on a regular basis as well (Noelle-Neumann 1999). More importantly, however, "by starting to read early children practice the ability to store information, think in abstract terms, and thereby lay the basis for structuring knowledge and tying incoming information to existing knowledge structures" (Noelle-Neumann 1999, 48, translation by the author). This, of course, is exactly the ability that is necessary for adults to extract relevant information from the steadily increasing flow of information.

Socialized media-use patterns might also have an influence on the levels of intrapersonal reflection among young people. Based on self-reports from children and teenagers as well as reports from mothers, Atkin and Gantz (1978, 195) found that "children who watch more news tend to seek more information afterwards" in order to understand what they have seen more fully. In addition to media-use patterns, however, what are potentially even more important are the communication patterns established in families. Chaffee and McLeod (1972), for example, distinguish two types of what they label "family communication patterns:" socio-oriented and concept-oriented styles of communication. Socio-oriented communication among family members encourages children to avoid controversy and arguments with others. At the same time, it discourages information seeking. This includes parents telling their children that "you will know better when you grow up" or "to give in on arguments rather than risk antagonizing others" (Chaffee and

McLeod 1972, 153). Concept-oriented communication patterns, on the other hand, encourage children to express their own ideas, challenge existing patterns, and expose themselves to controversial views. This includes items like encouraging a child to "always look at both sides of an issue before making up [his or her] mind" (Chaffee and McLeod 1972, 153).

In short, differential gains from the mass media might be a function of information-seeking patterns established during childhood and adolescence. As the mixed success of programs like deliberative polls shows, developing the habits of interpersonal and intrapersonal reflection as adults is harder than it is for children. Political socialization during childhood and adolescence might therefore be more important than ever before. The fact that media content is increasingly deprived of mobilizing information and is presented in a more complex and lengthy fashion reinforces the importance of teaching our children to become critical and open-minded citizens. Only then can widespread political participation become a meaningful reality.

NOTES

1. The combination of variables included in the equations plotted in figure 2.1 were available for election years only. In order to be able to show trends with equal time intervals, single nonelection years for which these variables were also available have been omitted.

2. The exact wording of the questions in the National Election Studies was:

During the campaign, did you talk to any people and try to show them why they should vote for [1984 and later: or against] one of the parties or candidates?

Did you go to any political meetings, rallies [1984 and later: speeches] [1978, 1980 1982: fund raising] dinners, or things like that [1984 and later: in support of a particular candidate]?

Did you do any [other] work for one of the parties or candidates?

3. Specifically, the trends shown in figure 2.1 are predictions based on ordinary-least-squares estimates, given the levels of various independent variables each year.

4. The data set (Study Nr. 6635) and specifics on sampling procedures and question wording are available from the ICPSR data archive [http://www.icpsr.umich.edu].

5. In order to test the interactive relationships hypothesized earlier in a multivariate model, it is necessary to build a hierarchical regression model that enters demographic, structural, and informational controls first, followed by the main effects of different types of media use and intrapersonal and interpersonal reflection, and finally by the interaction term. In order to avoid multicollinearity problems between the product term and its components, the main effect variables are standardized before the product term is formed.

6. It is important to note, of course, that the exposure measures of media use employed in this study are far from being ideal. In fact, Chaffee and Schleuder (1986) have argued that researchers should use attention rather than exposure measures of media use when tapping learning effects of mass media and related constructs.

3

Who's Voted In When the People Tune Out? Information Effects in Congressional Elections

Scott L. Althaus

It is something of an understatement to say that most Americans pay little attention to the world of politics. Survey after survey has shown that Americans often cannot provide basic facts about the players, issues, and rules of the game that structure American political life (Delli Carpini and Keeter 1996). For instance, when asked whether the Republican or Democratic Party was generally more conservative—surely an essential piece of information for connecting values with votes—only 57 percent of respondents in the 1992 National Election Study correctly chose the Republican Party. As the laws of probability tell us that half should have arrived at the correct answer by chance, the degree of public ignorance reflected in this finding is sobering indeed. Since democracy is, at least in theory, the form of government best suited for realizing and responding to the "will of the people," the fact that most people know (and care) very little about politics raises the possibility that democratic institutions function less well in practice than in premise.

This chapter examines the impact of political ignorance on the basic units of democratic input: individual votes cast in free elections. Do ill-informed people, regardless of their personal political views, tend as a group to favor certain kinds of candidates? If so, we might rightly question not only the ability of citizens to accurately communicate their needs, wants, and values through the ballot box but also the quality of representation provided by this most basic of democratic institutions.

POLITICAL KNOWLEDGE AND THE
QUALITY OF POLITICAL JUDGMENTS

The discovery by survey researchers in the 1940s and 1950s of widespread public ignorance about political affairs led several early and influential studies to suggest that the public's views on political matters were often shallow and misguided (Almond 1950; Berelson, Lazarsfeld, and McPhee 1954; Converse 1964, 1970). While this conclusion was often taken as axiomatic in subsequent research on public opinion and voting behavior, a number of studies in the past decade have suggested that the mass public's inattention to politics may have less bearing on the quality of its political judgments than previously thought. These studies emphasize that while most individuals tend to be ill informed about the political world, the availability of heuristic shortcuts (see Ferejohn and Kuklinski 1990; Lupia 1994; Mondak 1994; Popkin 1991; Smith and Squire 1990; Sniderman, Brody, and Tetlock 1991; Zaller 1992) and the filtering process of statistical aggregation (see Converse 1990; Page and Shapiro 1992) compensate for this lack of knowledge.

Yet recent work on information effects has demonstrated that the low levels and uneven social distribution of political knowledge in the mass public often cause election results and opinion surveys to misrepresent the mix of voices in a society (Althaus 1998, 1996a, 1996b; Bartels 1996; Delli Carpini and Keeter 1996). Correcting for unequal levels of political knowledge reveals that many collective policy preferences would look quite different if all citizens were equally well informed about politics. The present chapter illustrates this line of research by presenting new findings on information effects in congressional voting.

Two curiosities stand out in the modern history of congressional campaigns. First, Democratic candidates have tended to do better than Republicans. In the twenty-six sessions of Congress in the post–World War II era, Democrats have held majorities in the House in all but four sessions and majorities in the Senate in all but seven. A second puzzle is the high retention rate for incumbents, which between 1949 and 1998 averaged 92 percent in the House and 78 percent in the Senate (Davidson and Oleszek 1998, 66). Scholarly research has tended to explain these effects as a function of the resources and characteristics of the candidates running for office as well as features of the larger political environment. For instance, work on the Democratic advantage in congressional elections has focused on (1) the tendency for Republican candidates to run on issues that are popular in the national political arena—such as minimizing government interference in the economy—but uninspiring at the state or district level, (2) the fact that because Republicans have dominated the presidency in recent decades, the performance of Republican presidents influences retrospective evaluations made by voters in a way that tends to penalize Republican congressional candidates, and (3) the tendency for the Republican Party to field less-qualified candidates in Congressional elections than the Democrats (see Davidson and Oleszek 1998; Fiorina 1991; Jacobson 1990). Likewise, the incumbency advantage for members of Congress has been credited to the higher public visibility of incumbents relative to challengers, the declining quality of challengers, and the inherent resources of incumbency (such as the frank) and the ability to provide constituency service (see for example Davidson and Oleszek 1998; Gaines and Rivers 1996; Mayhew 1974).

While the resource and environmental advantages held by candidates can explain a great deal, we might also wonder whether individual characteristics of voters might incline them to support incumbents and Democrats. Previous research has tended to address the impact of voter characteristics by examining how aggregate differences in the partisanship, ethnicity, education level, and ideological makeup of constituencies might contribute to the advantages held by incumbents and Democrats. Little effort has yet been given to examining how individual differences in the cognitive resources used to process information about candidates might contribute to these tendencies. Political knowledge is among the most important cognitive resources for connecting our needs, wants, and values to our vote choices (Delli Carpini and Keeter 1996). This chapter takes a fresh look at the electoral advantages of incumbency and partisanship by examining how ill-informed voters as a group, regardless of their political leanings, tend to prefer certain kinds of candidates. The findings presented below suggest that the American electorate's low level of knowledge about politics biases the outcomes of congressional elections to favor Democrats running for the House, Republicans running for the Senate, and incumbents in both chambers of Congress.

POLITICAL KNOWLEDGE AND THE CONGRESSIONAL VOTE

While it seems clear that political knowledge is related to voting behavior, the precise nature of that influence is surprisingly hard to pin down. The challenge of determining which candidates might be advantaged by an ill-informed electorate can be illustrated by the voting patterns for House races in 1988. The National Election Studies (NES) data reveal that in 1988 51.9 percent of the votes for House candidates went to Democrats, and 80.1 percent to incumbents. Yet there is good reason to believe that these results have been influenced in some way by the relatively low levels of political knowledge in the American electorate because such knowledge seems to be associated with two regularities in voting behavior. To illustrate these regularities, respondents were grouped into quartiles based on their number of correct answers to fifteen factual political knowledge questions.[1]

The first association between knowledge and voting in these data is that ill-informed citizens are relatively more likely to support Democrats and incumbents than are more-knowledgeable citizens. As figure 3.1 shows, 66.7 percent of voters from the lowest knowledge quartile cast votes for Democratic candidates, compared to just 44.6 percent of voters from the highest knowledge quartile. In the same way, 85.7 percent of the least-informed voters cast votes for incumbents, compared to only 75.5 percent of the most-informed voters.[2] If we assumed that the effect of raising levels of political knowledge would be to make ill-informed people vote in the same proportions as the most-knowledgeable people (an assumption I will challenge below), we might infer that the distribution of votes among voters in the highest knowledge quartile would be a good indicator of "fully informed" voting patterns. Since only 44.6 percent of these most-knowledgeable citizens voted for Democrats and just 75.5 percent for incumbents, this comparison to the actual voting results would suggest that an electorate filled with ill-informed voters must advantage both Democrats (51.9 − 44.6 = +7.3 percentage-point bias favoring Democratic candidates in the actual distribution of votes) and incumbents (80.1 − 75.5 = +4.6 percentage-point bias favoring incumbents in the actual distribution of votes).

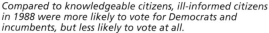

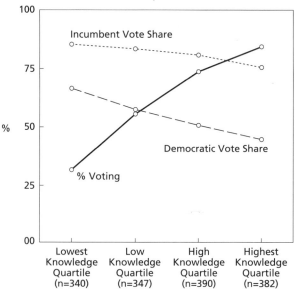

Figure 3.1.   1988 Voting Patterns for House of Representatives Candidates, by Political Knowledege Quartile

There is a second relationship between knowledge and voting that must also be taken into account: ill-informed citizens are much less likely than the well-informed to vote at all (Campbell, Converse, Miller, and Stokes 1960; Delli Carpini and Keeter 1996). Figure 3.1 shows that only 31.8 percent of the least-knowledgeable citizens cast votes in House races, compared to 84.6 percent of the most-knowledgeable citizens. What would happen if we could somehow factor in the "missing" votes from people who did not cast them? If we assumed for the sake of discussion that raising the public's level of knowledge would (1) lead everyone to cast a vote and (2) make abstainers vote in exactly the same proportions as the actual voters within each knowledge quartile, then we would find 54.4 percent supporting Democrats and 81.1 percent supporting incumbents. In this case, it would seem that an ill-informed electorate must advantage challengers (80.1 − 81.1 = −1.0 percentage-point bias against incumbents in the actual distribution of votes) and Republicans (51.9 − 54.4 = −2.5 percentage-point bias against Democrats in the actual distribution of votes), leading us to the opposite conclusion from that reached above.

Yet it turns out that both of these provisional assumptions are riddled with problems. First, less-knowledgeable citizens have different demographic characteristics than do the highly knowledgeable. In 1988, for example, 22 percent of respondents in the lowest knowledge quartile were African American, compared to just 5 percent in the highest knowledge quartile. Likewise, 37 percent in the lowest quartile called themselves Democrats compared to just 28 percent in the highest quartile, and those in the lowest knowledge quartile were much less affluent—at the 35th percentile of family income, on average—than those in the highest quartile, who have a mean family income level at the 68th percentile. Given traditional patterns of group support for the Democratic Party, the observed differences in voting patterns in figure 3.1 could result from demographic differences among voters just as much as from differences in levels of political knowledge.

Second, less-knowledgeable citizens are greatly underrepresented among the ranks of voters, and it is unclear both how much this level of nonvoting is due to low knowledge levels alone and how those nonvoters would actually vote if they were (hypothetically) to become better informed about the issues. As Anthony Downs (Downs 1957) demonstrated so ably, given the opportunity costs and the small expected rewards associated with voting, it makes sense that many people will find it unprofitable to cast a ballot, and that the degree of "rational abstention" should vary with the costs imposed on different kinds of voters. From this standpoint, even "fully informed" voters might well decide for good reason to stay home from the polls, since searching for information on which to base a vote choice is only one source of voting costs.

In the end, we can conclude from figure 3.1 only that political knowledge probably has some kind of relationship to the vote, without being able to specify what that relationship might be. There is no obvious way to tell whether the effect of low levels of knowledge is to skew election results to favor incumbents and Democrats, by leading ill-informed voters to disproportionately support these types of candidates, or to bias voting patterns in favor of challengers and Republicans by demobilizing ill-informed voters who seem likely to support incumbents and Democrats.

The tendency for political knowledge to produce such confounding effects on the vote choice means that looking at actual voting patterns can tell us very little about the overall effects of political knowledge on voting behavior. We require some means of sorting out the unique influence of political knowledge from the influence of demographic differences and other characteristics that distinguish the ill-informed from the knowledgeable citizen. A standard sort of multiple regression analysis can tell us a bit more than cross tabular data: we can learn the unique impact of political knowledge on actual vote choices. But if we want to know how voting patterns might be different if we could somehow control for the various influences of political knowledge, the standard approach will not get us very far. What about all of those nonvoters, whose preferences are missing in the actual data? And while the mere possession of knowledge or political expertise might have some sort of consistent effect on voting decisions independent of demographic or attitudinal influences, the unique effect of political knowledge in isolation is not all that telling. It is not very informative because the importance of political knowledge to the vote choice comes in large part from its association with beliefs about the world around us: the more knowledgeable we are about politics in general, the more likely we are to have accurate beliefs about the institutions of politics, the rules of the political game, and characteristics of the various candidates that are relevant to our vote choice—like issue positions and prior experience. As a result, the more knowledgeable we are about politics in general, the more likely we are to correctly associate our needs, wants, and values with our vote choices (Delli Carpini and Keeter 1996; Downs 1957). Thus, the primary effect of knowledge should be to *moderate* the relationships between demographic or attitudinal predispositions and the vote choice, rather than to serve merely as an additional source of influence.

What we need is some kind of counterfactual measure of what voting might have looked like if the uneven distribution of political knowledge were somehow taken into account or controlled for. The standard approach to this problem is to conduct experimental studies which attempt to isolate the unique impact of political knowledge on various kinds of judgments (see Fiske, Lau, and Smith 1990), inform members of a treatment group about some issue, and then compare their judgments about the issue to members of a control group that was given no information (see Kuklinski, Quirk, Schwieder, and Rich 1998), or compare the opinions of a group before and after being immersed in a deliberative environment that exposes respondents to relevant information about political issues (see Fishkin and Luskin 1999). While these approaches have yielded a rich variety of findings and have been especially useful in developing theories about the role of knowledge in cognitive processing, the artificial nature of these experiments distinguishes them from settings in which actual people make actual political judgments. As a result, research in this tradition has been much more successful in identifying the various relationships between political knowledge and voting than in suggesting how actual election results might be influenced by the low levels and uneven social distribution of political knowledge.

INFERRING "FULLY INFORMED" OPINIONS
FROM ACTUAL OPINIONS

Where traditional approaches fall short, a new method offers promise. This new method, which has been used to study the effects of political knowledge on political opinions (Althaus 1998; Delli Carpini and Keeter 1996) and presidential voting (Bartels 1996), uses multivariate regression to simulate how individual opinions might change if opinion givers were better informed about politics. In this approach, estimates of "fully informed" opinions are generated by assigning the distribution of preferences held by the more highly informed members of a given demographic group to all members of that group, simultaneously taking into account the influence of a wide range of demographic variables. For instance, if well-informed respondents hailing from union families express different policy preferences than ill-informed respondents from union families, this method assigns the mix of "fully informed" preferences to all respondents who come from union families. But instead of considering only the two-way relationship between union membership and policy preferences, this method looks at union respondents who are women, from a certain income level, who live in eastern states, who are married, own homes, of a certain age, and so on. If relatively better-informed people sharing all these characteristics have different preferences from their less-informed counterparts, the method identifies the relationship between knowledge and each characteristic in a way that suggests what each person's vote choice might be if he or she were more knowledgeable about politics.

Data for the simulations of "fully informed" voting preferences reported here come from the six National Election Studies conducted from 1988 to 1998. The self-reported voting decisions given by respondents following an election were used to analyze the effects of political knowledge on the vote choice. Each respondent's vote in a House or Senate election was coded into two categorical dependent variables. First, the respondent was coded as voting for the incumbent, for the challenger, or not voting at all (respondents living in states or districts with open-seat or uncontested races were treated as missing in constructing these incumbency variables). Second, the respondent was coded as voting for a Democrat, for a non-Democrat (typically a Republican candidate, but also including independents and third-party candidates), or not voting at all. Respondents living in states or districts with uncontested races were excluded, as—in the case of Senate voting only—were voters living in states with no Senate race that year. These outcome variables were then analyzed using multinomial logistic regression to assess the impact of political knowledge and a variety of demographic characteristics on the vote choice.[3] This technique estimates the probability that a particular individual would choose each of the three alternatives—for instance, the probability of voting for the incumbent instead of voting for the challenger or not voting at all. By factoring in the influence of knowledge on nonvoting, the approach used here has an important advantage over previous research on information effects in presidential voting, which considered changes in support for presidential candidates only among people who actually voted (Bartels 1996).

The simulation itself proceeds in four steps. In the first step, the vote choice variables are regressed on political knowledge, a variety of demographic characteristics, and a set of variables representing the interactions between knowledge and each of the demographic characteristics. By estimating the actual relationships between voting and each of the predictor variables, this step provides a set of coefficients that will be used to simulate each person's "fully informed" vote. Step two involves changing each respondent's score on the political knowledge scale to the highest possible value. As each of the knowledge scales used here is coded as the proportion of correct answers (ranging from 0 to 1), in this step all respondents were assigned a knowledge score of 1. In the third step, each respondent's predicted "fully informed" vote choice is calculated by plugging the coefficients obtained from step one into each respondent's actual demographic characteristics, substituting only the new values of the altered knowledge variable and interaction terms. This step produces, for each individual, a new set of probabilities for each alternative (that is, voting one way, voting another way, or not voting at all) that simulate the vote choice each person might make *if she or he were more knowledgeable* about politics. The final step collects all of the individual "fully informed" vote choices by taking the mean of the individual probabilities for each of the three alternatives. These average probabilities, which represent collective voting preferences controlling for individual differences in political knowledge levels, are then compared directly to the actual percentage of respondents in each category of the voting variables to reveal the impact of information effects. (For a more detailed discussion of the simulation method, see Althaus 1998.)

In short, this method takes into account the dual tendencies for less-informed voters to (1) support different kinds of candidates than knowledgeable voters and (2) vote at much lower rates than their more knowledgeable counterparts. It represents a way to statistically correct for the unique impact that political knowledge has on voting behavior. Using only the observed differences between well- and ill-informed respondents, this method imputes to all respondents the knowledge, beliefs, information processing strategies, and cognitive styles that influence the voting behavior of well-informed people. To be sure, the voting patterns produced by this transformation are only hypothetical. These "fully informed" preferences tell us not how people would "really" vote if they knew more about politics, but only the extent to which different outcomes are produced when slight changes are introduced into a mathematical model that mimics (in an extremely simplistic way) how people actually vote. Because there is no obvious way to tell whether these simulated "fully informed" preferences have any relationship to the vote choices that people would actually make if they were to become better informed about politics, I interpret the differences between actual and "fully informed" voting as merely indicating the relative impact of political knowledge on actual voting behavior. In other words, a large difference between actual and "fully informed" voting suggests only that the vote decision is heavily influenced by a voter's level of political knowledge, while a small difference suggests that political knowledge has little bearing on voter decision making.

INFORMATION EFFECTS IN CONGRESSIONAL ELECTIONS

To see what difference this statistical correction made for congressional voting in 1988, let's revisit the data introduced in figure 3.1 and include also the data for senatorial elections in that year. The left-hand graphs in figure 3.2 show actual voting patterns among respondents in each knowledge quartile for House and Senate elections (figure 3.1 is reproduced here as the graph for actual voting in House elections), and the right-hand graphs show "fully informed" voting patterns among the same groups of respondents after correcting for differences in political knowledge levels. The first thing to notice is the dramatic effect that raising everyone's knowledge level has on turnout, which is represented in these graphs by the heavy black line. While a small percentage of citizens in each knowledge quartile refrains from voting even in the "fully informed" data, imputing high knowledge levels to everyone creates voting levels that are nearly identical across quartiles. In both Senate and House voting, the percentage of people casting a ballot in the "fully informed" data rose among all quartiles to between 88 and 93 percent. In particular, the percentage of voters in the lowest knowledge quartile rose from

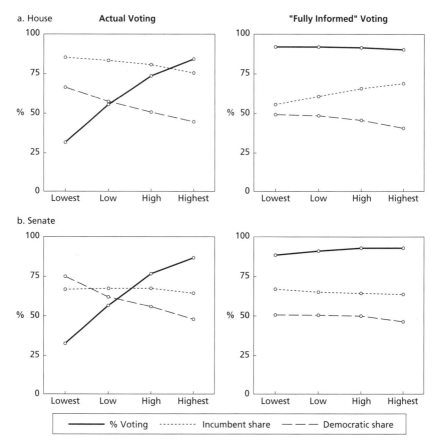

Figure 3.2.   1988 Actual and Simulated Voting Patterns for Congressional Candidates, by Political Knowledge Quartile

32.4 percent to 88.3 percent in Senate races and from 31.8 percent to 91.7 percent in House races, a nearly threefold increase over actual levels of turnout. In the actual voting data, 62.5 percent of respondents reported voting in House elections and 64.9 percent in Senate elections. Controlling for information effects in the simulated data raises these levels up to 91.1 percent and 91.4 percent, respectively. Not surprisingly, we find clear evidence that a lack of knowledge depresses turnout levels.

We might expect that a "fully informed" world would not only have more voters but would also contain voters who arrive at choices differently from those in the actual world. Looking first at changes in the levels of support for incumbents, the data show that correcting for information imbalances makes a large difference in voting patterns in House elections but hardly any difference in Senate elections. Compared to actual voting patterns in House races, "fully informed" votes are much less likely to go to incumbents, and the decline in support for incumbents is most precipitous among (what had been) the least-knowledgeable voters. While support for incumbents in the actual data ran 75.5 percent among the most-knowledgeable and 85.7 percent among the least-knowledgeable respondents, support for incumbents in the "fully informed" data dropped seven points to 68.6 percent in the highest knowledge quartile and 31 points to 55.0 percent in the lowest quartile. The collective differences are equally striking. As discussed in figure 3.1, the actual vote share for incumbents in 1988 was 80.1 percent when all voters were grouped together. Correcting for differences in political knowledge reduces this level of support to just 62.5 percent of the vote. In 1988, the incumbency bias in actual voting for House candidates was therefore nearly 18 percentage points (80.1 − 62.5 = 17.6). As modeled here, this bias was due solely to the effects of political knowledge on vote choice; House incumbents clearly benefit from campaigning before an ill-informed electorate.

In contrast to the patterns in House campaigns, figure 3.2 shows that there was almost no incumbency advantage for senatorial candidates in 1988. As the actual voting data contain few differences between ill- and well-informed votes in support for Senate incumbents (ranging from a low of 64.7 percent in the highest quartile to a high of 68.1 percent in the high-middle quartile), the simulated voting patterns are almost exactly the same as the actual data. Thus, a total of 66.8 percent of the vote among actual voters went to incumbents in the Senate, compared to a 65.0 percent share of the vote among "fully informed" voters, for a net incumbency advantage of just 1.8 percentage points. Because political knowledge levels were not an important predictor of incumbency voting in the 1988 Senate races, correcting for imbalances in political knowledge revealed only a small information effect. While the benefits of campaigning before an ill-informed electorate were realized by Senate incumbents just as they were for incumbents in the House, the net advantage was substantially smaller in Senate races for this year.

Like incumbents, Democratic candidates in 1988 also benefited from information effects in voting behavior. As shown in figure 3.2, correcting for uneven levels of political knowledge greatly reduces the tendency of less-knowledgeable voters to support Democratic candidates in both House and Senate races. Where actual voting patterns show Democratic support increasing as knowledge levels decline, "fully informed" voting patterns in both types of races show much more even levels of Democratic support across levels of (actual) political knowledge. As mentioned earlier, Democrats running for House seats won 66.7 percent of the vote among respondents in the lowest knowledge quartile, but only 44.6 percent of the vote among respondents in the highest quartile. In "fully informed" voting patterns, by contrast, Democrats won only 48.5 percent of the vote among respondents in the lowest (actual) knowledge quartile—an 18 percentage-point decline—and just

39.7 percent of the vote in the highest (actual) knowledge quartile. Taken together, the aggregate pattern of partisan bias introduced by information effects is similar in 1988 for both House and Senate races. Democrats running
for the House earned a total of 51.9 percent of the vote in the actual data and
45.1 percent of the vote in the "fully informed" data, yielding a net Democratic bias in actual voting of 6.8 percentage points. Democrats running for
the Senate netted a 56.7 percent share of the actual vote but only a 49.1 percent share of the "fully informed" vote, for a net Democratic bias of 7.6 percentage points in actual voting.

One other point to note about the patterns in figure 3.2 is that correcting
for information effects leaves simulated voters in each of the (actual) knowledge quartiles voting in essentially the same proportions for Democrats and
incumbents in Senate races but in different proportions for House races; that
is, "fully informed" support for incumbents in House races grows among the
higher (actual) knowledge quartiles, while support for Democrats decreases
among voters from higher (actual) knowledge quartiles. These differences in
voting patterns that persist after a statistical correction is made for uneven
knowledge levels are properly attributed to differences in such things as social characteristics, political attitudes, and other enduring predispositions of
voters associated with levels of political knowledge in the actual data. Re-
calling that citizens in the lowest quartile tend more than those in the highest quartile to be African American, less affluent, and more likely to identify
themselves as Democrats, it makes sense that "fully informed" voters in the
lowest (actual) knowledge quartile would still tend to support Democrats
more than those in the highest quartile. It is only after comparing simulated
to actual data that we can isolate these core patterns of enduring support
from the confounding effects of ill-informed voting.

With this insight into the dynamics of congressional voting in the 1988
elections, we can now examine whether these patterns of information effects
reflect general tendencies among voters or, rather, the specific dynamics of
that particular election year. Looking first at the impact of information effects
on turnout, figure 3.3 shows self-reported voting levels for House elections
in National Election Studies data from 1988 to 1998 (the pattern for Senate
elections is essentially identical, and so is not reported here). We can see that
turnout increases dramatically in the simulated voting data, averaging 84.9
percent across the six election years, compared to the 57.1 percent average
reported turnout in the actual data.[4] But while statistically correcting for uneven knowledge levels raises overall turnout levels dramatically, it does little to reduce the regular ebb and flow of voters in and out of the active electorate. Even among "fully informed" voters we find the familiar sawtooth
pattern of higher levels of turnout in presidential election years (the "on
years" of 1988, 1992, and 1996) and lower levels of turnout in midterm election years (the "off years" of 1990, 1994, and 1998). In the simulated data,

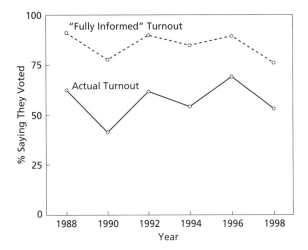

Figure 3.3.   Percentage of Respondents Saying They Voted in House Elections, by Year

on-year turnout averages 90.3 percent, compared to 79.6 percent among "fully informed" voters in off years. The size of the percentage-point difference between actual and simulated turnout in off-years (averaging a 29.9 percentage-point increase over actual turnout levels) is somewhat higher than that for the same difference in levels of on-year turnout (averaging a 25.7-point increase over actual levels), which is consistent with the expectation that uniformly high levels of political knowledge should have a greater influence on voting behavior in the years that turnout is typically lower. Yet the small size of the difference between these average increases suggests that the dynamic of "surge and decline" in congressional turnout (Campbell 1960) remains largely intact even after correcting for information effects on voting behavior.

In addition to suggesting that surge and decline in turnout is not primarily a function of the greater attention brought to congressional campaigns in presidential election years, these data from a full decade of congressional elections clarify the more general relationship between political knowledge and candidate choice. The findings reported in tables 3.1 and 3.2 suggest that there are some regularities in the effects of political knowledge on voter support for incumbents and Democrats running for Congress.

Turning first to the question of incumbency bias among ill-informed voters, table 3.1 confirms that the typical result of information effects is to advantage incumbents in the eyes of ill-informed voters. In House elections, the incumbency bias ran from a high of nearly eighteen percentage points in 1988 to a low of almost zero in 1998, while in Senate elections the incumbency bias ran from a high of fifteen points in 1992 to a low in

46 *Scott L. Althaus*

Table 3.1. The Incumbency Bias in Congressional Voting

	1988	1990	1992	1994	1996	1998
Senate						
Actual Vote Share	66.8	66.8	61.4	57.8	52.9	62.5
"Fully Informed" Vote Share	65.0	55.3	46.4	66.7	48.0	61.1
Incumbency Bias	+1.8	+11.5	+15.0	–8.9	+4.9	+1.4
House						
Actual Vote Share	80.1	78.7	73.5	68.5	72.3	68.5
"Fully Informed" Vote Share	62.5	73.5	68.4	57.8	64.7	68.3
Incumbency Bias	+17.6	+5.2	+5.1	+10.7	+7.6	+0.2

the following election of minus nine points against incumbents (that is, a net disadvantage). With the single exception of the Senate elections in 1994, the simulations suggest that "fully informed" voters in all of the other years reported here would have registered higher levels of support for challengers than was the case in actual voting. The typical result of ill-informed voting is to advantage incumbents, but table 3.1 shows that the size of this advantage varies greatly over time. Moreover, the size of the incumbency bias does not move in parallel between House and Senate races. For instance, in 1988 the incumbency bias for House candidates was nearly eighteen points, compared to just under two points for Senate candidates. But in 1992 it was senatorial candidates who benefited from the incumbency bias, which granted them a fifteen-point advantage, rather than House candidates, who were advantaged by only five points. This tendency illustrates that the incumbency bias is not solely a function of the general historical context in which these different elections were taking place.

Table 3.2. Partisan Bias in Congressional Voting

	1988	1990	1992	1994	1996	1998
Senate						
Actual Vote Share	56.7	56.1	54.2	42.7	52.3	55.2
"Fully Informed" Vote Share	49.1	67.8	59.4	39.2	56.2	56.4
Democratic Bias	+7.6	–11.7	–5.2	+3.5	–3.9	–1.2
House						
Actual Vote Share	51.9	61.2	57.9	48.0	47.8	50.7
"Fully Informed" Vote Share	45.1	53.1	54.6	42.3	49.1	51.4
Democratic Bias	+6.8	+8.1	+3.3	+5.7	–1.3	–0.7

Having said this, it also seems clear from table 3.1 that the larger historical context plays some role in shaping the incumbency bias among ill-informed voters. For instance, the 1994 congressional elections propelled the Republican Party to majority status in both the House and the Senate for the first time since the Eisenhower years. As a result of those elections, Democrats lost fifty-two seats in the House and eight in the Senate. Table 3.1 shows that the actual vote share for House incumbents reported by NES respondents was 68.5 percent, tying with 1998 as the lowest level of incumbent support for House candidates in these data. Yet the simulated data suggest that this low level of support would have been nearly eleven percentage points lower if a "fully informed" electorate had come to the polls. In this case, it seems that the voting behavior of an ill-informed electorate cushioned what could have been a much greater blow to the majority party in the House. At the same time, the net bias *against* senatorial incumbents in 1994 suggests that a "fully informed" electorate might have retained a Democratic majority in the upper chamber. It is possible that these patterns represent some sort of spillover effect from the House elections that penalized Senate incumbents in the same manner as House incumbents. Notice also the case of 1998, where both chambers of Congress had equally small incumbency advantages, the only such case in the six election years considered here. This pattern may well be due to the ongoing impeachment drama that defined the congressional elections that year, with heightened national attention on Congress's role in the impeachment leading to a smaller incumbency advantage. These possibilities are, of course, only speculations. Without a broader range of cases to study, it is impossible to identify the unique influence of election-year factors on the size of information effects. Yet the patterns in table 3.1 do suggest that the historical context in which congressional elections are contested may have some bearing on the size of the incumbency bias in actual voting.

The patterns of partisan bias brought about by information effects in actual voting are displayed in table 3.2. One pattern that stands out in this table is the tendency for ill-informed voting to advantage Democratic candidates running for the House but Republican candidates running for the Senate. For instance, the 1990 elections saw a net Democratic advantage of eight percentage points to House candidates and a net Democratic *disadvantage* of nearly twelve points for Senate candidates. Information effects advantaged Democrats in four out of six House elections, and advantaged Republicans in four out of six Senate elections. A second pattern to note in table 3.2 is that, if we set aside results from the 1988 elections, the consistent partisan biases brought about by information effects in congressional voting have tended to decline in magnitude over time. For instance, the net advantage given to Republican senatorial candidates by an ill-informed electorate shrank from nearly twelve points in 1990 to just over a point in 1998, and the net advantage to Democratic House candidates shrank from eight points in

1990 to become a slight disadvantage in the 1996 and 1998 elections. Since table 3.1 reveals no parallel pattern in incumbency voting, it is unclear what might account for this trend. The last thing to point out in table 3.2 is that information effects in the elections of 1996 and 1998 advantaged Republicans in both chambers. This may reflect nothing more than the consistent incumbency advantages enjoyed by Republicans during years when the GOP held majority status in both the House and Senate. Yet the finding that information effects can consistently advantage Republicans in both houses of Congress is an important finding for this study. In summary, tables 3.1 and 3.2 suggest that while incumbents tend to be favored over challengers in the eyes of ill-informed voters, information effects do not always bias these voters to favor Democrats over Republicans.

To provide a clearer picture of these general tendencies, table 3.3 presents the average incumbency and Democratic biases in ill-informed voting for different types of election years. Averaging the incumbency bias scores from the three off-years and the three on-years reveals that the incumbency advantage in ill-informed voting is much larger during presidential election years than midterm election years. Among House races, the size of the incumbency advantage nearly doubles in presidential year elections, and among Senate races the advantage given to incumbents shows a fivefold increase. These patterns are consistent with the notion, set forth by the "surge and decline" hypothesis (Campbell 1960), that on-year elections attract more ill-informed or inattentive voters than off-year elections, leading to greater support for incumbent politicians in on-year elections. Aside from differences between types of election years, table 3.3 also shows that the average size of the incumbency bias for members of Congress is comparable to that for incumbent presidents. Using a somewhat different simulation model, Larry Bartels (1996) estimated that incumbent presidents typically gain five percentage points more of the vote than they might if all voters were "fully informed" about politics. Averaging across all six years of congressional voting, it appears that incumbent senators draw on average four percentage points more support and incumbent representatives nearly eight points more support than they might if all voters were as informed about politics as the most-knowledgeable citizens.

Table 3.3. Average Percentage-Point Biases for Incumbents and Democrats, by Type of Election Year

	Average Incumbency Bias			Average Democratic Bias		
	Off-Years	On-Years	All Years	Off-Years	On-Years	All Years
Senate Voting	1.35	7.22	4.28	−3.14	−0.47	−1.81
House Voting	5.36	10.06	7.71	4.39	2.94	3.66

The comparable data on partisan bias shows that such effects tend to be smaller in presidential election years than in midterm election years. Republicans running for the Senate tend to do three points better in midterm elections but only a half point better in on-year elections than they might if all voters were "fully informed." In a similar way, Democratic candidates for the House tend to do more than four points better in off-year elections and three points better in presidential year elections because of the effects of ill-informed voting. Across all six years, however, the degree of partisan bias introduced by information effects tends to be fairly small. The average effect is less than a four-point bias favoring Democrats running for the House and less than a two-point bias favoring Republicans running for the Senate. As Democratic contenders for the presidency also appear to gain just around two percentage points more support from ill-informed voting (Bartels 1996), it would appear that a small degree of partisan bias brought about by ill-informed voting is the norm in federal elections. The important finding in this study is that such information effects do not uniformly advantage Democratic candidates.

A NEW AGENDA FOR RESEARCH ON INFORMATION EFFECTS

In examining the communication systems connecting governments with their citizens, political communication research has tended to focus on the "top-down" transmission of information from political actors to ordinary citizens. This chapter approaches the processes of political communication from a different direction: the "bottom-up" flow of information from ordinary citizens to political actors. By conceiving of political activity (like voting) as a channel for mass political communication, we can begin to clarify the reciprocal influences of media messages and public opinion on the quality of political representation in democratic societies. The growing body of work on information effects in collective preferences suggests that the low levels and uneven social distribution of political knowledge can have a profound impact on perceptions of the "will of the people," and ultimately on the responsiveness of governments to their citizens.

The ability to construct a new kind of dependent variable—counterfactual estimates of "fully informed" preferences based on the distribution of actual preferences in a population—allows researchers to reach beyond the traditional limitations of experimental methods to more fully identify the unique impact of political knowledge on the political judgments of individuals as well as on the collective preferences of groups. The standard ways of using experimental methods and multivariate analysis of survey data cannot reveal the substantive impact of ill-informed voting on actual election outcomes. The new approach used in this chapter illustrates one way, however limited, to begin assessing whether a population's low levels of knowledge might impair its ability to exercise popular sovereignty in democratic politics. In conjunction with the findings of experimental and cross-sectional studies, as well as with the findings of other methods for estimating "fully informed" opinions such as deliberative polls, the simulation approach described here can give us new insights into how political knowledge affects actual voting behavior, as well as the distribution of preferences expressed in opinion surveys. Yet the applications of this approach are not limited to assessing the effects of political knowledge. Constructed from actual survey data, hypothetical "fully informed" samples could be used to assess the effects of campaign activity, news exposure, partisanship, trust, efficacy, and any number of other variables on the real-world outcomes of democratic processes.

In this concluding section, I discuss three areas that encompass what I see as especially fruitful avenues for future research on information effects: identifying the environmental factors that generate or moderate these effects, identifying the kinds of judgmental or perceptual effects that are produced by low levels of political knowledge, and identifying the cognitive mechanisms by which these effects are produced.

When Do Information Effects Occur?

In order to properly understand the psychological mechanisms giving rise to information effects, future research must examine how different environmental and social influences mitigate or exaggerate the importance of political knowledge to political behaviors and opinions. Are the typical effects of ill-informed voting reduced in open-seat races, which tend to be more competitive and tightly contested? Are large information effects more likely to be associated with a strong national economy or the absence of military conflict, either of which might leave potential voters with fewer reasons to pay close attention to politics? The potential impact of the larger political environment on the voting behavior of ill-informed citizens also raises important questions about institutional design. For instance, imposing term limits on legislative bodies might counterbalance the tendency of less-knowledgeable voters to support incumbents, but at the same time heighten the tendency of ill-informed voters to support candidates from one party or another.

What Kinds of Effects Occur?

This chapter examined the effects of political knowledge on turnout and vote choice in congressional elections, yet this preliminary exploration raises more questions than it puts to rest. The limited number of cases studied here makes it difficult to sort out the impact of candidate partisanship from that of incumbency status on ill-informed voting. It is possible that the patterns observed in tables 3.1 and 3.2 might result primarily from the incumbency status of officeholders, with partisan advantage largely being an outgrowth of the majority status of a party in Congress. Unfortunately, the National Election Studies data used here include too few voters in each state and congressional district to make reliable comparisons across different races. As is the case with information effects in presidential voting (Bartels 1996), we are not yet sure how much of an impact incumbency status, party affiliation, and type of office sought by a candidate have on patterns of ill-informed voting.

Besides clarifying the influences of political knowledge on voting behavior, we still have much to learn about the relationship between political knowledge and other kinds of behaviors, judgments, preferences, and perceptions. For instance, recent work has shown that the public opinion as revealed in surveys tends to be more isolationist, hawkish, fiscally liberal, and socially conservative relative to the simulated opinions of a "fully informed" public (Althaus 1998; Delli Carpini and Keeter 1996). Yet, as researchers have only recently begun to explore these associations in depth, our understanding of the kinds of effects produced by deficiencies in political knowledge is still quite limited.

How Do These Effects Occur?

It may well turn out that the term "information effects" is an inappropriate label for describing regularities in ill-informed opinions or behavior, since the term suggests a unidirectional causal relationship that has yet to be established theoretically. We are still in the earliest stages of research on (what we might provisionally call) information effects, and thus far the small amount of work on this topic has not clarified how much these "effects" stem (1) directly from a lack of political knowledge itself, (2) from a lack (or abundance) of something else associated with political knowledge, or (3) from the interactions between knowledge and other elements affecting human cognition.

There are any number of relevant variables associated with political knowledge that might be contributing to the appearance of information effects. For example, highly knowledgeable people perceive a greater number of policy issues as important or salient than do less-knowledgeable people (Althaus 1996b). Perhaps the perceived salience of an issue or campaign, rather than knowledge itself, encourages well-informed people to engage in a more thorough and thoughtful analysis of a candidate's policy positions. Other "likely suspects" include the tendency of well-informed people to be more attentive to the news, to be attentive to different cues in the information environment than ill-informed people, and to rely on different information shortcuts for arriving at judgments (for a discussion of these and related factors, see Delli Carpini and Keeter 1996; Luskin 1990; Sniderman et al. 1991).

It also seems likely that the important contribution of political knowledge lies in its indirect effects on opinions and behaviors as a variable that interacts with or moderates the effects of other variables. As political knowledge (or expertise, as it is often called) has long been a topic of interest to political psychologists (Krosnick 1990), a great deal of research has confirmed important interactions between political knowledge and such things as the choice of information processing strategies (Fiske et al. 1990; Krosnick and Milburn 1990; McGraw and Pinney 1990; Sniderman et al. 1991), as well as the ability to store and retrieve information in long-term memory (Delli Carpini and Keeter 1996; Krosnick and Milburn 1990; Zaller 1992). Much more work is needed to connect these types of interactions to the appearance of information effects in individual and collective preferences. Only a new research agenda can establish those connections.

NOTES

1. The information measures used in this study are based on those originally constructed and tested by Delli Carpini and Keeter (Delli Carpini and Keeter 1993, 1996). These scales are primarily additive measures of correct answers to factual knowledge questions, where a correct answer is assigned a value of 1 and an incorrect response or no answer is given a value of 0. They also incorporate a subjective assessment of respondent knowledge level made by the survey interviewer at the conclusion of the interview. Three kinds of factual knowledge items were used to construct these scales: relative location tests in which correct answers are constructed by comparing responses to two different questions, open-ended questions asking respondents to identify the job or political office held by a public figure, and closed-ended questions testing knowledge of which party held majority status in both houses of Congress. An example of a correct answer to a relative location test is placing the Republican Party as relatively more conservative than the Democratic Party on a seven-point ideology scale, regardless of where on the ideology scale a respondent actually placed the two parties.

Besides the interviewer rating score (v555, reverse coded), the questions for the 1988 ANES information scale included identifying the offices held by Ted Kennedy (v871), George Shultz (v872), Margaret Thatcher (v875), Yasser Arafat (v876), William Rehnquist (v873), Mikhail Gorbachev (v874), and Jim Wright (v877); naming the majority party in the House (v878) and Senate (v879); correctly saying that the federal budget deficit had grown larger over the past eight years (v1036); identifying the relative ideological locations of the Republican and Democratic Parties (v234, v235), and locating the relative positions of the Republican and Democratic Parties on national health insurance (v321, v322), government services (v307, v308), defense spending (v315, v316), and job assurances (v328, v329).

2. Data on incumbency voting excludes voters in districts with open-seat or uncontested races. This results in slightly smaller numbers of voters in the incumbency data. For the incumbency data in figure 3.1, there are 337 people in the lowest knowl-

edge quartile, 335 in the low middle quartile, 362 in the high middle quartile, and 349 in the highest quartile. The percentage voting in figure 3.1 is the percentage voting in all contested elections.

3. The simulations reported here account for the impact of political knowledge, years of formal education, family income (in percentiles), age (in years), as well as the following categorical variables: Republican Party affiliation and Democratic Party affiliation (excluding "leaners"), ethnicity (blacks = 1, all others = 0), gender, union membership, region of the country (dummy variables for South, Midwest, and East), and urbanity (dummy variables for urban and rural residents).

4. As is well known, these self-reported turnout percentages are much higher than those found in the historical record. For instance, over this same time period, the *Statistical Abstract of the United States* shows that only between one-third and one-half of the voting-age population actually participated in elections for the House of Representatives. The tendency for certain kinds of respondents to misreport that they voted has been shown to overstate the apparent effects of independent variables, such as education level, on voting behavior, leading many scholars to recommend using validated vote measures instead of self-reported vote measures (Presser and Traugott 1992; Silver, Anderson, and Abramson 1986). Since the National Election Studies no longer constructs a validated voting record for each respondent, it is unclear how much the self-reported voting patterns of respondents are skewed by social desirability effects, demand effects (in presidential election years) of being included in the preelection sample, or other factors that could plausibly lead to actual increases in turnout as well as to overstating actual voting behavior (for a discussion of these issues, see Abelson, Loftus, and Greenwald 1992). As previous research has shown that politically knowledgeable respondents are especially prone to say they voted when in fact they did not (Presser and Traugott 1992), the likely impact of such misreporting in the present analysis would be to exaggerate the apparent importance of political knowledge to voter turnout. Since there is no way to check whether misreporters tended to support similar kinds of candidates over the time series analyzed here, it is unclear how much such misreporting might influence the estimates of information effects in levels of support for different types of candidates.

4

The Collision of Convictions: Value Framing and Value Judgments

Dhavan V. Shah

An often-strident language of rights and morals seems to dominate contemporary political discourse. As Americans, we tend to articulate our most important concerns in ethical terms, often treating political issues as a collision of opposing convictions. Such talk, some argue, has become the primary language of democratic political culture, permeating both the public and private spheres (Glendon 1991; Sniderman, Brody, and Tetlock 1991). Anecdotal evidence supports this view. The catalog of value-charged controversies has grown considerably over the last half century, with opposing perspectives drawing upon the same language of life, liberty, equality, and justice to advance their beliefs. Indeed, debates over rights and morals now animate policy disputes as diverse as gun control, capital punishment, health care, immigration, trade and environmental policy, social welfare, labor practices, the treatment of women and minorities, assisted suicide, and, of course, abortion.

This focus on rights and morals raises normative concerns suggested by classical democratic theory. Ideally, citizens' evaluations of political alternatives are supposed to be informed by a thoughtful deliberation of available information, yet this standard may be distorted by a public increasingly conditioned to evaluate political leaders and to reach electoral decisions on the basis of ethical criteria. It is suspected that the conflict over basic principles produced by this mode of speech leads citizens to think and act in single-minded, absolutist terms, thereby increasing the likelihood of simplified political reasoning and a general impoverishment of the political process. Anxiety over the implications of "rights talk," as some have referred to it, can be seen in the growing concern about "hot button" issues and their potential to be used to construct "issue publics" that can be manipulated by politicians (Bennett 1993; Edelman 1993; Glendon 1991).

These normative concerns may be somewhat misplaced, and I argue instead for rethinking our assumptions about the invocation of values in political debates. This latter perspective recognizes that while political appeals focusing on rights and morals may be increasing, they are not new; rather, the construction of issues as an ethical debate is a hallmark of democratic political systems. In the United States, this discourse can be traced back through Supreme Court decisions and the Constitution to the legal, theological, and philosophical writings of the Victorian age, and can be credited throughout U.S. history with providing a means for the disenfranchised to articulate claims against dominant groups. Perhaps the prevalence of this moral and ethical speech in contemporary politics—and citizens' responsiveness to it—reflects an emerging regard for postmaterialistic values in Western democracies (Abramson and Inglehart 1995). As Taylor (1985, 1989) asserts, the need to express basic symbolic concerns is a fundamental aspect of the modern democratic identity. This shift in focus from the level of mass discourse to individual psychology further suggests that the rise of "rights talk" may actually foster more integrative political reasoning as value conflicts emerge across, as well as within, issues that implicate individuals' most cherished concerns (Tetlock 1986, 1989).

Regardless of the implications for democratic politics, the media are certainly implicated in this dynamic. It is widely acknowledged that news coverage provides the primary context for public access to policy discussions and that the process of news production encourages journalists to frame issues around certain enduring values (Ball-Rokeach and Loges 1996; Gans 1980). Notably, issues regularly discussed by the media in terms of "deeply held values," such as abortion and gay rights, have been found to influence voting behavior in both national and state elections (Abramowitz 1995; Haider-Markel and Meier 1996). Scholars contend that citizens are often concerned with the symbolic importance of such issues and use them to assert their values to the broader community (Klein 1984; Olson and Carroll 1992; Sears and Funk 1991). Relatively unexamined, however, are the ways in which citizens' thoughts and actions are influenced when "rights talk" is the rule, rather than the exception, of political discourse—that is, when a majority of campaign issues are framed as a conflict over basic morals and principles.

This chapter discusses and then expands upon a program of research exploring how such shifts in news discourse interact with individuals' cognitions and motivations to shape political evaluations. To date, this line of experimental inquiry has examined how the introduction of a conflict over rights and morals into campaign discourse—that is, the framing of a single issue in symbolic, *ethical* terms within a political environment otherwise characterized by the instrumental, *material* discussion of issues—can not only shape individuals' interpretations of issues but also can encourage voters to make attributions about candidate character and modify their decision-making processes (Domke, Shah, and Wackman 1998a, 1998b, 2000; Shah 1999; Shah, Domke, and Wackman 1996, 1997, forthcoming). This study explores the repercussions of shifts in issue framing—from a focus on *material* concerns to one focusing on *ethical* concerns—for citizens' electoral reasoning when campaign discourse is dominated by "rights talk."

NEWS FRAMING AND POLITICAL PREDISPOSITIONS

Work on news framing may prove invaluable in understanding how the language of rights and morals, together with citizens' value preferences, encourages certain interpretations of political issues and particular patterns of political reasoning. This perspective begins with the assertion that media reports are socially constructed and, as such, foster certain conceptions of policy issues based on what is emphasized and omitted in news coverage (Ball-Rokeach, Power, Guthrie, and Waring 1990; Entman 1992). Scholars studying the sociology of news agree that enduring norms of newsworthiness, production routines, and extramedia influences lead journalists to organize—to frame—their reports in predictable ways (Dennis and Ismach 1981; Shoemaker and Reese 1996). Particularly important, Gans (1980), who spent time in leading print and broadcast newsrooms, concludes that news workers principally frame stories around certain enduring values to satisfy elites, ease news production, and structure audience understanding.

Often unacknowledged in analyses focusing on the production and content of news, however, is the fact that individuals "do not slavishly follow the framing of issues presented in the mass media"; rather, people "actively filter, sort, and reorganize information in personally meaningful ways in constructing an understanding of public issues" (Neuman, Just, and Crigler 1992, 76–77). When confronted with information, individuals are thought to first locate relevant schema to guide processing. Research suggests that recency and frequency of use influence which schemata are activated. For unfamiliar objects, recently activated schemata prompted by contextual cues may guide information processing (Chaiken 1980; Higgins and King 1981); for more familiar objects, however, relevant schemata are highly—even chronically—accessible due to frequent activation (Fazio 1989; Krosnick 1988). In particular, values, with their centrality in individuals' beliefs systems, may be closely associated in memory with "constellations of knowledge" about many issues, increasing the likelihood that they will be activated for use in information processing independent of contextual cues (Anderson 1983; Hurwitz and Peffley 1987; Price and Tewksbury 1996; Rokeach 1973).

Similar insights are available from research on the cognitive demands of survey response. Synthesizing this work, Zaller and Feldman (1992) assert that most people are internally conflicted with multiple, often opposing, "considerations" on most political issues. Thus, when expressing an opinion on a survey, individuals do not exhaustively search their memories; rather, they sample from their available cognitions to construct an attitude "on the fly," oversampling schemata that are easily brought into conscious thought. The ordering and wording of survey items has been found to activate certain considerations that, along with a person's political predispositions, guide political judgments (Kinder and Sanders 1990; Krosnick 1991a; Tourangeau and Rasinski 1988). In other words, individuals do not deterministically yield to the conception of the issue suggested by the framing of a survey question; rather, values and motives, along with textual cues, help structure citizens' "statements of political preference" (Zaller 1992, 23).

Consistent with this research, the influence of shifts in media frames on the process and outcome of social and political evaluations have been found to be mediated by motivational considerations (Green and Blair 1995; Nelson, Clawson, and Oxley 1997).[1] In particular, my colleagues and I have discovered that the *ethical framing* of political issues activates considerations about rights and morals in the minds of some citizens, who then use these standards in making other, more distant campaign evaluations. Specifically, individuals who encounter an issue framed in ethical terms become more likely to view not only that issue moralistically but also other issues—even issues typically understood in economic or pragmatic terms (Shah 1999; Shah et al. 1996, forthcoming). Such individuals also apply these ethical criteria to candidate character evaluations such that attributions about the morality, honesty, and compassion of candidates (or lack thereof) tend to increase when an ethically framed issue is part of the political conversation (Domke et al. 1998a, 2000). These findings share some commonality with research on "value-choice" frames, which asserts that political candidates and politicians struggle over the construction of issues "to legitimate to themselves and to communicate to others why their choice is more moral or competent than their opponents'" (Ball-Rokeach and Loges 1996, 279; Ball-Rokeach et al. 1990). In sum, theories of human motivation should receive greater attention when trying to understand the linkage between news frames and judgmental processes.

MOTIVATION AND DECISION MAKING

Motivational approaches to personality and attitudes suggest that mental systems serve both a "schematic" function, providing individuals with a frame of reference for understanding and ordering attitude objects, and an "expressive" function, affirming core values and defending one's self-image (Herek 1986; Snyder and DeBono 1987, 1989).[2] Particular attention has focused on phenomena that demonstrate and maintain an individual's sense of self, with some scholars positing that the expression of core values allows individuals to support their self-concepts (Greenwald and Breckler 1985; Rokeach 1973). Especially relevant for this research, Tetlock (1989, 130) argues that individuals' reasoning about political issues is "powerfully shaped by the fundamental values they are trying to advance in particular policy domains."

These insights, then, suggest that voting may be a means for individuals to validate core aspects of their self-conceptions, or more specifically, the values they believe to be at stake in a given political context (Abelson 1988; Steele 1988). Candidates who stand in opposition to an individual's core values may be evaluated unfavorably because compromising such values would be threatening to his or her sense of self. Thus, when core values become the focus of news frames and thereby contribute to an individual's issue interpretations, motivational factors may influence how much, as well as what, information is used by that individual in forming political judgments.

Research evidence provides some support for this perspective. When a single issue is framed by media *and* interpreted by voters moralistically, it plays an overriding role in the candidate selection process, leading individuals to truncate their decision making. In contrast, when individuals interpret available issues in practical terms, they favor more integrative styles of decision making (Domke and Shah 1995; Domke et al. 1998b; Shah et al. 1996, 1997, forthcoming). My research associates and I have observed this effect across a range of subject populations (for example, evangelical Christians, military reservists, union members, and undergraduate students) and issues (for example, abortion, euthanasia, gays in the military, and health care). We conclude that the effects of value frames on the vote-choice process are mediated by individuals' ethical issue interpretations. As Tetlock (1986, 819) asserts, it is threatening to individuals' self-esteem to concede "that they are capable of cold-blooded trade-off decisions" that require them to compromise on issues closely tied to basic values.

This perspective contrasts sharply with the core assumption of compensatory models of decision making which hold that all choices are based upon a willingness to engage in trade-offs—comparing one valued attribute to another—to determine which alternative has the greatest overall worth (Billings and Marcus 1983; Hogarth 1987; Payne, Bettman, and Johnson 1992). Compensatory models assume that positive and negative evaluations on several criteria can offset one another and that individuals can make concessions among valued attributes (Beattie and Baron 1991; Wright 1975). Notably, these multiple-criteria models—with their weighting and summing of decision criteria—share theoretical commonality with rational choice models of voting behavior (Herstein 1981; Hinich and Pollard 1981).

Both compensatory and rational choice models, however, have been criticized precisely because of their assumptions that all decision makers are highly calculative (Green and Shapiro 1994; Onken, Hastie, and Revelle 1985; Rabinowitz and Macdonald 1989). Not surprisingly, noncompensatory strategies, in which positive evaluations are unable to offset negative evaluations, have also been theorized. These models recognize that decision makers often use an overriding or contingent criterion (Payne, Bettman, and Johnson 1992; Wright and Barbour 1975). Similarly, psychologists contend that although individuals occasionally optimize—considering all available information when confronted with a choice—they more commonly satisfice by focusing on key attributes and integrating just enough information to make a decision (Krosnick 1991a; Simon 1979).

As this research suggests, decision-making strategies exist along a continuum from compensatory to noncompensatory processing. Particularly important for this study, Tetlock (1986, 1989) attempts to explain individual variation in political reasoning and decision making by way of a *value-pluralism model*. The model assumes that people prefer—for both cognitive and motivational reasons—simple solutions, which minimize effort and strain, to more complex reasoning. However, individuals do not avoid trade-off decisions in all cases. Indeed, the pressure to think in trade-off terms may be heightened when competing values are assigned equally high priorities in a person's belief system. I argue that as the number of issues an individual interprets in terms of core values increases, so does the potential for conflict among these issues and the pressure to think in trade-off terms. Accordingly, the relationship between issue interpretations and political reasoning may be highly conditional, depending on the number of issues interpreted ethically and the value conflicts that emerge among them.

UNANSWERED QUESTIONS

My research explores two sets of questions. The first concerns the influence of value frames and individuals' value preferences on issue interpretations. The second concerns the mediating role of subjects' issue interpretations on the vote-choice process and the inherent complexity of this relationship when multiple issues are interpreted in ethical terms.

A primary assumption of my research is that news frames, by selecting and emphasizing certain aspects of an issue, help shape citizens' understanding of the issues. In particular, the framing of issues around certain values functions as a heuristic (or self-teaching device) for a wide variety of people— from the politically unsophisticated to the politically knowledgeable (Hurwitz and Peffley 1987; Kinder and Sears 1985). I contend that two overarching value frameworks are used in this way: *ethical values*, which become most explicitly apparent in symbolic discourse about rights and morals; and *material values*, which are often manifest in instrumental discussions over economics and expediency. Parallel to these distinctions, voters are likely to form distinct interpretations of issues based on the activation of different sets of considerations. Individuals may assign an ethical interpretation to an issue, understanding it in terms of such things as liberty, equality, justice, and other noble principles. Conversely, individuals may assign a material interpretation to an issue, understanding it in terms of pecuniary and pragmatic concerns, including, but not limited to, personal self-interest (see Abramson and Inglehart 1995; Green and Blair 1995; Sears and Funk 1991; Shah et al. 1997). Since schemata related to ethical concerns are closely associated with one's self-conception, they should be quite prominent in a voter's mind, increasing the likelihood that exposure to the ethical framing of an issue will foster an ethical interpretation of many issues. Stated as a hypothesis, this prediction reads:

H1: Individuals receiving one issue with an ethical value frame will judge more issues ethically than individuals receiving that same issue with a materialist frame.

Much research, however, suggests that individuals, rather than being passive receivers of political messages, have personal experiences and basic motivations that act to regulate their understanding of political issues (Gamson 1992; Zaller 1992). In particular, values, by allowing citizens to interpret issues based on internal standards closely tied to their sense of self, shape attitudes towards political options. Thus, individual differences in issue interpretations may vary according to the importance people give to certain values, regardless of how the issue is framed. To be clear, this is not to argue that frames are without influence; rather, it is to say that individuals holding one of the conflicting values are more likely to understand the issue in value-based terms than are individuals who have no clear value preference (Tetlock 1986, 1989). This view also recognizes that values used to interpret one issue may "transfer" to other issues in the political environment, particularly if the issues share common underlying dimensions. Stated as a hypothesis, this prediction reads:

H2: When confronted with an ethical issue, individuals who strongly favor one of the conflicting values will interpret more issues ethically than individuals who have no clear value preference.

Further, this program of research suggests that individual interpretations of issues may serve as a critical mediating factor between value frames and value preferences, on the one hand, and voters' decision-making strategies on the other (Domke and Shah 1995; Domke et al. 1998b; Shah et al. 1996, 1997). When individuals do not form an ethical interpretation of an issue, candidates are typically evaluated on pragmatic grounds. In such instances, individuals most likely allow candidates' stands on various issues to balance, offset, or compensate for one another, since compromising on practical or material issues is not threatening to the self-concept.

In contrast, compensatory processing seems less likely when individuals interpret issues ethically. In such cases, people will focus on that issue during elections because their sense of "right and wrong" is critical to maintaining their self-conception. In evaluating candidates, then, such people will first consider each candidate's position on the issue in question, thereby shaping the manner in which they process information to arrive at an electoral decision. That is, voters with an ethical interpretation seem especially likely to use a noncompensatory decision-making process.

However, as discussed above, informational and dispositional factors may lead individuals to interpret more than one issue in ethical terms. Such multiple evaluations may attenuate the relationship between looking at things ethically and using the noncompensatory decision-making model. Indeed, as the number of issues being interpreted ethically increases, so does the difficulty of finding a candidate who has taken suitable positions on all of the ethically interpreted issues. In such instances, I suspect, voters will feel pressured to think in terms of trade-offs. This is not to say that they will act like "materialists," but they seem likely to take just enough additional information into account to make a choice—that is, *satisficing*, not *optimizing* (Simon 1985; Krosnick 1991a). Stated as a hypothesis, this prediction reads:

H3: People's interpretations of the issue environment will mediate the effects of value frames such that noncompensatory decision making will be (a) likely to occur when issues are interpreted ethically and (b) particularly likely to occur when only one issue is interpreted ethically.

AN EXPERIMENTAL INQUIRY

The core strategy in this program of research is the controlled presentation of political information environments. As a starting point for this particular study, a variety of political issues were content-analyzed for the presence of (1) ethical and (2) material news coverage, using a computer-aided technique (Fan 1994; Jasperson et al. 1998; Shah et al. 1999).[3] Stories about these issues were randomly sampled from four sources—Associated Press, United Press International, *New York Times,* and *Washington Post*—for a sixteen-year period from 1981–1996. Results indicate that welfare reform, the focus of this report, was typically discussed in material terms—70 percent of content—with coverage centered on cutting welfare benefits to reduce government spending and the logistics of moving recipients from welfare to work. However, a substantial amount of coverage was ethical in nature—30 percent of content—with coverage focused on social justice for vulnerable populations and the value of personal responsibility that some believe welfare recipients need to learn. Analyses also revealed that ethical coverage of welfare reform rose during the sixteen-year period of study (Shah 1999).[4]

Using insights gained from this analysis, experimental manipulations were developed that paralleled the ethical and material framing of welfare reform in news coverage.[5] These manipulations were embedded in otherwise controlled political information environments. Each environment included newspaper articles that presented contending views of three Democratic congressional primary candidates on five issues.[6] In this study, all subjects received the same articles on four issues—assisted suicide, education, gun control, and tax cuts. Two of these issues—education and tax cuts—were consistently discussed in material terms, whereas the remaining issues—assisted suicide and gun control—were consistently discussed in ethical terms. Alternating the framing of welfare reform created two experimental conditions during which subjects were presented with a minority of two or a majority of three ethically framed issues. In carrying out the experiment, candidates' positions and policy implications were the same in both conditions; only the rationale underlying candidates' positions, or the news frame, was varied.[7]

The experiment included 121 undergraduate students. After reading the articles, subjects completed a questionnaire about their voting process that began by asking them which one of the three candidates they would vote for in the primary election. Two measures were used to assess subjects' decision-making strategy. First, a series of open-ended questions asked subjects to describe their candidate choice process.[8] Guided by research on compensatory and noncompensatory strategies, we coded responses into these two categories. In brief, if subjects (a) indicated that they eliminated a candidate because of his stand on a particular issue, or (b) based their decision on certain overriding criteria, they were coded as noncompensatory. Conversely, if subjects indicated that they weighted candidates' stands on a variety of issues, allowing them to compensate for one another, to arrive at a vote choice, they were coded as compensatory.[9] Next, subjects responded to seven statements corresponding to compensatory and noncompensatory aspects of decision making. These items were used to build the second measure of decision-making strategy. Subjects rated their agreement with the statements using a five-point Likert scale, ranging from "strongly disagree" to "strongly agree."[10]

Individual interpretations of issues were measured next with five open-ended questions, one for each issue. The questions asked subjects to engage in a thought-listing procedure exploring how each issue related to their current life situation and their ethics and morals, as well as their concerns about costs, practicality, and the health of society. Issues were individually coded as having received primarily an ethical interpretation, material interpretation, or as consciously ignored/not mentioned. An issue was coded as receiving an ethical interpretation if the individual primarily discussed it within the framework of personal principles, basic rights, or religious morals. An issue was coded as receiving a material interpretation if the individual primarily discussed it in terms of economics, pragmatics, or self-interest.[11] Individual-issue codings were combined to create a variable assessing the number of issues interpreted ethically.

The next portion of the questionnaire focused on a series of seven-point scales that placed the different values brought into conflict by the political information environment at opposing ends of a continuum. Subjects were asked to indicate whether they favored one of the values, and, if so, the degree to which they preferred it (see Handy 1970; Tetlock 1986). In this way, the conflicts that were most likely to occur within this simulated congressional primary—between the values implicated by the issues of assisted suicide, gun control, and welfare reform—were presented to subjects.[12] Notably, the mean scores on these measures of value preference did not differ significantly across experimental conditions, indicating that value preferences were unaffected by the framing of the welfare reform issue.

These scales were used to construct measures of "differential value strength," consistent with the value-pluralism model of ideological reasoning (Tetlock 1986, 1989). To create these variables, the conflicting values implicated by the issues of assisted suicide, gun control, and welfare reform were subtracted from one another. These scales were then collapsed to create measures of "value strength." Notably, as the theory guiding this research predicts, the value strength measure for each issue was significantly related to an ethical interpretation of that issue.[13] Several demographic and orientational variables were also assessed, including age, gender, education, parents' education, household income, and political party identification.

CLARIFYING FRAMING EFFECTS

To simultaneously examine the predictions outlined above, a path model was developed that included the following variables: value frame of welfare reform, value strength toward welfare reform, number of issues interpreted ethically, and decision-making strategy.[14] A number of variables were controlled throughout this analysis to defend against potential confounds: age, gender, education, parents' education, household income, political party identification, and the value strength measures for the issues of assisted suicide and gun control.[15]

The data presented in figure 4.1 lends support to the theory advanced in this chapter. The effect of value framing and value strength on decision making appears to be largely mediated by individuals' issue interpretations. Moving through the model, direct effects were observed for news framing of welfare reform and the strength of value preferences on the number of issues interpreted ethically.[16] The size and direction of the coefficients indicate that ethical interpretations of issues rise considerably when individuals either encounter an issue framed in ethical terms or when they hold a clear value preference. In sum, these results provide support for hypotheses 1 and 2.[17]

Issue interpretations, in turn, were found to have a direct effect on the decision-making strategy, providing some support for hypothesis 3. Results

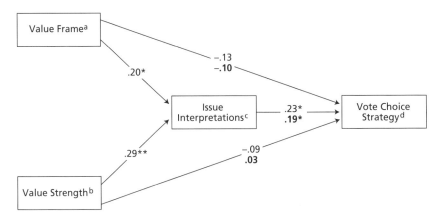

Notes:
Coefficients are equivalent to standardized partial regression (ß) weights. Analysis controls for age, gender, education, parents' education, household income, political party identification, value strength toward assisted suicide, and value strength toward gun control. In paths directly leading to the vote-choice strategy, coefficients in regular typeface are for the open-ended decision-making measure and coefficients in bold typeface are for the closed-ended decision-making measure. Significance tests are one-tailed.

[a]Value frame of welfare reform: 0 = material value-frame, 1 = ethical value-frame.
[b]Value strength toward welfare reform: low = value pluralism, high = value preference.
[c]Interpretation of issue environment: 0 = no ethically interpreted issues, 1 = one ethically interpreted issue, 2 = two or more ethically interpreted issues—explained variance = .21.
[d]Decision-making strategy: Open-ended measure coded as 0 = compensatory, 1 = non-compensatory—Explained variance = .09; Closed-ended measure coded as low = compensatory, high = non-compensatory—explained variance = .15.
* p<.05; ** p<.01.

Figure 4.1. Path Analysis of Mediational Role of Issue Interpretations for Value Framing and Value Strength

across two very different measures of the decision-making process indicate that individuals who interpreted issues in ethical terms were significantly more likely to make a noncompensatory vote choice.[18] Further, no direct effects from value framing or value strength were observed on the vote-choice strategy.

It must be acknowledged that forcing these variables into a path model may not do justice to the complexity of the relationship between ethical issue interpretations and noncompensatory decision making. Therefore, an additional analysis was conducted to explore whether evaluating multiple issues ethically increases the pressure to think in trade-off terms, leading to more integrative forms of decision making. To test this prediction, a comparison was made between the number of issues subjects interpreted ethically and their decision-making strategy (see table 4.1). As expected, noncompensatory decisions were particularly likely when an individual formed an ethical interpretation of a single issue—71 percent noncompensatory—but grew less prevalent when two or three issues were interpreted in ethical terms—46 percent noncompensatory on average. In contrast, when no issues were interpreted ethically, compensatory processing was the norm, with only 5 percent opting for a truncated choice.

As a second test of this relationship, with the decision-making strategy index as the dependent variable, analysis was run to compare the means of subjects with differing interpretations of the issue environment (see table 4.2). The findings closely parallel the results generated by the open-ended measure of the decision-making strategy. Individuals who look at things materialistically had the lowest index scores, indicating use of a more compensatory strategy ($\underline{M}$ = 4.0). In contrast, individuals forming an ethical interpretation of a single issue had the highest decision-making strategy index score ($\underline{M}$ = 10.2), indicating the use of a more noncompensatory strategy. Such noncompensatory decision making grew less prevalent when two ($\underline{M}$ = 9.3) or three or more ($\underline{M}$ = 7.4) issues were interpreted in ethical terms.[19] These findings suggest that individuals interpreting multiple issues in ethical terms use a decision-making strategy that is more effortful than is typical of individuals interpreting a single issue in ethical terms.

Table 4.1. Ethical Issue Interpretation by Open-Ended Decision Strategy

| Decision Strategy | Number of Ethically Interpreted Issues | | | |
	Zero	One	Two	Three+
Compensatory	95%	29%	50%	63%
Noncompensatory	5%	71%	50%	37%
Totals	100%	100%	100%	100%
	(n = 21)	(n = 34)	(n = 44)	(n = 19)

X^2 = 23.6, d.f. = 3, p < .001

Table 4.2. ANOVA of Ethical Issue Interpretations on Decision Strategy Index

	Number of Ethically Interpreted Issues			
	Zero (n = 21)	One (n = 35)	Two (n = 45)	Three+ (n = 20)
Index Mean#	4.0	10.2	9.3	7.4

F = 5.8, d.f. = 3, p < .001

Notes: Values with the same subscript are significantly different from one another at p < .05 (one-tailed) in LSD post hoc tests.
(#) coded as low = compensatory, high = noncompensatory.

IMPLICATIONS AND DIRECTIONS
FOR POLITICAL COMMUNICATION

The findings presented here support the perspective that value frames *and* value preferences influence issue interpretations, and that these interpretations shape electoral decision-making strategies. The path model presented in this chapter indicates that the impact of value framing is limited, with the strongest effects occurring on the most basic cognitive operations. Framing was found to have a pronounced influence on issue interpretations but limited effects on the "higher order" political judgment of electoral decision making. Results indicate that when media present an issue as a clash of rights or morals, ethical interpretations of issues rise; in contrast, when coverage of the same issue focuses on economics or pragmatics, material interpretations are favored. Thus, the frame of a news story—by emphasizing certain aspects of the issue while ignoring others—tells audiences how to process that story. It appears, then, that individuals have a variety of ways to form conceptions of political issues and that they very much rely on contextual cues when making these judgments.

However, people do not passively respond to the content of political messages. Indeed, my analysis indicates that value strength is related to issue interpretations. Thus, issues tend to be interpreted in terms of rights or morals if there is a clear preference for a particular core value. It seem likely, then, that when one of the values brought into conflict by an issue holds a preeminent place in the mind of a voter, it not only makes an ethical interpretation of that issue more likely, it also increases the probability that other issues will be interpreted in ethical terms. For example, a clear preference for the value of "personal responsibility" may not only prove useful in interpreting the issue of welfare reform but may also help shape how issues like education or gun control are conceived (since they share similar underlying dimensions). In other words, both values *and* media frames shape individuals' issue interpretations.

Issue interpretations, in turn, were found to have considerable sway over individuals' political reasoning. Results suggest that compensatory voting decisions are particularly likely to occur when an individual interprets issues in material terms. For these individuals, issues are likely to compete in a relatively equal manner since no single decision criterion is linked to an individual's core identity. Conversely, noncompensatory decision making is most likely when an individual forms an ethical interpretation of a single issue. It appears, then, that due to the strong linkage of ethical concerns to the self-concept, voters place the ethically interpreted issue at the center of their candidate evaluation. In this context, their own stands on the issue function as a filter through which candidate information will first be processed, thereby encouraging noncompensatory decision making.

As more and more issues are interpreted ethically, however, it becomes increasingly difficult for many people to find a candidate who reflects their principled preferences. Value conflicts increase the pressure to think in trade-off terms, encouraging individuals to adopt more integrative styles of political reasoning. This suggests that in electoral contexts where numerous issues are discussed and interpreted in terms of rights and morals, a limited pool of candidates (and thus a constrained range of options) may make it hard to satisfy the "irreducible pluralism of [voters'] moral intuitions" (Fiske and Tetlock 1997, 257). In these cases, ethically dissonant interpretations of the issue environment tend to increase—that is, individuals experience conflict among their value preferences because they are unable to find a candidate who satisfies all of their ethical concerns. In contrast, it may be substantially easier for individuals encountering only one ethically interpreted issue to find a candidate who advances their most basic concerns—a focus on a single ethical criterion minimizes the potential for conflict and, therefore, virtually guarantees that individuals forming an ethical interpretation can locate a candidate who affirms their convictions.

The broader research program of which this study is a part, as noted earlier, also indicates that the highlighting of ethical concerns in news discourse has an impact on citizens' judgments about the integrity of political candidates. Although these data are not presented here, the implications of a relationship between value framing of issues and candidate character evaluations are considerable. In particular, this linkage suggests that image-based voting represents the outcome, in part, of perceptions encouraged by individuals' exposure to subtle shifts in the framing of campaign issue information. That is, the value framing of issues also may trigger priming effects that begin with voters' thoughts about issues and issue positions and then "carry over" to shape evaluations of the integrity of political candidates. Given that issue-based evaluations of candidates appear to contribute to image-based voting, this research questions the long-standing dichotomy between the roles of political issues and candidate images in electoral behavior (Domke et al. 1998a, 2000).

Research on the implications of "rights talk"—a discourse that is often generated by politicians—for the evaluations of candidates and elected officials is only beginning to emerge as an area of study. This chapter suggests that such work deserves greater attention. In addition to the implications of issue framing for candidate character evaluations, future research should also explore the efforts of politicians to "value frame" issues in ways that highlight traits they wish to emphasize to the electorate. If the relationships observed in this program of research are any indication, such efforts may not only serve to shape evaluations of the sponsoring politician, and may also alter the criteria on which opponents are judged. Indeed, the framing of issues in ethical terms may play an important role in political perception.

Further, these findings suggest that scholars who claim that "rights talk" has impoverished American political discourse—causing citizens to think and act in simplistic terms—ignore the complexity of the relationships among political discourse, media frames, issue interpretations, and political judgment and reasoning. First, core values appear to allow people to form value-based judgments about issues, intervening between political discourse and political judgments. Moreover, even when individuals interpret issues in ethical terms, this does not always lead to truncated political judgments. Indeed, as the number of issues an individual interprets ethically increases, so does the pressure to think in more integrative terms. This suggests that an expansion of the catalog of issues discussed in ethical terms may actually foster more compensatory vote choices, as individuals consider additional information to resolve emergent value conflicts.

However, it does appear that thinking about issues in ethical terms can, in certain circumstances, lead people to engage in truncated forms of electoral decision making. The unconditional nature of basic rights and religious morals, and their close linkage to the self, may motivate some individuals to apply an ethical decision heuristic in their political judgments. In such instances, citizens may make decisions that are not instrumental from the standpoint of personal self-interest and do not appear to be integratively complex, but nonetheless serve to satisfy and affirm their sense of self. Bellah et al. (1985) refer to these drives as "habits of the heart," Taylor (1989) speaks of "moral intuitions," whereas Abelson (1988) discusses "convictions." Regardless of the term, the desire to assert one's fundamental beliefs is arguably an efficient and normatively sound method for selecting a candidate, since such a method of choice reflects an individual's basic symbolic concerns.

Thus, warnings about the harmful consequences of a political discourse that focuses on rights and morals may be misplaced. Scholars and social critics voicing these concerns fail to consider how fulfilling and efficient such decisions can be. Instead, academic discussion on this topic, and its focus on societal-level dynamics, tend to obscure the normative promise and peril of both instrumental and expressive approaches to political life. Although adoption of a utilitarian perspective would seem to result in more deliberative political information processing, it runs the risk of "emptying life of meaning" by dislocating judgments from our most valued concerns (Taylor 1989). On the other hand, a deontological perspective seems to foster political judgments that are grounded in intuitions and deeply held values, rather than a sober evaluation of the sufficiency of alternatives. As such, this approach likely leads to political decisions that sacrifice some deliberative quality for a pursuit of what is "morally correct." Future research should attend to these issues when formulating assumptions about the implications of rights talk for political life.

Moreover, to further validate the theoretical relationships and implications suggested by this research, future research should explore the linkages among frames, interpretations, candidate evaluations, and decision making across a wider variety of issues *and* across a broader range of people. It is possible that the relationships observed here are restricted to the particular set of issues selected for presentation to a highly constrained research population. Other issues presented by the media both ethically and expediently, issues such as tobacco regulation, the environment, trade and labor practices, and election finance reform, could be used to confirm the implications of media framing and individual issue interpretations.

This replication should be conducted with a wholly different research population. Part of my research program is to examine how various groups of voters—military reservists, evangelical Christians, union members, undergraduate students—respond to the same experimental manipulations (see Shah et al. 1996, 1997, forthcoming). Studies including specific subgroups allow for a contextualized analysis of these cognitive processes, which are not easily examined by traditional methodologies. Expanding the range of issues and subpopulations included in this research would provide a more nuanced understanding of voters' judgmental processes, adding to basic research in political psychology.

Finally, my research associates and I have devoted most of our effort to exploring the implications of value framing for candidate evaluations and voting behavior. Future research needs to look beyond this context to examine the effects of value framing on individuals' political knowledge, opinion expression, civic engagement, and political participation. It seems likely that the phenomena that foster attributions to candidate integrity and truncated decision making might also encourage greater levels of learning about certain issues, make the expression of minority opinions more permissible, and sponsor greater levels of involvement in public life. This is because individuals who come to understand an issue as linked to core values are driven to defend their self-conception by acting upon this set of concerns. An expansion of the implications of value framing to consider these other possible consequences of political discourse would substantially improve our study of the invocation and effects of values in politics.

NOTES

This research was supported by a doctoral dissertation fellowship from the graduate school of the University of Minnesota, as well as the Ralph D. Casey Dissertation Research Award from the School of Journalism and Mass Communication and a dissertation research award from the Center for the Study of Political Psychology. I owe special thanks to David Domke, my research partner throughout this program of study, and Daniel Wackman, my advisor. I must also acknowledge the thoughtful suggestions offered by Eugene Borgida, Ken Doyle, Ronald Faber, Lew Friedland, Robert Hawkins, Lance Holbert, Nojin Kwak, Jack McLeod, Wendy Rahn, Mark Snyder, John Sullivan, and William Wells, at various stages in this research program.

1. Like these scholars, I define framing as the presentation of an equivalent set of considerations in the context of different themes, or organizing principles (see also Lau, Smith, and Fiske, 1991; Kahneman and Tversky 1984; Tversky and Kahneman 1981; Tversky and Kahneman 1986). This conception of framing is substantially narrower than the usage of the term in the work of Iyengar (1991) and Capella and Jamieson (1997), both of whom, I argue, confound differences in news frames with variances in the substantive content of news.

2. Throughout this chapter, I use the term *core values* as synonymous with ethical values due to the strong link between concern about rights, morals, and basic principles and the self-concept.

3. The InfoTrend computer-aided content analysis method (see Fan 1994) was used to analyze the retrieved stories for the principal ways in which the issues were framed in news media. Unlike a number of other computer methods, in which both the input and analysis techniques are preset (and therefore limited) by the software search strategies, InfoTrend utilizes a programming language in which the researcher enters words, word relationships, and phrases to extract meaning from the text. Researcher-defined dictionaries are used to locate words in the text and then the machine implements a series of iterative-specified decision rules to extract ideas.

4. The coding unit for this content analysis was the paragraph. A total of 1,344 paragraphs were coded, 407 (30.3 percent) as ethical and 937 (69.7 percent) as material. When the raw counts and media shares of particular types of coverage were plotted, analyses show that welfare reform, though predominantly discussed in material terms, has increasingly been discussed in ethical terms. When it was a topic of debate in the 1980s, a vast majority of coverage adopted a material frame. However, when the issue reemerged in the 1990s, ethical framing of the issue became more conspicuous. For plots of these data, see Shah (1999).

5. Space permits only a brief description of the content features of one issue. Notably, the issues of assisted suicide and gun control were also analyzed. As with welfare reform, insights gained from content analyses of these issues were used to develop the research stimuli (Shah 1999).

6. This combination of candidates and issues was chosen in an effort to balance concerns about information overload with the ability to distinguish decision-making strategies. Further, for each issue, two of the three candidates held the same liberal-leaning position, with candidates taking turns in disagreement. Having candidates share issue positions increased the difficulty of decision making, since candidates often tied; in such cases, subjects would have to use at least one more issue to reach a decision (which worked against the hypotheses).

7. In the articles, a number of variables (for example, political party affiliation, gender of candidates and journalists, and subject familiarity with candidates, as well as order of issue and candidate information) were controlled or randomized to guard against potential confounds. For examples of these types of stimulus materials and other methodological procedures, see Shah et al. (1996).

8. Research suggests that questions about information processing can effectively elicit a "memory dump" if asked immediately after a task has been carried out (Ericsson and Simon 1984; Zaller and Feldman 1992).

9. Of the 118 usable responses, coders agreed on 91 as compensatory or non-compensatory (α = .77). For examples of the types of responses coded into these categories, see Shah et al. (1997) and Shah (1999).

10. Following data collection, these statements were subjected to confirmatory factor analysis. The compensatory items loaded strongly negatively and the noncompensatory items loaded strongly positively, supporting the conceptualization of decision-making strategies as one-dimensional. This solution accounted for 51.7 percent of the variance in the items. Compensatory items were reverse coded and responses to these items were used to build an additive "decision-making strategy" index (α = .84.) Notably, the decision-making index correlated .68 ($p < .001$) with the open-ended decision-making measure, increasing confidence that the two measures tapped the same construct.

11. Of the 121 usable responses, two coders agreed on 627 of 705 individual-issue codings (α = .89). For examples of the types of responses coded into these categories, see Shah et al. (1997) and Shah (1999).

12. Each value was pitted against three potentially conflicting values to create measures of value preferences. Analysis was performed on the resulting scales, yielding internally consistent measures for "the right to bear arms," "a peaceful and safe society," "the sanctity of life," "freedom of choice over one's body," "personal responsibility," and "providing for the needy." The mean inter-item correlation for each value preference measure is as follows: "The right to bear arms" (r = .37); "A peaceful and safe society" (r = .25); "The sanctity of life" (r = .35); "Freedom of choice over one's body" (r = .53); "Personal responsibility" (r = .42); and "Providing for the needy" (r = .46). Due to the sensitivity of Cronbach's alpha to the number of items comprising a scale, reliability coefficients are not reported.

13. For example, to create the differential value strength variable for welfare reform, the scale measuring support for "personal responsibility" was subtracted from the scale measuring support for "providing for the needy." For each controversy, the

resulting measure ranged from +18 (a liberal value orientation) to –18 (a conservative value orientation). Negative scores on each differential value strength scale were recoded to their absolute value so that a high scale score indicated a preference for a one of the conflicting values and a low scale score indicated value pluralism. Correlations between value strength and an ethical issue interpretation are r = .16 (p < .05) for assisted suicide, r = .23 (p < .01) for gun control, and r = .25 (p < . 01) for welfare reform.

14. Prior to testing the hypotheses, a manipulation check was run to determine whether the framing of the welfare reform issue influenced subjects' interpretation of that issue. To examine this, a cross-tab was run between the experimental conditions and subjects' interpretations of the welfare reform issue. As expected, subjects receiving welfare reform with an ethical frame were significantly more likely to interpret the issue in an ethical manner than subjects receiving welfare reform with a material frame. Results indicate that 40 percent of the sixty subjects receiving the ethical frame of welfare reform ascribed an ethical interpretation to the issue, compared to only 23 percent of the sixty-one subjects receiving the material frame of welfare reform (X^2 = 4.1, d.f. = 1, p < .05). It should be noted that the framing of welfare reform was by no means deterministic; a majority of subjects did not adopt the ethical framing of the issue in their individual issue interpretation.

15. This causal modeling analysis was performed using OLS regressions to estimate path coefficients. Overall, the regression models explained 21 percent of variance in issue interpretations and between 9 percent (open-ended measure) and 15 percent (closed-ended measure) of variance in the decision-making strategy. Although one of the measures of the criterion variable, the open-ended decision-making strategy measure, was dichotomous, linear regressions were run in order to allow comparison of 1) the beta weights—particularly their direction—for each predictor variable, and 2) the amount of variance explained across the two dependent measures. When using the open-ended measure as the dependent variable, logistical regressions were also run to compare the results, and there were no distinguishable differences between the linear and logistical regressions.

16. The framing of welfare reform (ß = .20; p < .05) and the strength of value preferences (ß = .29; p < .01) combined to account for an additional 11 percent of variance beyond the 10 percent explained by the exogenous variables.

17. Additional analysis indicates that these effects were not restricted to interpretations of the welfare reform issue. Indeed, among individuals exposed to the ethical framing of welfare reform, 85 percent interpreted one of the controlled issues (assisted suicide, education, gun control, and tax cuts) in ethical terms, as compared to 71 percent of subjects exposed to the material framing of welfare reform (X^2 = 3.7, d.f. = 1, p < .05). Likewise, individuals with a clear preference for one of the two values implicated by welfare reform were more likely to form an ethical interpretation of one of the controlled issues than individuals with a pluralistic orientation (r = .25, d.f. = 105, p < .01), even when accounting for age, gender, education, parents' education, household income, political party identification, and the value strength measures for the issues of assisted suicide and gun control.

18. When the open-ended decision strategy measure served as the criterion variable, the issue interpretation scale explained an additional 4 percent of variance beyond that accounted for by variables earlier in the model (ß = .23; p < .05). Similarly,

when the closed-ended decision strategy measure functioned as the criterion variable, the issue interpretation scale explained an additional 3 percent of variance (β = .19; p < .05).

19. Least significant difference (LSD) post hoc tests confirm these differences. The mean decision-making strategy index score of individuals who did not interpret any issues in ethical terms was significantly different from all other individuals. Further, the mean index score of individuals who interpreted a single issue in ethical terms was significantly different from individuals who interpreted three or more issues in relation to core values.

5

A Unified Method for Analyzing Media Framing

Adam F. Simon

Political communication scholars are generally aware of the history of media effects research, which has gone from failure to ever-brightening success. Beginning in the aftermath of World War II, initial research into this area largely met with failure. Attempts to isolate the persuasive effects of propaganda went well in the laboratory but fared poorly in the field (Hovland 1959). Accordingly, Klapper (1960) coined the term "minimal effects" to describe the net impact of political communication. Little changed until the 1970s when two new research paradigms appeared. The first, agenda setting, gave birth to a well-developed literature featuring a relatively firmly grounded theory of media effects based on human cognition. Framing, the second paradigm, is potentially more powerful and yet the theory of framing is much less well developed (for other critiques of framing research, see Entman 1992; Brosius and Eps 1995; and Scheufele 1999a). In this chapter, I lay out a theory based on the associative network model of human memory (which uses a statistical approach called spatial modeling) that can unite research on framing and framing effects. Based on this theory, I also outline a new method for studying framing using computer-aided content analysis.

Agenda-setting theorists argue that the media exert their influence subtly, telling people not what to think, but "what to think about" (Cohen 1963). Despite a massive number of studies (see Rogers, Dearing, and Bregman 1993 for a review), the theory behind agenda setting is relatively straightforward. Specifically, it stipulates that increases in the amount of media coverage accorded to an issue or event will cause the public to have increased concern for that subject. The notion of priming is closely related to agenda setting, holding that the media set the criteria for evaluating public officials and events. Under priming, the more prominently a factor is featured in the information stream, the greater its weight will be in subsequent judgments (Iyengar and Kinder 1987). Again, the idea underlying priming is that discourse's influence is subtle. Rather than altering preferences directly, priming presumes an indirect effect, where only the weight with which different considerations influence judgment becomes powerful. In both of these cases, the factor governing the magnitude of the effect is simply the amount of communication relevant to the subject at issue.

The idea of framing—and its potentially more powerful research paradigm—appeared around the same time. Goffman's (1974) seminal work presented an avenue for studying the media's influence by looking at the organization of messages. The underlying presumption was that this organization affected subsequent thinking about a given subject. Particulars of his definition are discussed below, but it is safe to say that framing research represents a more comprehensive way to approach political communication. Most importantly, the framing paradigm explores the actual content, as opposed to the mere presence, of communicative behavior (see Nelson, Oxley, and Clawson 1997). This means that in studying framing we can explicate the behavior of both message senders and receivers more fully. At the same time, while it turned out to be relatively easy to fully specify and document the agenda-setting and priming effects, the framing phenomena have proven more elusive. There are many, albeit related, ways of defining and studying framing, but to this point, there has been little in the way of theoretical cohesion or methodological unity among such approaches.

DEFINING FRAMING

What then is framing? There are several intertwined answers to this question, all of which tend toward two poles. For lack of better labels, I call these the positivist and the constructivist views. There is considerable overlap across both approaches. In general, framing involves the organization and packaging of information. As Goffman (1974, 21) puts it: "we actively classify and organize our life experiences to make sense of them." These "schemata of interpretation" are labeled frames; they enable individuals to "locate, perceive, identify, and label." In another early work, Gitlin (1980, 7) defined frames as the "persistent selection emphasis and exclusion" which allows journalists to efficiently package information. The emphasis here is on the organization of discourse in the service of transmission and understanding.

Economists have also taken up the use of the term. Like other researchers, they also believe that framing entails the organization of information in choice situations. Their definition stems from Kahneman and Tversky's (1984) widely read work, which argues that placing information in a unique context leads certain elements of an issue to get a greater allocation of an individual's cognitive resources. Kahneman and Tversky (1984) were mainly interested in the principle of descriptive invariance, a key tenet of rationality, which implies that as long as the essential parameters of a decision task are unchanged, the decision will be stable. In other words, rational people will not respond differently to different descriptions of the same choice.

Kahneman and Tversky (1984) showed that framing effects violate this invariance principle. Consider this example:

> Imagine the United States is preparing for the outbreak of an unusual Asian disease, which is expected to kill 600 people. Two alternative programs to combat the disease have been proposed. Assume the exact scientific estimates of the consequences of the program are as follows: If program A is adopted, 200 people will be saved. If program B is adopted, there is a one-third probability that 600 people will be saved, and two-thirds probability that no people would be saved. Which program would you favor?
>
> Now imagine the same situation with these two alternatives: If program C is adopted, 400 people will die. If program D is adopted, there is a one-third probability that no one will die, and a two-thirds probability that 600 people will die. (see Fiske and Taylor 1991, 378)

The college student participants studied in this research (as well as many other participant populations over the years) favored Program A to Program B by 72 to 28 percent. However, the same participants also favored Program D to Program C by 78 to 22 percent, even though the rational expectation of the outcome was the same in both situations. Kahneman and Tversky (1984) assign responsibility for this effect to framing, arguing that when the situation is framed as a gain (200 people will live), people are risk-averse, but if it is framed as a loss (400 people will die), people are risk-seeking.

While this example represents framing at its most basic level, it is not very useful from the standpoint of contemporary political communication research. This example was constructed so that each situation would contain exactly the same information. In the real world of everyday politics, however, most alternative choice situations do not follow this principle of descriptive invariance. In the real world, framing almost always adds or subtracts information as it changes the alternatives. To cite one example, Iyengar's (1991) work contrasts thematic and episodic frames surrounding the issue of poverty. Thematic frames organize aspects of this problem in relationship to poverty's impact on the entire society, often using statistics to describe the number of people afflicted. This kind of information is absent from the episodic frame, which organizes information around poverty's specific effects on individual people. In this case, the statistics are replaced with individuating information, therefore violating the invariance principle.

Positivist Studies of Framing

Most political researchers are prepared to move away from the economic approach to framing. Instead, they tend to look at frames as categories of informational alternatives. In this vein, Nelson and Kinder (1996) present work in which the information presented is either group-centric or not. In their study, randomly assigned participants were exposed to one of two competing messages. One message was group-based and the other was not. In one condition, for instance, the disease of AIDS was linked to homosexuals. A post-test then assessed participants' policy attitudes. On the whole, audiences exposed to group-centric frames were much more likely to cast their responses in group terms, and their attitudes toward the group significantly influenced their political judgments.

As can be seen from these examples, positivistic researchers work mainly in laboratory settings using experimental techniques. As such, their definition of framing is predominantly inspired by work in psychology (although it should be noted that constructivist scholars also favor this definition; see for example, Tuchman 1978, Neuman, Just, and Crigler 1992).

When psychologists examine framing effects, they are generally referring to the relationship between context and information as it determines meaning. Minsky (1975) defined a frame as a template or data structure that organizes various pieces of information. Thus, frames are discursive or mental structures that are closely related to the ideas of "scripts" and "schemas" as well as other constructs from the literature on social cognition (see Fiske and Taylor 1991 for a complete review). In fact, some researchers do not distinguish between frames and schemas (Lodge and Hamill 1986) or between frames and other information-processing phenomena (Popkin 1994).

This emphasis on the internal processes of human memory continues to play a large role in almost all assessments of framing. Robert Entman, one noted authority on framing, makes memory structures central to his definition of framing, calling them "mentally stored clusters of ideas that guide individual's processing of information" (Entman 1992, 53). He also says that "to frame is to select some aspects of a perceived reality and make them more salient in a communicating text, in such a way as to promote a particular problem definition" (1992, 52). Thus, for Entman, framing an issue in two ways leads to the creation of two different (but related) memories, each coding a particular version of a problem. Again, the emphasis is on how different organizations of information—contextual material, for instance—govern the internal processes of information storage and, hence, the determination of meaning.

Experimental designs are ideal for positivist studies of framing effects. Iyengar (1991) as well as Nelson and Kinder (1996) all focus their studies on the consequences of framing on individuals (see also Price, Tewksbury, and Powers 1997). The mechanism underlying framing is assumed to be the mental processes of individual receivers. The researchers' choice of experimental manipulation, however, sometimes gives this research a reductionist quality. Such scholars tend to ignore the uniqueness of individual messages when opting for hard coding of message content into specific categories. They do so, of course, because these techniques make it easier to gather quantitative evidence about framing effects.

By the same token, practitioners following this experimental/individual paradigm have avoided answering some basic questions about framing itself. Most of this research operationalizes frames as mutually exclusive dichotomies—that is, a given unit of discourse is either thematic or group-centric or not. On the face of it, this does not represent a substantial obstacle so long as the dichotomies retain their meaning when imported into the world of everyday politics. On the other hand, this tendency does obscure some critical issues. In the first place, what is the universe of frames? Often, the message options presented to subjects in framing experiments arise from little more than the researcher's intuitions about which kinds of mental organizations are interesting. To my knowledge, no experimental research has attempted to systematically enumerate all possible frames and sample from that universe. The absence of a scientific basis for selecting frames leads to a second, more pressing, concern: even if one were to argue that the message dichotomies researchers use in their experiments exhaust all the discursive possibilities, we still have no theory as to how one frame relates to another.

In the positivistic world, there is little allowance for what might be called "shades of gray." Moreover, the only account that can be provided for observed effects is that certain signifiers are either present or absent and that they do or do not influence subsequent thought and action. To date, positivist experimental research has failed to offer a theoretical account of the differences between frames that give rise to the effects it has observed. In short, while the positivist paradigm of experimental research shows that framing occurs and that it can affect subsequent political evaluations, we do not yet know how or why these effects occur.

Constructivist Studies of Framing

Another line of research approaches framing from a constructivist standpoint and is especially common among sociologists and communication researchers. Gamson and Modigliani (1987) take this approach when stipulating that frames are the "central organizing idea or storyline that provides meaning" (1987, 143) or "a central organizing idea for making sense of relevant events and suggesting what is at issue" (1989, 57). Of course, there is no simple relationship between what a speaker intends in a message and how it is understood due to the active nature of discourse comprehension in audiences (van Dijk 1988). Nevertheless, their general idea is that a frame is an ever-present discursive device that "channels" the audience as they take in particular communicative acts.

Constructivist researchers generally focus on careful accounts of frames within particular message domains. Gamson's (1992) work provided an example of this style when he carefully looked at the alternative themes deployed by news organizations and news consumers when selecting issue domains. Researchers like Gamson usually exclude the study of framing effects in individuals, although there are important exceptions. For example, Neuman, Just, and Crigler (1992) experimentally studied individual decoding processes from a constructivist standpoint. By and large, all of the researchers in this tradition are most interested in capturing the flavor of discourse, especially news programming, by examining the variety of frames present within it, and so they typically prefer content analysis as their tool for studying framing. Although such researchers do create complex categorization schemes, they take special pains to avoid reductionism. Human coders who are trained to observe the subtlety of frames and the idiosyncrasies of human language use such approaches. Thus, for the most part, this research strain has an interpretive and descriptive bent.

The problems with the constructivist approach stem mainly from its ambition. This is not to say that it is insufficient as a descriptive enterprise—this research is well suited for such purposes. On the other hand, one would be unsatisfied with this approach if one wanted definitive answers or a paradigm characterized by rigorous theory. Probably the main obstacle to the systematization of the constructivist strain of research is its lack of foundation. Also, no such foundation is likely to appear soon because contemporary understandings of human language are not up to the task of providing a rigorous theory of meaning (Pinker 1999). Accordingly, it seems more appropriate to call practitioners of content analysis craftspeople as opposed to scientists. The difficulty is not so much in ensuring reliability or ease of replication but robustness—the ability to apply particular findings to more general settings. Present studies in the area almost always rely on handcrafted coding schemes that are purposefully built for the research problem at hand. While this state of affairs has its advantages, it also means that it is hard to compare results across studies or to quickly develop new research paradigms. From another vantage point, therefore, a more general theory of framing is lacking.

At the same time, researchers are more divided over another issue concerning constructivist approaches, an issue that looms large in the minds of some positivists as well. The nature of the method—content analysis—is suitable for only relatively small samples of material. For each implementation, a suitable number of coders have to be trained and long hours spent on the process of explicating meaning. The result is a large number of studies based on relatively small discourse samples. Often, this raises questions about selection bias and robustness. Finally, many researchers also lament the lack of hard data. In general, then, the results of constructivist studies are not deeply quantifiable and that makes it hard to make comparisons across such researches.

TOWARD A COMMON DEFINITION AND THEORY

It is worthwhile to consider the large degree of overlap between the various definitions of framing just surveyed and the increasing need for common ground for theory building. To my mind, Nelson et al. (1997b) provide the best and most comprehensive common definition of framing: "the process by which a source defines the essential problem underlying a particular social or political issue and outlines a set of considerations purportedly relevant to that issue" (1997b, 222). In other words, "framing is the process by which a communication source . . . defines and constructs a political issue or public controversy" (1997a, 567). For me, this definition avoids some of the concerns raised earlier while pinpointing the very heart of framing—the construction of political issues.

Nelson et al. go on to suggest that "media frames influence opinions by stressing specific values, facts or other considerations, endowing them with greater apparent relevance to the issue than they might have under an alternative frame" (Nelson, Clawson, and Oxley 1997a, 569). Their view, then, is not so different from others we have discussed (except for the economist's version I dismissed earlier). Gamson and his colleagues should be comfortable with this definition because it highlights the media's role in framing symbolic issue constructions. At the same time, it subsumes all the more positivist definitions, while being broad enough to cover many different experimental treatments. This definition is not, however, precise enough to resolve all ambiguity or to precisely define research hypotheses. To narrow the definition somewhat, I digress a bit to discuss the workings of human memory because I believe the associative aspect of human information storage is the foundation upon which framing research should be grounded in the future.

Human Memory As It Applies to Framing

The associative network approach—the most common and well-developed model of human memory—provides a good basis for further specifying the framing phenomenon. This model uses a "net" metaphor to describe the workings of human memory (see Collins and Loftus 1975 for details). In brief, the model places concepts at the nodes where strands of the net intersect. What these concepts correspond to in real-world terms is somewhat controversial—they may be propositions, single ideas, or some other unit standing in as a memory code (Fiske and Taylor 1991). For the purpose of discussing framing, let us assume, based on theory (Anderson 1990), that each node contains a concept. These concepts might be drawn from everyday political discourse, for instance, where "taxes" might be a typical node entry. The strands of the net represent associations between concepts, thereby forming the basis for extended memory and knowledge. To illustrate, we might see "taxes" connected to "government." Information entering this system is coded as new nodes or associations, and this entering information might well strengthen existing associations.

This idea of associations is critical to understanding framing. A model of framing can be built on the premise that to frame a message in a given way entails that it contains some associations and not others. For example, a message describing taxation as a way to achieve equitable income distribution would strengthen or create associations between the nodes "taxes," "equality," and "income." In this way, the concepts of taxes, income, and equality are framed together, at least according to Entman's (1992) definition. This idea can be applied to message content as well. To say that a message constructs an issue, we are really saying that it has built-in associations among the concepts it treats. Thematic frames of poverty, for example, associate society with destitution. At the same time, to say that an individual exhibits framing effects is to say that that individual has experienced new or strengthened associations between certain concepts—for example, that there are more poor people today than before.

For the time being at least, and in the company of language researchers, we can safely assume that phrases or individual words represent the basic units of meaning in human languages and that they therefore compose the nodes in which we are interested. Using this logic, we can incorporate the idea of a "designator," which Pan and Kosicki (1993) convincingly argue is central to the idea of framing.

> Lexical choices of words are made to designate one of the categories in syntactic or script structures. The results of this choice called "designators" function to establish a correspondence between the signifier and signified as well as allocating the signified to a specific cognitive category. For example when Nicaraguan antigovernment rebels are designated "freedom fighters," a clear ideological orientation is presented. Choosing a particular designator, then, is a clear and sometimes powerful cue signifying an underlying frame. (Pan and Kosicki 1993, 62)

I would add that the combination of designators and associations between designators is sufficient to fully describe the contents of a particular frame or framing effect.

Framing, then, constructs thinking about an issue or event by forming associations between an object of judgment and a particular context in memory. Yet we must recognize that the concepts of "object" and "context" are somewhat arbitrary. We can illustrate the ever-changing relationship between object and context, or signified and signifier, with an example drawn from visual perception. Consider the famous optical illusion which when perceived one way is simply a vase and yet in an instant can change into two faces meeting. Both perceptions depend on what the observer has taken to be the background or the foreground.

Similarly, the relationship between object and context can be arbitrary. In Nelson and Kinder's (1996) study of AIDS policy, for example, attitudes toward the group influenced the policy attitudes more strongly when the issue was framed in group terms. On the other hand, it is also probably reasonable to think that the reverse is true—that attitudes toward the policy influenced the group attitudes more strongly when the issues were framed in policy terms. Because of these uncertainties, I will avoid the language of object and context, as well as the terms signifier and signified, and simply argue that framing effects are the sum of concepts and associations.

A SPATIAL REPRESENTATION OF FRAMING

We are now ready to precisely define framing in spatial terms. The first panel in figure 5.1 portrays a standard spatial modeling setup of a simple election with one voter, two candidates (D = Democrat; R = Republican) and two issues. This definition easily expands in complexity (especially to multiple-issue dimensions) but this simple arrangement will suffice for the purposes of illustration. Let us assume that the voter lies at the center of the space at the point of origin, in Cartesian coordinates (0,0). Further, let us place the Democratic candidate at coordinate (0,–.5) and the Republican opponent at (.5,.5).

The most important feature of the first panel is the circle that represents the voter's preferences. Given that voters usually prefer candidates closer to them, distance is critical. The circle represents all points at which the voter is indifferent to the Democratic candidate. Notice that in the first panel the voter prefers the Democrat to the Republican by a slight amount. Further, we can think of Dimension X and Dimension Y as representing the two issues (or concepts) to be involved in this illustration of framing. The key background assumption in the first panel of figure 5.1 is that the two dimensions are orthogonal; in other words, the dimensions meet at a 90-degree angle so that changes along one dimension will *not* influence changes along the other.

Using the definition of framing as the built-in association between two concepts, we can see the effect of framing Dimension X in terms of Dimension Y (or vice versa) in the second panel of figure 5.1. Here, framing is taken to be an increase in the association between Dimension X and Dimension Y.

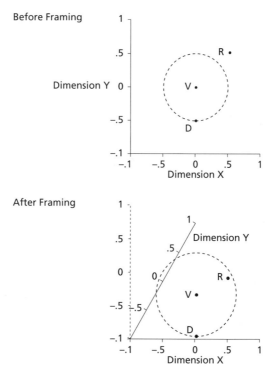

Figure 5.1.   A Spatial Representation of a Framing Effect

Whereas in the first panel, the two dimensions are orthogonal, in the second panel the two dimensions are correlated, as the angle between them is 60 degrees (instead of 90 degrees). To take a real-world example, in order to document a framing effect, we first have to decide who is responsible for setting up the frames. In most political communication contexts, candidates and the media are the most likely actors.

To see how framing works in practice, let us imagine that a candidate is making a speech on the economy. The candidate can choose to frame this issue in terms of inflation or unemployment, but let us assume the candidate has chosen to emphasize unemployment. Thus, in our example, issue X is the economy and issue Y is unemployment, and the speech itself, which associates the two issues, would represent the bottom half of figure 5.1, where the two issues have become correlated. Note that the magnitude of the correlation is determined by the degree of the angle between X and Y, that represents the strength of the association between the economy and unemployment, which can be determined by noting the proximity of these two ideas in the speech. This theoretical treatment of framing as the "simultaneous construction of issues" leads to a more precise empirical treatment.

Distinguish Framing from Priming and Persuasion

The spatial approach makes it easy to theoretically distinguish framing from other, closely related effects, namely priming and persuasion. Priming pertains to how prominently a factor is featured in a message or information stream; the more prominent it is, the greater its weight in subsequent judgments by audience. In spatial terms, two dimensions can again be used to capture the priming effect. The upper panel of figure 5.2 presents a pre-priming situation that is identical to the preframing situation depicted in the upper panel of figure 5.1.

Let us assume that in the upper panel the voter weights each dimension equally. Now let us assume that one candidate "primes" the electorate, changing the relative magnitude of the voter's weights. Assume, for example, that D is able to change the weights to 1/3 for Dimension X and 2/3 for Dimension Y. As presented in the lower panel of figure 5.2, the voter is now twice as concerned about issue X versus issue Y, thereby changing the relative scale of these issues. The change effectively moves the Democrat closer to the voter.

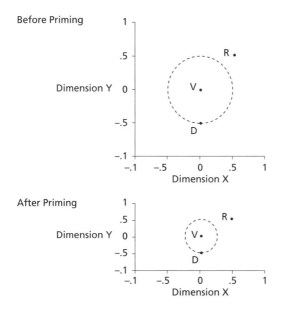

Figure 5.2.   A Spatial Representation of a Priming Effect

To take a real-world example, let us say that a candidate must decide between talking about the economy and talking about education. Given the candidate's position relative to the median voter and his opponent, the candidate decides to prime the audience about the economy, which would become issue Y. Thus, by taking time to discuss the economy, the candidate changes the situation to the one represented in the bottom half of figure 5.2—where issue Y, the economy, now dominates the voter's arena.

In contrast to McCombs et al. (1997) who talk about framing as a "second-level agenda-setting" process, we can see a clear differentiation here between priming and framing. Framing involves the recasting of issues relative to one another, while priming is only reflected in changes in the voter's level of concern. It is equally easy to distinguish framing from persuasion.

Psychologists generally define persuasion as any message-induced change in attitudes or beliefs (Petty and Cacioppo 1986). Thus, in common usage, all communicative activities can be in some sense "persuasive." Finding out something new about a candidate, for instance, can be called persuasion if the new information changes voters' intentions. (Intentions are what vote choice is called in the context of survey research, as in: "Whom do you intend to vote for in the upcoming election?") A narrower conception of persuasion is required to distinguish it from priming and framing. When used here, direct persuasion refers to the power of messages to alter the positions of candidates or voters themselves, over a given issue space. Because neither the demonstration of framing nor of priming showed any movement in these positions relative to a constant set of coordinates, persuasion did not occur in either case illustrated here.

On the other hand, while we can now analytically distinguish these effects, it remains difficult to distinguish them observationally. For example, in just looking at the lower panels in figures 5.1 and 5.2, we see a given constellation of candidate and voter positions, but we cannot properly attribute these positions to framing or priming without knowing something about the process that brought these new constellations into being. Finally, we must consider the question of how to study framing in everyday discourse.

A COMPUTER-BASED METHOD FOR MEASURING FRAMING

We can leverage our theoretical discussion of framing to provide an entrée into a more rigorous way of measuring framing in everyday political life. This new method will have a number of practical advantages over existing research in the constructivist and positivist veins. Especially in the face of the constructivist's small sample sizes and the artificiality of much positivist and experimental research, a new method for procuring content data on framing is warranted. Computer coding offers an ideal way to study framing on an appropriately large scale. Before discussing the method itself, I discuss the strengths and weaknesses of computer coding.

Computer coding has assets and liabilities, like all methods. By far the greatest strength is its ability to digest and analyze large volumes of information compared to the larger expenditure of resources involved in human coding. The computer can proceed systematically through all the discourse in a particular arena with enviable speed, thereby keeping researchers from being misled by an unrepresentative sample of message content. Such an approach ensures high reliability and an intense focus, both of which are the result of eliminating human coders from the research cycle. This particular method also takes advantage of natural data in that it examines the texts in their original form, thereby avoiding the filtering that always takes place in experimental research.

At the same time, there are weaknesses in this method. The chief disadvantage is that the computer is simply unable to understand human language in all its richness, complexity, and subtlety as can a human coder. Computer coding schemes also tend to be overly rigid and usually less detailed than human coding. In short, the efficiency of coding by computer must outweigh the very real disadvantages that can come from unthoughtful use of the method. Whatever method is used, the researcher must publicly declare the choices that drive the coding process to ensure transparency as well as replicability, both of which are hallmarks of the scientific method.

More to the point, computer-based methods are particularly well suited to the study of associations that form the basis for framing phenomena. Too, they can represent an advance over previous computer methods that depend largely on word counts and thesauri. The "associational" approach does track these measures, but it also examines the *co-occurrences of designators* in an exhaustive way, a way that human coders would find difficult to track.

The method itself has two stages, the first of which I call the "tokenizing" stage. During this phase, an exhaustive list of all the meaningful units in the discourse are compiled. This portion of the research will depend on existing algorithms, which are quite good at this particular task. For example, the computer will assess all the word clusters within an arbitrary limit, say fifteen words or fewer. The researcher would scan these lists and replace meaningful words or phrases with a token that would summarize that meaning. The point of this exercise is to take advantage of the redundancy in the English language and to minimize the amount of text under consideration—hopefully with no loss of meaning. For example, in standard political texts, the phrase "President of the United States, Bill Clinton" has the same meaning as "President Clinton"; both phrases can be replaced with "Clinton" with little loss in generality. The tokenizing process can also be aided by the use of thesauri, which would replace sets of words with just one word. The list of replacements—which phrases and words were replaced by which tokens—would be the primary document produced by this stage of the analysis.

The innovative aspect of this technique comes in the second stage, where the distance between tokens in the text is assessed, thereby serving as a measurement of framing. For example, if a given idea unit is immediately adjacent to another one, that implies that the two are "framed" much more strongly than one further away in the text or not present at all. The researcher would search for all meaningful frames in the list of associations, using the average distance between tokens as a measure of their association/ framedness. This technique, therefore, can trace a large number of varied texts in a relatively efficient manner. When used judiciously, then, the model and the empirical examination should be able to shed light on a number of important research topics that heretofore have remained outside of the scope of "large N" content-analytic studies.

On the whole, the technique described here is designed to provide a measure of framing in specific texts, so its research applications are as plentiful as the idea of framing itself. The measures thereby produced could constitute an independent variable; for example, they could be linked up with public opinion data to look at framing effects. They could also serve as a dependent variable. The characteristics of different news organizations could be compared by examining how different kinds of journalistic output are framed, for instance. The technique could also be used to study framing as a process across discourse domains. The "intensity" of a frame at one point in time could be compared to its intensity at other times in the same text or in other discourses. The technique can also be applied to other textual material. Open-ended survey questions could be coded using this method, or it could be used to verify the content of experimental manipulations. On the whole, the application is only limited by the researcher's imagination and, of course, his or her ability to draw prudent conclusions about the framing devices noted.

To conclude, let us examine a potential study that would employ this new method, one that looks at the role of framing in the formation of public policy. The quality of public policy is an issue of great interest to scholars of the political process and to policy practitioners as well. However, while consensus exists over "good policy" as a goal, there is less understanding about what makes policy beneficial. In part, we know that the goodness of a policy is determined by its outcome. Policies that are effective in helping those they were designed to assist, or solving the problem for which they were targeted, are considered better than those that fall short of these goals. Another common criterion for good policy is efficiency—policies that accomplish their goals more quickly with lower resource expenditures, are generally viewed as superior to those that are slower to show results and are more expensive. A third criterion for good public policy is legitimacy. In a system of representative democracy, policies that are enacted according to proper procedures and that represent the beliefs and goals of the public are believed to be normatively better than policies that do not meet these standards. More specifically, because democratic theorists link the legitimacy of governmental action to the quality of the deliberation that accompanies it, the goodness of a particular policy may be a function of the quality of public deliberation surrounding it. The key to evaluating deliberation's quality, then, is to be able to assess the argument put forward on its behalf. If we consider each frame to correspond to a particular argument (see Simon and Xenos 2000), then we could use our computer-based method to study the dynamics of public deliberation.

The study I imagine would address the role of deliberation in the formation of public policy. At its heart lie two questions. First, how does deliberation over policies actually occur? Second, what is the effect of this deliberation on policy making and policy outcomes? The goal of this project would be to model how certain frames come to be dominant in the discussion of a given policy and to discover the effects of variations in the type and strength of frames on the final policy outcome. A topic receiving a substantial amount of attention in the media (and by political actors) would provide sufficient deliberative content for the analysis I propose here.

To examine the role of deliberation, we would need a conceptual model describing how deliberation through framing functions in the creation and enactment of particular policies. The main idea is that public deliberation is a process that begins with the making of political arguments—which involves framing—in an attempt to win support for specific pieces of public policy. The rest of public deliberation consists of two processes. First, individual frames representing specific proposals are examined and revised until they either receive support or disappear from the public agenda. Second, successful frames are grouped together, uniting their supporters until such time as a majority, or at least a plurality, collects around a particular set of proposals. Because public deliberation leaves its record in the discourses created by political entrepreneurs in legislatures and by the members of the mass media as well, these texts can become the basic data used in analyzing the process of policy formation. In short, such a study of framing effects would shed light on some issues basic to political inquiry by using the insights and methods of political communication to transform a case study into one that gets at the very roots of human cognition, language behavior, policy formation, and democratic deliberation itself.

6

Voter Uncertainty and Candidate Contact: New Influences on Voting Behavior

Lynn Vavreck

On a crisp New England autumn morning in 1999, the sun barely shining through high clouds, John McCain, Arizona senator and candidate for president, made his first trip to New Hampshire. He had declared his candidacy only a week earlier. The light drizzle did not seem to keep people away from this early morning "New England Town Meeting"—McCain's first of what would become a record 117 such events. A quick look around the room revealed middle-aged and more senior residents of the town, many standing because all the seats were taken. The smell of coffee and sugary doughnuts hung in the air as neighbors discussed with one another their business. On this day, John McCain was polling single digits in New Hampshire (Kranish 1999).

In a matter of days, the GOP frontrunner, George W. Bush, announced that he would skip the New Hampshire debates scheduled for late October. Pat Buchanan, another candidate, allowed his potentially anti-Semitic views to be discussed nationwide, and Elizabeth Dole, the only woman in the race, dropped out, along with former Vice President Dan Quayle. All of this happened while McCain was on a book tour promoting his bestseller, *Faith of My Fathers.* McCain's share of the vote surged to 23 percent in only a few days (Price 1999). After the New Hampshire debate, McCain's share rose to 31 percent. After the holidays, McCain was polling 42 percent (Dartmouth College/WMUR Poll 1999). He won the New Hampshire primary with 47 percent of the vote.

How might modern scholars of voting behavior describe McCain's rise to popularity? Possible explanatory factors would include social groups (Lazarsfeld, Berelson, and Gaudet 1944; Berelson, Lazarsfeld, and McPhee 1954), short-term forces motivating defection among Democrats (Campbell,

Converse, Miller, and Stokes 1960), issue positions (Downs 1957; Nie, Verba, and Petrocik 1976; Fiorina 1981), electoral viability and momentum (Bartels 1988), effective use of symbols and signals (Popkin 1991), emotions (Marcus and MacKuen 1993), social interactions (Huckfeldt and Sprague 1995), campaign advertising (see Lau, Sigelman, Heldman, and Babbitt 1999), or other campaign-related activities (Franklin 1991; Vavreck 1997; Shaw 1999).[1] The rich history of voting behavior research provides no shortage of possible explanations for McCain's insurgent rise.

If young scholars are to contribute new agendas to mainstream voting research, they will do so only by benefiting from the work of luminaries who have led the way. Still, it is possible to see gaps and opportunities for future work. I propose a new look at an old agenda: presidential election campaign effects. I see this opportunity as significant in light of recent work on ambiguity and information uncertainty that may call into question long-standing presumptions among candidates and consultants about the dynamics of electioneering. I have two arguments to make in the following pages: Primarily, recent work in American politics shows that uncertainty about candidates' issue positions affects voters' choices among candidates (Bartels 1986, 1988; Alvarez and Franklin 1994; Vavreck 1997; Alvarez 1997). Given these findings, I argue that campaign activities can affect election outcomes in theory, but this possibility has not been sufficiently integrated into a broader search for campaign effects in practice. My second argument follows from the first—we must investigate the effects of more traditional forms of campaigning, such as direct and indirect voter contact with candidates, in light of these findings about uncertainty.

THE LITERATURE ON DECISION MAKING

The early work in voting behavior perpetuated the minimal effects hypothesis (or the minimal effects straw man, as I sometimes like to refer to it), which stated that campaigns persuaded and converted voters only at marginal levels (Lazarsfeld, Berelson, and Gaudet 1944; Berelson, Lazarsfeld, and McPhee 1954; Campbell, Converse, Miller, and Stokes 1960). Because these early efforts at uncovering campaign effects found little conversion among voters (despite their careful panel and cross-sectional survey designs, probability samples, and attention to persuasive messages), scholars turned their attention to explaining the stability of voters' preferences in terms of partisan affiliation and group interactions. As a result, several campaign elements were largely overlooked by scholars. By looking only for persuasion and conversion among voters, researchers failed to examine changes in voters' levels of certainty about candidates' issue positions and how these changes may have affected their voting decisions. The dynamics of the information environment of a campaign did not play an integral role in these early investigations.

Not only did voting decisions seem to have little to do with campaign information explicitly but Campbell and his colleagues confirmed what the Columbia research team had unearthed: there was a great divide between average citizens and political elites in their engagement in politics, level of political information, and ideological connectedness (Campbell, Converse, Miller, and Stokes 1960, chapter 10). One might imagine that the pioneers of voting research released a grand sigh of relief upon realizing that campaigns did not matter much to an electorate that could not or would not process political information in a sophisticated manner anyway.

Due to this finding, research on voting behavior began to focus on the voters' abilities, or lack thereof, to comprehend and utilize important political information when rendering a decision. Certainly, the decade after Campbell and his colleagues published *The American Voter* (1960) seemed to discredit that volume's claim that citizens were disinterested in politics. Issues seemed much more important to voters in the 1960s and 1970s, and party affiliation perhaps much less. This might well explain Lyndon Johnson's landslide victory in 1964 followed by his decision not to run for reelection in 1968, Hubert Humphrey's astoundingly dismal campaign season, or George McGovern's rejection by moderate Democrats in 1972.

The scholarly interest in issues during the 1960s and 1970s was fertilized by the rise of a clever and promising paradigm in political science—rational choice—that viewed economic decision making and political decision making as similar. Rational choice theorists used the notion of utility maximization to explain behavioral outcomes in both disciplines. Anthony Downs published *An Economic Theory of Democracy* in 1957 but its influence on political science came much later, during the 1970s and 1980s, as scholars such as Plott (1967), Fiorina (1981), Enelow and Hinich (1984), and countless others examined how issues may affect decision making.[2]

While scholars were busy investigating the role of issues in elections, the minimal effects straw man grew stronger in exile. In public opinion research, scholars began demonstrating that the media had interesting effects on people's perceptions about issue importance (Iyengar and Kinder 1987). But in voting behavior research, the general assumptions about issues were that people had clear issue positions, knew where the candidates stood on these issues, and could act instrumentally to further their interests. It was only a matter of time, however, before Larry Bartels (1986) synthesized rational choice work (Enelow and Hinich 1984; Shepsle 1972) with public opinion research on agenda setting and priming (Iyengar and Kinder 1987) into an empirical test for the effects of issue uncertainty on voting; soon, others followed his lead (Franklin 1991; Alvarez and Franklin 1994; Alvarez 1997). It turned out that voters did indeed have uncertainty about candidates' policy positions and this uncertainty had an influence on their decisions. As a result, interest in campaign effects was reborn.

If uncertainty about candidates' policy positions was important to voters as they made up their minds, then candidates could do things in their campaigns to reduce voter uncertainty and, hence, lead to a rise in the polls. Some candidates, for example, might be better communicators; some might have clearer campaign plans; others might try to be too much to too many and suffer on election day. The possibilities for campaign effects were many, and some scholars set off to suggest once more, as Lazarsfeld and his colleagues had done forty years earlier, that campaigns mattered. Nevertheless, this time the larger theoretical construct was clear: campaigns mattered because issues mattered in elections.

The marked progress of this line of research, however, did not lead scholars interested in campaign effects to investigate these matters theoretically. What emerged from the decades of work on voting behavior and the rebirth of campaign studies was a proliferation of research, often without clear theoretical mooring. The most prodigious area has been the study of advertising (Ansolabehere and Iyengar 1996; Finkel and Geer 1998; Geer 2000; Kahn and Kenney 1999a; West 1997; Freedman and Goldstein 1999; see Lau et al. 1999 for a complete list of citations). In addition, media studies have been numerous (Patterson 1993; Paletz 1999; Sparrow 1999; Cook 1999; Page 1996; Hetherington 1996). Debates (Hart and Jarvis 1997), campaign events (Holbrook 1996; Shaw 1999, 2000), and candidate discourse (Hart 2000; Vavreck 2000; Spiliotes and Vavreck 2000) have also received attention from scholars.

These discrete analyses, however, have failed to start from or synthesize a theory about how and why campaigns affect voters. Furthermore, they have mainly been narrow in their search for campaign effects. Even researchers investigating the role of information have overlooked campaign interactions between candidates and voters that are not easily captured by survey methods or content analyses. The study of campaigns needs two elements in its new research agenda: (1) theoretical motivation to guide the analyses and (2) a broader conception of campaign stimuli from which to search for effects.

A THEORY OF CAMPAIGN EFFECTS

Researchers interested in voting have always suspected that campaigns mattered. After all, elections are the mechanism that connects those who govern to those who are governed; campaigns, presumably, are about how the governed learn what their governors might do if elected. However, the mere existence of campaigns does not make them important to voters, and the fact that candidates and journalists behave as if campaigns mattered is not enough to sustain a serious line of academic inquiry into their supposed effects. As a result, scholars must ask: why do we suspect that campaigns matter? To answer that question, we must turn back to the literature on voting behavior to find a theory of campaign effects.

The spatial model (Downs 1957) seems a good place to start since it is among the simplest theories of voting. Under certain assumptions, the spatial model yields important insights into the importance of campaigns.[3] The model assumes that voters prefer what they know to what they do not know (voters are risk-averse), and that voters have policy positions which they know with certainty and that candidate positions removed from voters' preferred positions (in absolute terms) are increasingly less appealing to voters.

Interestingly, the spatial model allows voters' perceptions of candidates' positions on issues to be unclear. As voters compare candidates' policy positions to their own preferred position on an issue, they take into account how sure they are about where the candidate stands on that issue. Because of the assumptions of the model, uncertainty about candidates' positions makes the candidate less appealing to a voter. This outcome is a direct result of the risk-aversion assumption—we prefer what we know to what we do not know; as a result, candidates who are vague and ambiguous are punished at the polls.

Candidates can affect how confident voters are about their policy positions by simply talking about their issue positions in campaigns. Therefore, the model suggests that campaigns can matter because candidates can influence voters' preferences through their campaign discourse about specific positions. This latter assumption, of course, has clear implications for future research in the subfields of political communication and electoral behavior.

The 2000 New Hampshire primary presented a good opportunity to test this theoretical prediction. As George W. Bush campaigned around the country calling himself a "compassionate conservative," voters became increasingly confused about what that phrase actually meant. A *Washington Post* reporter (Milbank 2000) writes, "Once more the compassionate conservative, Bush gushes . . . about 'hope in people's hearts,' a 'universal call to love one's neighbor' and 'miracles of renewal.' 'I'm a uniter, not a divider,' Bush says for possibly the millionth time. His 'compassionate conservatism' theme, a vague but pleasant message that got him through the early primary process [disappeared] . . . 'Somehow,' says a top Bush advisor, 'we lost our mojo.'"

Meanwhile, John McCain was navigating the Granite State taking position after position on virtually any issue voters or reporters asked him to discuss. His "Straight Talk Express" bus tour was designed to capitalize on the fact that he was willing to speak openly about anything, even detailed public policy. Speaking about the bus, a *Baltimore Sun* reporter (Gamerman 2000) writes, "It has attracted scads of free press—plenty of it favorable—created an image of accessibility and lent the campaign a hit-the-highway independence that

matches the message. A ride on the bus is de rigueur for the big names in journalism . . . the media Pooh-Bahs like the cozy familiarity of the bus, and for
impassioned voters, a glimpse of the vehicle itself seems to be enough."

Bush's vague strategy seemed to fail him in early stages of the primary
process while McCain's open strategy had positive effects. This anecdotal evidence supports the notion that voters like policy information about candidates. What impact did Bush's failure to debate in New Hampshire's first
town hall have on his ratings among voters? How did it affect how much voters knew about him in terms of policy? Did McCain's 117 town hall meetings
really solidify his victory? What kind of an effect did actually meeting John
McCain have on how much voters know about his politics? These are the
kinds of questions campaign scholars should be asking in the years ahead in
light of theoretical predictions about issue uncertainty.

Most of the studies that have investigated the impact of informational clarity on campaign effects have used individual-level survey data describing
where voters place candidates on important issues. Very little has been done
to investigate how voters gather this important information (except to note
that the media is an important conduit for the delivery of candidate discourse
in campaigns). Certain types of campaign activities, however, might be better at delivering this information than others. By looking deeper into the
campaigns—at activities like phone banks, direct mailings, town hall meetings and other forms of direct voter contact—we may be able to learn more
about how voters learn about candidates' specific policy positions. We may
also be able to compare these types of information-disseminating activities
to others that we have long studied, such as news and paid advertising.

AN APPLICATION OF THE THEORY: CANDIDATE CONTACTS

The study of primaries is well suited to test some of these hypotheses about
different kinds of campaign effects. Analyses of primaries, however, are not
new to voting behavior (Polsby 1983; Bartels 1988; Geer 1989; Norrander
1988, 1993; Abramowitz 1989). The proliferation of primaries in the 1970s
was accompanied by an increase in studies about them (and those who participated in them), but scholarly attention to primaries has dropped off since
most of the initial works in this area were published, even though primary
elections provide an abundant variety of activities and effects.[4]

Primary elections provide a unique and fertile opportunity to investigate
voting behavior because the influence of party identification is (usually) held
constant in these intraparty contests, although the increase in open and blan-
ket primaries now affects the impact of party identification in a new way.[5]
The New Hampshire primary presents a special opportunity for voting behavior analysts in that (1) its "first in the nation status" holds at bay the in-

fluence of electoral momentum and (2) there are often a good number of viable candidates.

Primaries also provide the opportunity to contextualize the study of candidate behavior and voting behavior in meaningful ways. From a researcher's vantage point, the contained geographic area of most primaries makes collecting data on elite behavior, news content, independent groups, advertising, direct mail, phone banks, and candidate behavior in general much more feasible. If one wants to know how candidate contact affects learning about issues, the small-state primary is an ideal setting in which to work.

DIRECT VOTER CONTACT

One particularly compelling aspect of state-by-state primary elections is the opportunity for voters to meet candidates personally. A famous story about the New Hampshire primary tells the tale of a voter who can't make a vote choice. "How will you vote?" a pollster asks her. She replies, "I don't know, I've only met each candidate three times." Such stories about voters dutifully gathering information in order to make a vote choice are abundant in New Hampshire. In fact, a colleague of mine got a personal phone call in his office from a sitting United States senator who wanted to "chat with him" until he was convinced to get out and vote for Al Gore. Retail politics, or candidate contact, is a signature New Hampshire political trademark.[6] One might imagine that this kind of political experience is more intense than the typical campaign experience of hearing about the candidate on the news. Up close and personal campaigning should generally provide voters with more information about candidates than other types of campaigning. Thus, I investigate here whether this kind of up close and personal politicking has any impact on voters' favorability ratings of the candidates and on their uncertainty about candidates. Data from the 1996 New Hampshire primary can help to answer this question.[7] Does meeting a candidate directly affect voters' opinions of the candidate in 1996?[8] The results are presented in table 6.1.

Table 6.1. Favorability Ratings Controlling for Contact

	Did Not Meet Candidate	Met Candidate	Total
Unfavorable	32.48	30.31	32.36
Neutral	41.85	17.11	40.52
Favorable	25.67	52.58	27.12
Total	100	100	100

Notes: $N = 8,989$. Pearson chi-square(2) = 192.4474 Pr = 0.000. Cell entries are percents of voters in each category.

The answer to this question appears to be a resounding yes.[9] Among voters who met candidates during the primary, 52 percent had favorable ratings of the candidates they met; by way of comparison, only 25 percent of voters who had not met a candidate had favorable ratings. Table 6.1 details that the shift to favorable opinions among voters who meet candidates seems to be coming from voters who would otherwise have neutral ratings, as is evidenced by the fact that the percentage of voters with unfavorable ratings is similar regardless of whether or not the voter was contacted (32 percent v. 30 percent). The most striking finding from table 6.1 is the comparison between the neutral opinion categories. Among those who met a candidate, only 17 percent felt neutral about the candidate; compare this to those who did not meet a candidate, of which 41 percent had ambivalent feelings. Candidate contact does appear to influence overall ratings of the candidates—possibly moving people from the neutral category to the favorable category.

In terms of uncertainty about the candidates, I predicted that voters who had contact would be more certain about the candidates. In this survey, respondents were asked to give up to five open-ended responses to a question asking them what came to mind when they thought of a specific candidate. Of some interest is the fact that no one in the sample gave five comments about any of the candidates. As shown in table 6.2, the highest number of comments delivered was four—and the average number of comments made was 2.5. I assume here that fewer comments correlate with higher uncertainty about the candidate, and test for whether meeting the candidate increased the number of things that voters could say about that candidate when asked.

Once again, meeting a candidate translates into an ability to say more things about that candidate—an indirect reduction in uncertainty. Among voters who did not meet the candidates, there is a steady drop-off in the ability (or desire) to say things about the candidates when pressed. The plurality of voters who did not meet candidates offered no comments about those

Table 6.2.   Number of Open-Ended Comments Controlling for Contact

	Did Not Meet Candidate	Met Candidate	Total
0	39.86	10.01	38.27
1	23.56	27.05	23.75
2	20.41	27.05	20.72
3	9.99	20.08	10.53
4	6.18	16.60	6.73
Total	100	100	100

Notes: N = 8,989. Pearson chi-square(2) = 236.5134 Pr = 0.000. Cell entries are percents of voters in each category.

candidates (nearly 40 percent of noncontact voters had nothing to say). In contrast, most voters who did meet a candidate could say at least one, and often two, things about that candidate (54 percent of voters who met a candidate could say either one or two things about the candidate they met). Thirty-six percent of contacted voters could say three or four things about the candidate they had contact with versus 15 percent of voters who had no contact. Meeting the candidate appears to deliver some information to voters they do not otherwise get. That is, a high dose of political information about a specific candidate may well reduce voter uncertainty about that candidate.[10]

We can also use these data to learn a little bit about what kind of information candidate contact provides. By content analyzing the open-ended responses, it is possible to determine whether those who met the candidates were saying qualitatively different things about those candidates compared to those who did not meet them. Table 6.3 presents these results as they appear in Vavreck, Spiliotes, and Fowler (1999).

The list of things voters say about the candidates looks relatively similar regardless of whether they had direct contact.[11] In the case of Pat Buchanan, however, voters who met him talked more about his issue positions (24 percent of the comments were about issues) than voters who did not meet him (18 percent). For voters who met Lamar Alexander, comments on his issue

Table 6.3.   Impact of Meeting Candidate on Open-Ended Comment

	Met Candidate	Did Not Meet Candidate
Dole	1. Experience/Ability (26.35%) 2. Right Track/Wrong Track (16.89%) 3. Personality/Character (16.49%)	1. Experience/Ability (23.96%) 2. Personality/Character (17.36%) 3. Right Track/Wrong Track (15.23%)
Buchanan	1. Issues (23.65%) 2. Ideology/Party (21.18%) 3. Personality/Character (18.72%)	1. Ideology/Party (27.29%) 2. Personality/Character (19.91%) 3. Issues (18.58%)
Forbes	1. Issues (31.56%) 2. Experience/Ability (19.26%) 3. Right Track/Wrong Track (15.98%)	1. Issues (29.07%) 2. Experience/Ability (19.38%) 3. Background/Qualifications (16.78%)
Alexander	1. Experience/Ability (22.50%) 2. Issues (18.75%) 3. Personality/Character (17.08%)	1. Experience/Ability (16.98%) 2. Personality/Character (16.11%) 3. Campaign Characteristics (15.99%)

Note: Cell entries are percents of total mentions that fall into each category (top three listed).

positions were the second most prevalent topic; for voters who did not meet him, issue discussion was not among the top three topics mentioned.

INDIRECT VOTER CONTACT

There are other forms of contact about which scholars know very little, especially as they relate to voter uncertainty. Those other ways might include slightly less direct forms of candidate contact—for example, direct mail or phone calls to voters during campaigns. How do these types of contact influence citizens' favorability and uncertainty? Tables 6.4 and 6.5 itemize mail and telephone contact ratings from voters.

Just as with direct contact and favorability, these indirect forms of contact produce the same increase in affinity for the candidate from whom a person has received a phone call or piece of mail. Among voters who received direct mail from a candidate, favorability ratings were 20 percent higher (24 to 44 percent). A similar increase (26 to 46 percent) is seen among those who received a phone call from a campaign. As before, and in the case of mail and phone calls, the movement toward a favorable rating seems to be coming from voters who had neutral ratings of the candidates. The unfavorable ratings hold steady at roughly 32 percent.

In the interest of parsimony, I will not present the results for the relationship between the number of open-ended comments and indirect contact, but I can report that the same trend holds—voters who experience *any* kind of contact can say *more* things about the candidates who contact them.

There are actually two possible conclusions that can be drawn from these brief, descriptive tables. Either contact really does affect voters in desirable ways or the candidates are doing a terrific job of targeting their supporters. Indeed, the causal order in these relationships may be unclear. For example, one might conclude based on the above data that receiving phone calls about Bob Dole increases voters' knowledge about him. On the other hand, one might conclude that the Dole campaign calls only

Table 6.4.   **Candidate Mail and Favorability Ratings**

	No Mail	*Recieved Mail*	*Total*
Unfavorable	32.5	31.39	32.36
Neutral	42.85	24.04	40.52
Favorable	24.65	44.57	27.12
Total	100	100	100

Notes: N = 8,989. Pearson chi-square(2) = 228.6406 Pr = 0.000. Cell entries are percents of voters in each category.

Table 6.5.   Candidate Calls and Favorability Ratings

	No Call	*Recieved Call*	*Total*
Unfavorable	32.38	32.03	32.36
Neutral	41.59	21.77	40.52
Favorable	26.03	46.20	27.12
Total	100	100	100

Notes: N = 8,989. Pearson chi-square(2) = 113.8027 Pr = 0.000. Cell entries are percents of voters in each category.

people who are likely supporters (and have neutral ratings) and who may already know a lot about Dole. In the latter scenario, the increased knowledge about Dole is the *cause* of the contact, not the *effect* of it. Controlling for this kind of influence was our mission in another work (Vavreck, Spiliotes, and Fowler 1999) and looking at these internal factors proved fruitful (see note 10).

Either way the relationship works, it is interesting to speculate about what this means in terms of McCain's rise in 2000. Given that much of his support came from Independent (nondeclared) voters and that he held 117 town hall meetings in the state, the findings from 1996 suggest that McCain's campaign could have targeted those undeclared voters and, once "contact" was made, the targeted voters' favorability ratings and knowledge about McCain went up. In other words, the data suggest that it is likely that being in New Hampshire so often actually helped McCain at the polls, while Bush's absence from the state may have hurt him.

WHERE WE ARE GOING

Campaigns can matter—or so the spatial model suggests—especially in terms of how much uncertainty voters have about candidates' policy positions. This preliminary attempt to investigate whether old-fashioned, traditional forms of campaigning can help voters learn about candidates' positions suggests that direct and indirect forms of candidate contact may indeed assist voters in assessing their policy preferences. Quite clearly, we learn more about candidates when they come into our homes (and when we cannot change the channel on them) and when we go to meet them in our communities. These suggestive findings, however, lead to a more expansive research agenda concerning candidate discourse in campaigns, an agenda that is directly relevant to any question about how much voters learn about candidates.

Voters cannot learn what candidates do not tell them. If candidates do not take positions on issues during campaigns, if they provide little clarity about what they believe and why, it is not surprising that voters will have high levels of uncertainty about candidates. Even as the spatial model predicts that positional clarity on the part of candidates can help them electorally, candidates may believe that ambiguity is still the best strategy (since it allows the candidate to be "all things to all people"). Clearly, no candidate can win an election without taking any positions on issues, but it takes careful research to determine *how much* ambiguity and clarity a campaign can afford.

This type of research requires more than content analyses of campaign rhetoric. It also requires information on the frequency of campaign communication (especially in terms of advertising buys) and may even be best served by participant observation techniques or in-depth interviews with candidates and consultants during campaigns. The difficulty, of course, is that candidates and consultants often do not want to talk with researchers during elections and, after the elections, the observations are not as valuable (hindsight being 20/20).

The final step in this new research agenda is connecting the behavior of candidates in campaigns (the variation in clarity and ambiguity across candidates, elections, and years) to changes in voting behavior, with specific attention to voters' levels of uncertainty. From this type of work, we are likely to gain practical insight into what kinds of candidates or campaigns are "better" for voters (that is, which provide more issue information). These findings will speak directly to the campaign reform agenda actively afoot in the United States today.

Theoretically, we are likely to discover how well the spatial model explains the behavior of candidates in campaigns (we have already examined it in terms of voting behavior). By linking the two sets of data (candidate and voting behavior), we may learn how well the spatial model is able to predict changes in voting behavior associated with nuanced changes in candidate behavior. If the model fails to explain candidate behavior and seems to have no bearing on whether candidates win elections, more theoretical work will be called for, with particular attention paid to the assumptions underlying the model in its original formulation.

The future of voting behavior is surely as rich as its past, as scholars begin to use various methodologies and data (in-depth interviews, snowball samples of elites, participant observation of candidates and journalists, textual analyses of campaign discourse, information on advertising content and frequency) to supplement the attitudinal measures often found in conventional survey analyses. These multimethod, abundantly contextual components can only increase our systematic knowledge of voting behavior. I believe strongly that if we want to know how campaign discourse affects voters, we must roll up our sleeves and get out among the candidates, journalists, and citizens, watching and listening to them. Only then can we understand the underlying beliefs and behaviors suggested in previous survey work. More detailed, more contextual knowledge can help us design surveys that will be more sensitive to the subtle forces informing people's political attitudes. Even more importantly, it may suggest new ways of designing campaigns so that more people know more about the candidates on election day.

NOTES

I thank my coauthors Linda L. Fowler and Constantine J. Spiliotes for shaping my interest in the effects of retail politics and allowing me to preview a small portion of our joint work in this chapter. I appreciate the efforts of Linda L. Fowler and Tami Buhr in gathering these data and making them available. I must also thank Daron R. Shaw and Bartholomew Sparrow for helpful comments on this chapter. Finally, for his curiosity and enthusiasm about my work, and his generosity in sponsoring a conference for junior scholars from which I benefited greatly, I thank Roderick P. Hart.

1. For an excellent review and interpretation of the history of voting behavior research to date, see chapter 1, "A Subjective History of Voting Research," in Bartels (2000b).

2. Generally speaking, utility maximization implies that given a choice among alternatives, voters or consumers will select the option that maximizes their return on some previously specified dimension.

3. Those assumptions are: Voters have quadratic utility functions, are utility maximizers, and that preferences can be expressed with a Euclidean distance measure.

4. This is perhaps because the last National Election Study primary election survey was done in 1988.

5. The opportunity for out-partisans to vote in the other party primary could provide new tests for strategic or sophisticated voting hypotheses.

6. Direct candidate contact is defined not only as a personal meeting but also as attending a candidate's rally or political meeting.

7. These data were collected by Dartmouth College and WMUR television during the 1996 election and were generously made available by Linda Fowler and Tami Buhr. For further details about these data and survey design, see Vavreck, Spiliotes, and Fowler (1999).

8. For the purposes of these analyses, the effects of candidate contact are constrained across all candidates. Thus, meeting a candidate means meeting any candidate from 1996. The effect of meeting a candidate is always matched up with the appropriate candidate's favorability rating or open-ended comments. It was necessary to constrain the effects in this way because there were simply not enough voters meeting many of the candidates. In other words, variation on the contact variable would have been quite low for some candidates in the survey.

9. The obvious endogeneity between how much you like a candidate (or how much you know about a candidate) and whether you go to meet him (or he comes to meet you) is not lost on me. In another work (Vavreck, Spiliotes, and Fowler 1999), I have described the endogeneity issues in detail and used two-stage least squares to

estimate endogenous probit models on contact and favorability; and on contact and uncertainty. The results are robust to this appropriate control.

10. While the theory specifically talks about issue information, this table presents results for issue and trait information as the results show more interesting differences among contacted versus noncontacted voters. Very few voters actually volunteer explicit issue information in the open-ended format.

11. It would have been helpful in this regard if the data had differentiated among the different "issues" that people listed for each candidate. Not having access to the original raw data limits my ability to distinguish these categories any further.

7

Declining Trust and a Shrinking Policy Agenda: Why Media Scholars Should Care

Marc J. Hetherington

"Trust" Most Important Consideration for New Hampshire Voters in Republican and Democratic Primaries

—Gallup Poll, February 1, 2000

As the above headline from a Gallup Poll news release suggests, the degree to which people trust or distrust political figures is critical to understanding political outcomes. While this particular reference is to the trustworthiness of specific candidates running for president, general trust in government is important as well. Indeed, that voters put such stress on candidates' trustworthiness perhaps reflects how untrustworthy they view the government. In the public's view, it might take someone like Frank Capra's Mr. Smith, an individual imbued with the morals of a Scout leader, to tame Washington's scandal-ridden mess.

Trust in government is a concept that has often attracted the attention of political communication researchers. Beginning with Michael Robinson's (1976) video-malaise argument, scholars have focused on the role the media play in undermining political trust, or, put another way, in creating political cynicism. A sampling of scholarly work in political communication from just the last decade highlights this concern. Citing an overly negative reporting style, Thomas Patterson (1993, 22) suggests in *Out of Order* that "[a] number of unfavorable developments in recent years have eroded the public's faith in its political leadership. Yet there can be no doubt that the change in the tone of election coverage has contributed to the decline in the public's confidence." In *The Spiral of Cynicism*, Capella and Jamieson (1997) argue that the media's use of strategy-oriented coverage encourages the electorate to view all politicians as self-interested. They present an army of results, almost all of which implicate the news media in creating a cynical environment. "If any conclusion is supported by the pattern of findings, it is that strategy frames for news activate cynicism" (159).

In *Seducing America*, Hart's (1994) explanation for Americans' cynical feelings about politics moves beyond the news media to the nature of television itself. Television, he argues, has changed the language we use to talk about politics and not for the better: "Each day, television presents us with an infinite set of pigments for painting politics black" (22). Worse yet, it does so in a way that makes us feel good about feeling bad. "Being cynical also means that I am articulate, that I can give voice to the incongruities of life, that I can speak of multiple things simultaneously. Ultimately, of course, being cynical means that I am media-savvy" (81). As a result, these more cynical feelings are hard to shake because people do not want to shake them.

Missing almost completely from this work, indeed missing from almost all empirical political communication research, is whether or not increasing political cynicism has broader implications. Cynicism sounds bad, but does it matter? Admittedly, quantifying cynicism has proven elusive (Lodge and Tursky 1979; Muller and Jukam 1977), but the dominant strain in the literature is that cynicism is a ritualistic reaction to the common themes of current politics (Citrin 1974). Besides, even as trust measures continue to plummet, elections continue to occur regularly, presidents continue to send the military to faraway places like Kuwait and Bosnia with little public recrimination, and, even in the angry 1990s, Bill Clinton achieved the highest second-term approval ratings of any president in the survey era despite his personal foibles.

In fact, a report from the Pew Research Center (1998) entitled "Deconstructing Distrust" concluded that "It is difficult to pinpoint the specific negative behavioral or attitudinal consequences of distrust. It has not diminished Americans' sense of patriotism, nor has it created a climate of opinion that is conducive to acceptance of illegal anti-government activities. . . . For the most part, Americans remain open-minded about government" (12–13).

While media scholars express much dismay about political cynicism and distrust, they have been hard-pressed to find evidence that growing cynicism matters. On its face, trust in government seems like an important concept. For scholars to express so much concern about it, however, we need some reason to motivate this work beyond that trust *ought* to be important. In this chapter, I provide a theoretical argument and empirical evidence that the concerns raised by political communications researchers are not unfounded. We do, however, need to be careful about where we search.

SOME EVIDENCE THAT TRUST MATTERS

Because political elites characteristically try to maximize their political advantage, observing what themes they think will move public opinion is a good starting place for research. Importantly, elites often choose words that imply the significance of political trust. For example, public support for health care reform was extraordinarily high in the months preceding and immediately succeeding Bill Clinton's election in 1992. Opponents, however, managed to turn opinion against the reform effort. With their "Harry and Louise" ads, the insurance industry, in particular, targeted public fear about the government administering a large new bureaucracy.

Of course, people do not generally fear things they trust, which suggests that the concerns raised about new federal responsibilities were intended to tap the public's lack of faith in government. Given the risk-averse nature of human beings (Kahneman and Tversky 1979), raising the specter of fear is often an effective strategy. In the end, public opinion about Clinton's health care plan soured, allowing opponents to defeat his initiative easily.

In addition, when candidates run their campaigns, they frequently invoke themes designed to tap Americans' flagging trust in government. Observing eighteen individual congressional campaigns, Fenno (1978) found that, in trying to build constituent trust, sitting members of Congress often attacked the institution. Antigovernment rhetoric was also at the core of the 2000 presidential campaign, particularly John McCain's. The popularity of outsiders, insurgents, and reformers suggests that such rhetoric resonates well with the public. Even the sitting vice president at the time (Al Gore) attempted to cast himself as an outsider to some degree. It should come as no surprise, then, that anti-Washington rhetoric was the modal appeal used in senatorial campaign advertisements between 1988 and 1996 (Globetti 2000). Such rhetoric also comes with a cost. In addition to priming people to think about political races in terms of trust, anti-Washington appeals actually generate even further political distrust (Globetti and Hetherington 2000).

Although this reasoning makes sense, it is a departure from how political trust has been treated by many scholars heretofore. Studies examining trust in the mid to late 1960s and 1970s attempted to explain its steep decline. In the social science vernacular, these scholars and their successors treated trust as a dependent variable and tried to see what caused it and why it often varied from situation to situation. Such a focus has two problems. First, although understanding what caused the change is important, political trust should, logically speaking, occur at the same time as, or prior to, many of the opinions and behaviors that scholars used to explain it. For instance, is public dissatisfaction with the president a cause of declining political trust or is a lack of political trust a cause of dissatisfaction with the president? In fact, both are true (Hetherington 1998).

Second, by treating trust as an outcome rather than a cause, scholars unintentionally rendered it somewhat unimportant. If political trust doesn't affect anything, why bother understanding its surges and declines in the first place? Obviously, by confronting the problems of causal ordering, the effects of political trust become clear. Trust does, in fact, have a wide-ranging impact on the American polity. For one thing, it affects the size and content of the public policy agenda.

WHY POLITICAL TRUST SHOULD MATTER

A simple analogy about professors and their research assistants helps illustrate why trust should affect people's political opinions and behaviors. Professors who have little trust in their assistants will, on average, assign them menial work like copying articles and inputting data. In contrast, professors who have a moderate amount of trust in their assistants will ask them to analyze articles and gather new evidence. Finally, those with high levels of trust in their assistants will allow them to analyze findings and coauthor papers. That is, the amount of trust profoundly affects behavior. The same logic applies to a range of interpersonal interactions. If you trust your neighbors, you will be more comfortable lending them money or allowing them to supervise your children than if you do not trust them. While your trust may not be justified 100 percent of the time, you will, at a minimum, make different decisions than if Charles Keating or Hannibal Lecter were living next door. In both cases, trust affects the range of duties and responsibilities assigned.

Although political trust and interpersonal trust are distinct concepts, the same theoretical dynamics should hold in the political realm. If people do not trust the government, they will be less inclined to let it near their money and their kids. This should be particularly true when the government proposes programs that impose costs but do not provide direct benefits in return. When people send their tax dollars to Washington, they have little personal experience with the people or institutions that will spend it. In the case of programs that redistribute income, moreover, most taxpayers will not receive money or services in return. Trust is, therefore, necessary for people to accept these arrangements.

Research in psychology and economics also underscores the importance of trust in shaping behavior and decision making. Psychologists have found that trust is an important element in reducing "transaction costs" and encouraging sociability (for a review, see Kramer 1999). For example, when organizations and workers possess assets that are difficult to quantify but may be mutually enriching, trust between the two can facilitate their exchange (Uzzi 1997). In addition, by encouraging sociability, trust encourages the "cooperative, altruistic, and extra-role behavior in which members of a social community engage, that enhance collective well being and further the attainment of collective goals" (Kramer 1999, 575).

From an information-processing perspective, attitudes must be accessible if they are to influence other attitudes or inform behaviors (for example, Fischhoff, Slovic, and Lichtenstein 1980). Quite clearly, the present political media environment should make trust very "accessible." Television news, the public's most important information staple, is disproportionately negative (Patterson 1993). Regular features like the *Fleecing of America, Reality Check,* and *Your Money, Your Choice,* all of which uncover some form of government waste or malfeasance, cut to the core of what political trust means.[1] The tendency of reporters to treat politics like a game only encourages people to question the motives of those in the political world (Capella and Jamieson 1997).

For those who avoid political news, anti-Washington messages are pervasive elsewhere in the media. A recent Pew Foundation study reports that better than 10 percent of Americans say that they receive at least some political information from late-night talk shows, and close to half of those under thirty do so as well (Pew Foundation 2000). Those turning to these and other pop culture outlets find talk show hosts like Jay Leno and David Letterman constantly questioning the ability and ethics of those in political life. Rarely, if ever, do they make positive references about politicians or the government. Although these portrayals are often very entertaining, they will, at best, serve to keep people's trust considerations at the tops of their heads, and, at worst, further undermine public confidence.

Finally, political trust is attractive as an explanation for other political opinions and behaviors because it is easy to use. Given that most Americans lack political expertise, they are unlikely to know the intricacies of policy proposals, much less base their support on them. On the other hand, people need not know much about the minutiae of government to develop an impression of how much they trust it, and this impression may then act as a simple decision rule for supporting or rejecting governmental activity. All things being equal, if people perceive the architect of policies to be untrustworthy, they will reject its policies; if they consider it trustworthy, they will be more inclined to embrace those policies.

The Costs of Misspecification

The theoretical case for treating political trust as an explanatory variable is strong. Trust plays a central role in the contemporary political dialogue, and one need not be a member of the *Capitol Gang* to use it. By focusing on its determinants and ignoring its effects, however, scholars have generally ignored the potential implications of declining political trust. The focus of this chapter centers on one such implication: In ignoring the consequences of political trust, we have perhaps ignored the most compelling explanation for why the public policy agenda has shrunk markedly over the last forty years.

Even the most cursory comparison of the policy outputs of the 1960s and 1990s suggests a profound shift. Thinking about the 1960s, especially before the escalation in Vietnam, generally conjures up a time of great optimism about what government might accomplish. In the area of race relations, the 1960s saw the Civil Rights Act of 1964, the Voting Rights Act of 1965, and open-housing and accommodation laws with real strictures. To aid the poor and the elderly, Lyndon Johnson's Great Society gave us programs like Medicare and Medicaid and extended the reach of programs like AFDC. The federal government also made its first large-scale commitment to public education both in terms of funding public schools and in implementing new programs like Head Start. In the 1960s, the government actually went to war against poverty.

Contrast the outputs of the 1960s with those of the 1990s. More recent policy efforts have had more modest goals and often have emphasized transferring powers away from the federal government. Bill Clinton, for example, only found his stride when he started to think small rather than big, pursuing what advisor Dick Morris referred to as "bite-sized" initiatives. When Clinton tried to think big, as with comprehensive health care reform, he almost always failed.

One important exception, ironically, was the sweeping Welfare Reform initiative, which actually took power away from the federal government. Indeed, if the Clinton presidency has a lasting legacy beyond the economic prosperity of the 1990s, it will most likely be this particular dismantling of the welfare state. It was not Newt Gingrich but rather former McGovern operative Bill Clinton who proclaimed that the era of big government had ended. From a policy perspective, then, it is clear that things have changed substantially since the 1960s. Importantly, levels of political trust have declined as well (Orren 1997), suggesting that the two trends are causally linked.

ALTERNATIVE EXPLANATIONS

Of course, other variables might help explain this shrinking public policy agenda. The public's ideology seems to matter quite a lot in terms of state government outputs (Erikson, Wright, and McIver 1993; Hill and Leighley 1992). That is, states with more liberal constituencies tend to produce more liberal policies, while those with more conservative constituencies produce the reverse. Some might therefore argue that a truncated policy agenda results from a "right turn" in American national politics. Such an explanation has certainly received ample journalistic attention.

While this scenario seems plausible, there is in actuality very little evidence of a "right turn" (Stimson 1999; Mayer 1992). Longitudinal data from the National Election Study (NES) illustrate this point. Figure 7.1 shows

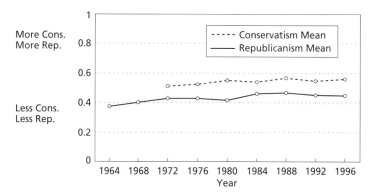

Figure 7.1.   Changes in Key Political Variables, Presidential Years, 1964–1996

changes in the mean score of the NES's seven-point liberal/conservative self-placement question, which I call conservatism, and its partisanship question, which I call Republicanism.[2] One won't find too many flatter lines in public opinion than these two. Although both partisanship and ideology have crept slightly to the right over the last thirty-five or forty years, the differences are not substantive. If one compares the beginning and ending points of the series, conservatism has increased by only about four percentage points and partisanship by eight. Such modest movement could not bring about the fundamental change in what the public wants or, more to the point, doesn't want, the federal government to do.

In addition to self-placement on a single liberal/conservative scale, I also examined people's self-placement on a range of different issues to see whether they suggested a right turn. That is, people might not be more inclined to identify themselves as conservatives because they reject such labels, but they might increasingly favor the more conservative position on questions about government services and spending, government guaranteed jobs, the proper role of women in society, and the like. The same five issue items that the NES asked in 1994 were also asked in the 1984 NES. The difference between the means is small but statistically significant in the *liberal* direction.

This brings me to a theoretical digression, but an important and often neglected one. When political scientists use cross-sectional data—data collected at a single point in time from a single group of respondents—they most often assume that an attitude has to be stable for it to be considered a cause of other attitudes and behaviors. Cross-sectional data provide no obvious temporal ordering to variables since all are measured at the same time. Thus, the best we can often do is to suggest that some are prior to (but not necessarily the cause of) other, less stable opinions.

For example, party identification's stability in the NES's 1956–1960 Panel Study was one of the primary reasons that scholars identified it as the most critical political attitude (Campbell et al. 1960). People who were Democrats in 1958 tended to be Democrats in 1960. Hence, even if scholars only had the 1960 data available, they could infer that a person's party identification, which was in place well in advance of the presidential election, caused him or her to vote for a given presidential candidate, rather than the reverse. Although others have shown a certain amount of interaction between party identification and vote choice (Fiorina 1981; Franklin and Jackson 1983), the stability of party identification strongly suggests its causal primacy.

Although useful, this emphasis on stability has important limitations. Absent stark changes caused by generational replacement (young people replacing older people), the distribution of variables that are stable on the individual level also tends to remain relatively stable on the group level. Static attitudes are very good at explaining other phenomena in a cross section, but if they do not change in the aggregate, they cannot tell us much about why other things change over time.

The reason for their failure brings to mind another old saw in data analysis: one cannot explain a variable with a constant. That is, if you want to understand why something important has changed, you cannot rely on things that haven't changed as explanations. In our present example, we have seen the policy agenda shrink substantially between the 1960s and the 1990s. Although it is true that those who are more conservative and Republican in a given cross-sectional survey are less supportive of government spending and policy innovation (see for example Jacoby 1994), figure 7.1 shows that the number of Republicans and conservatives has not increased substantially since the 1960s. Hence, ideology and partisanship cannot explain change in the policy agenda.

What we need to identify, then, is an attitude that is relatively stable within individuals, but one that has seen its distribution in the aggregate change substantially over time. Political trust is such a variable. Even during periods of dramatic aggregate change, it remained relatively stable for most individuals (Markus 1979). Indeed, Markus (1979) concludes that political trust's persistence on the individual level, despite the upheavals of the 1960s and 1970s, was perhaps his most striking finding. In addition, Krosnick (1991b) finds that, after correcting for measurement error, trust is at least as stable as all other major symbolic political attitudes (with the exception of partisanship). Even without correcting for measurement error, the correlation between trust for individuals measured one year and then measured again two years later (its test–retest correlation) compares favorably with test–retest correlations for variables such as conservatism, political efficacy, and a citizen's average self-placement on a range of issues. To the extent that political trust has changed on the individual level, almost all of it has been in the same direction, and this sizable deterioration is precisely what makes it interesting.

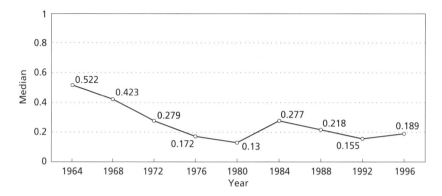

Figure 7.2.   **Change in Median Political Trust, Presidental Years, 1964–1996**

Figure 7.2 shows just how steep the drop has been. Compared with the four and eight percentage-point changes in partisanship and ideology, respectively, the median level of trust dropped by roughly 35 percent between the mid-1960s and mid-1990s.[3] Compared with most political attitudes, a change of this magnitude can only be considered an earthquake. Given the theoretical properties discussed above, these results suggest that declining political trust is a real contender as an explanation for the shrinking policy agenda.

POLITICAL TRUST AND THE PUBLIC POLICY AGENDA

When we consider the effect of political trust on the public policy agenda, we should consider both its indirect and direct effects. The indirect effect follows from previous scholarship. In trying to explain the causal dynamics between trust and other variables of normative importance (like feelings about the president and Congress), I posited and tested a mathematical model (Hetherington 1998). By taking into account a range of reciprocal relationships, I was able to demonstrate that, contrary to previous research, trust did more than simply reflect dissatisfaction with incumbent officeholders and political institutions. Instead, trust had an impact on evaluations of officeholders as well. In fact, trust had a larger effect on evaluations of both Ronald Reagan and Bill Clinton than vice versa.

This relationship is significant because levels of presidential support have important effects on the political process. Brody (1991), for example, observed that contemporary presidential approval ratings tend to peak ten to fifteen percentage points below where they did in the 1950s and early 1960s. Estimating a model of presidential approval using data from both the 1980s and 1990s and correcting for the post-1964 decline in trust, I found that political trust explained this ten to fifteen percentage-point difference. If I artificially raised trust back to its 1964 level, Reagan's second-term approval ratings were almost identical to Eisenhower's, and Clinton's first-term numbers approximated those of first-termer Johnson. In other words, it is declining political trust that makes presidents less popular today.

Trust, therefore, indirectly affects the scope of the public policy agenda through its effect on presidential approval. Neustadt (1960) helps us understand why. Lacking strong formal powers, the president's primary power is the power to persuade. When the public supports the president, this power increases, thus providing him more leeway with Congress and other elites. For example, when presidents need votes from key congressional members, they will have more success securing them if their personal popularity is high in certain congressional districts. Conversely, lower levels of approval will make it more difficult for a president to win key policy battles (Ostrom and Simon 1985).[4]

This discussion suggests that the simultaneous relationship between trust in government and presidential approval provides an indirect drain on how aggressive a president can be in pursuing policy goals. It also suggests further consequences. Less-popular presidents will get less done, which will lead to more political dissatisfaction, which will lead to less approval, and, ultimately, to even less policy innovation.

In addition to this indirect effect, trust in government should have a direct effect on the public's appetite for policy innovation, but only in certain cases. Trust is most necessary for policies from which Americans do not receive direct benefits but for which they are asked to pay. Not coincidentally, these are the only policies where public support has actually waned during this so-called—but wrongly identified—right turn, an era when declining trust has been most consequential.

TRUST AND SACRIFICES

It also seems reasonable that trust should have an impact on public support for programs requiring people to make sacrifices. In other words, trust's impact should be particularly influential for those policies conferring benefits on one group while imposing perceived or real costs on another. The group paying the costs does not realize a direct benefit from the policy and therefore has both less personal incentive to support it and little to no personal experience with which to evaluate it. For example, middle- and upper-income individuals will need to trust the government more if they are to support increased spending on food stamps and welfare. Similarly, white Americans will need more trust to support programs like affirmative action and other programs that explicitly assist racial minorities (Hetherington and Globetti

1999). Finally, all Americans will need trust to support foreign aid since no Americans directly receive such funds and few even directly witness where the money goes.

In contrast, support for policies that involve public goods, such as public schools, crime reduction, defense, and the environment, should require little or no trust. In the case of schools, crime, and the environment, even the distrustful can readily support spending or government involvement because, even if the benefit is discounted by poor administration, greater government involvement will likely provide at least some benefit to all. In the case of defense, the public could not hope to accomplish the task without the government, so the public has no choice but to tolerate losses.

Interestingly, a fault line in public support for spending falls almost exactly along these lines. While this fault line has been apparent for some time (see Free and Cantril 1968), the gulf has recently grown wider. Large majorities continue to support at least present levels of spending, if not increases, on *distributive* programs, despite the supposed "Republican Revolution" of 1994 and the ideological right turn that allegedly accompanied it. In contrast, the only areas where a large chunk of the American public thinks that spending ought to be cut is on *redistributive* issues or spending targeted toward racial minorities. The percentage of Americans who support cutting redistributive spending has also been increasing of late.

Figure 7.3 shows this graphically. Since 1984, the NES has asked people if they had a say in the federal budget whether they would increase, decrease, or keep spending the same on a range of items. I have graphed the percentage of people who choose the "decrease" option in several issue domains.

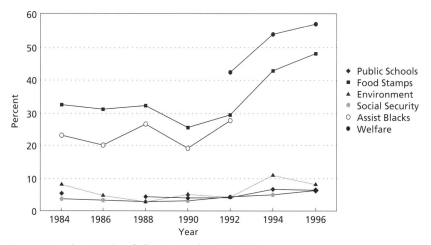

Source: American National Election Study, 1984–1996

Figure 7.3. Public Support for Decreasing Federal Spending, 1984–1996

First, note that Americans are much more likely to suggest decreasing spending on food stamps, welfare, and assistance to black Americans than they are to suggest decreasing spending on the environment, social security, and public schools. Second, note that only on the redistributive items has a greater percentage of Americans embraced spending cuts between 1984 and 1996.

These results are important for two reasons. First, table 7.1, which employs data from 1984–1996 as well, shows that conservatism on the individual level is negatively correlated with increasing spending in *all* these areas. That is, the more conservative a respondent is, the less supportive of additional spending the respondent becomes. On many occasions, these correlations are quite large for individual-level data. Hence, if the public were truly becoming more conservative, the correlations presented here suggest that support for spending, whether distributive or redistributive, should have decreased for all of the items. It has not. It has only decreased on redistributive issues. This further undermines conservatism as an explanation.

Second, and most important for my argument, table 7.2 shows that trust in government is positively correlated with support for several, but not all, of these spending programs. That is, the (more/less) trustful people become, the (more/less) they prefer to spend on these programs. Unlike conservatism, trust is only correlated with the spending domains, which figure 7.3 shows to have experienced a decrease in support for spending over time. So, for example, trust has a correlation of .10 or better nine times, and eight of those instances involve redistributive programs where people have to make sacrifices. Moreover, the one-to-one relationships between trust and these variables have been generally increasing over time. Specifically, trust's correlation with spending on food stamps nearly tripled during the 1990s, and its correlation with support for spending on welfare nearly doubled between 1992 and 1994.

These results are also compelling when we move outside the cross section and consider whether the direction of change in political trust over time

Table 7.1. Bivariate Pearson Correlations between Conservatism and Support for Spending on Various Programs

	1984	1988	1990	1992	1994	1996
To assist blacks	−.24	−.25	−.21	−.25	—	—
Food stamps	−.29	−.24	−.20	−.23	−.21	−.31
Foreign aid	—	—	−.08	—	−.12	−.11
Welfare	—	—	—	−.22	−.25	−.31
Public schools	−.26	−.23	−.16	−.19	−.27	−.28
Environment	−.21	−.14	−.17	−.21	−.28	−.31
Social Security	−.17	−.19	−.11	−.09	−.10	−.13

Source: American National Election Studies, 1984–1996.

Table 7.2.   Bivariate Pearson Correlations between Political Trust and Support for Spending on Various Programs

	1984	*1988*	*1990*	*1992*	*1994*	*1996*
To assist blacks[a]	.06	.09	.10	.09	—	—
Food stamps	−.05	.03	.05	.06	.11	.14
Foreign aid	—	—	.21	—	.17	.24
Welfare	—	—	—	.07	.13	.10
Public schools	.01	−.03	.02	.07	.07	.09
Environment	−.05	−.06	−.01	.02	.06	.04
Social Security	−.09	−.10	−.05	−.01	−.01	.01

Source: American National Election Studies, 1984–1996.
Note: In 1986, the NES asked only two of trust index's four components.
[a] Among Whites only

matches the direction of support for spending over time. Recall from figure 7.2 that trust declined between 1984 and 1996. Next, recall from figure 7.3 that support for redistributive spending has also declined during the same period. Hence, both the increase in the size of the correlation coefficients and a decline in trust coincide with a decrease in support for spending on food stamps, welfare, and assistance to black Americans.

Although these correlations are not enormous, they do suggest that trust will have an independent effect even after proper statistical controls are implemented, and, in fact, they do (see Hetherington and Hess 1998). Indeed, the effects are quite significant. Given the size of the changes in support for spending on food stamps, in particular, it is clear that more is at work here than just the effect of political trust. In all likelihood, some external event, perhaps Clinton's embrace of welfare reform, had an even larger impact. Of course, a Democratic president embracing welfare reform is also probably the result of his realization that the electorate has become much less trustful of government and thus less supportive of these programs.

In sum, if segments of the public have to make tangible sacrifices, whether it be tax dollars for programs that will not benefit them directly or privileged status on questions of race, they will need more trust in the government that administers these programs if they are to support them. These results, along with the results regarding trust and presidential approval, make clear that trust in government has both an indirect and a direct effect on policy innovation.

THE CONFUSION OF TRUST AND CONSERVATISM

Some may be tempted to conclude from these results that political trust is simply a more precise measure of ideology than the liberal–conservative continuum presented in figure 7.1. Skeptics might further suggest that a better measure of ideology is a respondent's mean position on an array of issues. I investigated these possibilities, finding that trust and ideology, however measured, are two very distinct concepts. For example, the correlation between trust and ideological self-placement over the 1984–1996 period is, on average, .057 points from zero.[5] If one substitutes the mean issue position on seven-point issue scales for ideological self-placement, its correlation with trust is also less than .10. In short, while the concepts are related to some degree, they are clearly not the same thing.

It is easy to confuse the policy goals of the distrustful and the conservative because both seem to want less government. My results, however, suggest there is a critical distinction to be made here. Whereas conservatives desire spending cuts across the board, distrust is only important on spending for programs with relatively small, often disliked constituencies. Hence, conservative politicians should be most successful when talking about spending cuts on redistributive programs, which should tap both distrust and conservatism. When conservatives move beyond redistribution, the electorate may not be sufficiently conservative in principle for them to rally much public support.

The Republicans' successes and failures in the mid-1990s are instructive in this regard. After the "Revolution" of 1994, the GOP maintained high levels of public support when they focused their efforts on areas like reforming Congress, cutting spending on social programs, and reforming welfare. In short, they were successful in areas where both trust and conservatism are important. When they moved to areas like eliminating the Department of Commerce and the Department of Education, however, they enjoyed less success. Although these latter positions were surely embraced by ideological conservatives, there were not enough of them to ensure success. When Gingrich and associates decided to shut down the government rather than compromise with the president on a budget, they sealed their own fate. By fighting an ideological war rather than one focused on improving the public perception of government, they demonstrated that they were not Mr. Smiths at all. They had violated people's expectations about how the government should work.

It is easy to understand why the Republicans misinterpreted their mandate. The "Contract with America" was both about reforming Congress and reducing the number and types of things government does. When talking about the latter, people, on average, tend to think about issues of redistribution rather than the general scope of government (Jacoby 1994). When the Republicans sought to implement their ideology, they moved beyond the true nature of their mandate. They have not done particularly well in a federal election since.

CONCLUSION

This research demonstrates that political communication researchers are clearly correct to be concerned about the effect the mass media have on public trust in government. Patterson (1993) identifies the late 1960s and early 1970s as the period when the news media turned from being skeptical about the motives of politicians to being cynical, causing presidential candidates and the government in general to receive far more bad news than good. Although the evidence of the connection between negative media and declining trust requires additional attention, the trends toward negative news and declining trust in government do coincide to some degree. Even if news consumption is not a direct cause of political cynicism, the present media environment, at a minimum, reinforces and activates cynicism (Capella and Jamieson 1997).

That our media play such a role is problematic. Political trust limits the range of policies those in government can pursue. While this particular relationship is surely of normative import, the public policy agenda is not the only thing that trust affects. I have shown elsewhere that trust in government has a sizable effect on presidential vote choice and third-party voting (Hetherington 1999), support for devolutionary policies (Hetherington and Nugent 2000), support for a range of racial policy preferences (Hetherington and Globetti 1999), and support for Congress as a political institution (Hetherington 1998). In addition, trust affects external efficacy (Miller, Goldenberg, and Erbring 1979) and thus voter turnout, at least indirectly.

Although this research agenda on trust has shown promise thus far, I believe the surface has only just been scratched. At the risk of being overly technical, I suggest that the most fertile direction for future research in this area centers on measurement. Quantifying concepts like "trust in government" is a daunting, but extraordinarily important, enterprise because, to the extent that variables are measured with error, their estimated effects on other attitudes and behaviors will be misunderstood. Given the well-known measurement problems in the trust scale as it is presently conceived, it is almost certain that I am underestimating its impact here. In addition, the fact that media researchers have uncovered only modest relationships between media usage and political trust may also result from measurement problems.

Conceptually, scholars have most often defined political trust as a general evaluation of how people think the government is doing, all of which depends on what they think government *should* be doing in the first place (Miller 1974). The measure that I use here, taken from the NES, is an average of responses to four questions: 1) how much do people think they can trust the government, 2) how much money do they think the government wastes, 3) how many people in government are crooked, and 4) do people perceive that the government is run for all people or for a few big interests.

How well do these measures approximate the concept of political trust? Many have persuasively argued that they have shortcomings (see for example, Lodge and Tursky 1979; Muller and Jukam 1977). While my research suggests that trust in government is related to important attitudes and behaviors, they may not get to the heart of institutional legitimacy. Witness, for example, the overwhelming level of support President George H. W. Bush had for the use of American military force in the Persian Gulf, even as political trust was at a low ebb. A public that viewed its institutions as increasingly illegitimate would surely have reacted much differently to the use of force in a faraway place. While I think my research suggests that the drop in political trust (as measured by the NES) is far more than "ritualistic," it provides us less insight on weightier issues like legitimacy.

Similarly, the word choice and format of these questions are problematic. While having a forty-year data series is a rare commodity in the study of political attitudes, the terms used in the questions are beginning to lose meaning. This is especially true of the word "crooked," which is used in one of the items. In addition, the fixed-choice options the questions provide limit the amount of variation that researchers might find in respondents' levels of trust. Perhaps questions that, for example, place "government run for a few big interests" and "government run for the benefit of all people" as two poles on a continuum would allow for finer distinctions. Surely, most ordinary Americans do not see the political world in the stark categories available to them in the present measures.

Given how well trust performs even in its less-than-optimal form, improving how it is measured could provide great rewards. Conceptually, trust has all the properties that someone studying political behavior could want. Having a general feeling about government does not require much expertise, so trust is an attitude that will be available to almost every American. Since references to trust in government are ubiquitous, moreover, the issue of trust will remain relevant for Americans who follow either politics or popular culture. It is not surprising, then, that trust has become an influential determinant of public opinion and political behavior. Indeed, if political behavioralists are interested in understanding why politics has changed fundamentally between the 1960s and the 1990s, one would be hard-pressed to find a better explanation than declining trust in government.

NOTES

1. Trust is a gut-level evaluation of government based on people's expectations about how the government ought to operate.

2. The NES started to ask the conservatism question only in 1972. I would not expect that conservatism would have changed radically between the mid-1960s and early 1970s.

3. The measure is the mean score of people's responses to four questions about the government in Washington. The exact wording is in the appendix.

4. Of course, not all presidents will use such leeway to implement more policy. A conservative like Ronald Reagan would tend to do the reverse.

5. The sign on the correlation differs by which party controls the White House. Given that trust mirrors the party of the president to some degree, the sign is positive when Republicans are in control and negative when Democrats are in control.

APPENDIX: MEASURING POLITICAL TRUST

People have different ideas about the government in Washington. These ideas don't refer to Democrats or Republicans in particular, but just to the government in general. We want to see how you feel about these ideas. For example:

1. How much of the time do you think you can trust the government in Washington to do what is right—just about always, most of the time, or only some of the time?

   Just about always
   Most of the time
   Some of the time

2. Do you think that people in government waste a lot of the money we pay in taxes, waste some of it, or don't waste very much of it?

   Not very much
   Some
   A lot

3. Would you say the government is pretty much run by a few big interests looking out for themselves or that it is run for the benefit of all the people?

   For the benefit of all
   Few big interests

4. Do you think that quite a few of the people running the government are crooked, not very many are, or do you think hardly any of them are crooked?

   Hardly any
   Not many
   Quite a few

8

Imagining Political Parties: A Constructionist Approach

Sharon E. Jarvis

What is the significance of the word *Democrat* in the United States? Or *Republican*? Or *Liberal* or *Conservative* or *Independent*? Are these labels descriptive or nebulous? Helpful or harmful? Important or trivial? In other words, what do these terms mean, and what does it matter when they are used to refer to elected officials, candidates, citizens, or voting blocs?

Political scientists have produced an impressive body of literature on American political parties, describing why they form and what they do, tracing them throughout history, and explaining their ideological perspectives. These scholars have conceptualized and measured parties in the United States and abroad, as well as theorized about them in explanatory, predictive, and normative ways. They have studied the role of the party in three places—in the government, as an organization, and in the electorate—and have both applauded and denigrated its role in the body politic. All the while, however, these researchers have left a critical avenue of partisanship unexplored: the ways in which parties are talked about and made sense of—parties as cast in political discourse.

As Murray Edelman (1977, 142) has written, people are more likely to experience the "language about political events rather than the events themselves." This statement is particularly relevant to political parties in the United States, for Americans are much more likely to be subject to the discourse of partisanship via candidate statements and media reports than to actually attend partisan meetings or fundraisers. Thus, to add to what is known about partisanship, I propose a new avenue of research: listening to how parties are constituted in political conversations. Specifically, this chapter addresses the fit between the field of political communication and constructivism, presents findings from a longitudinal content-analytic study focusing on the meanings of parties, and raises questions for future inquiry. In essence, I suggest that listening to the discourse of parties can both inform our understanding of these groups and reveal the priorities, tensions, and latent assumptions surrounding them. Given the centrality of these institutions at the turn of the twenty-first century—not to mention debates in the scholarly literature regarding party decline and resurgence—both endeavors seem important (see Bartels 2000a).

THE CONSTRUCTION OF PARTIES

To better understand political parties, this chapter advocates examining public communication practices, the primary way modern citizens become involved in public affairs. This chapter attempts to piece together how parties have been *constructed* in public discourse, a project inspired by a host of scholars, including Raymond Williams (1976), Richard Merritt (1966), Daniel Rodgers (1987), Celeste Condit and John Lucaites (1993), and, of course, Murray Edelman (1964, 1971, 1977). All of these researchers have analyzed the meanings of certain key words and symbols in political communication, noting how these terms have changed over time and influenced public life. As Condit and Lucaites assert, people "understand their lives together in large measure through the stories they tell about the past" (1993, 1) and whatever a certain term means, "it is necessarily a function of the interaction between its past and present usages for a particular rhetorical culture" (1993, 218).

This approach borrows from many disciplines. Key concepts from the fields of linguistics and sociolinguistics served as an initial springboard for this project, including the notions that (1) all languages change with time because the meanings of words expand, contract, and shift from their original meanings (Fromkin and Rodman 1974), and (2) language helps us understand our social situations (Berger and Luckmann 1966) and shape our personal thoughts (Kress and Hodge 1981).

Edward Sapir's work (see Whorf 1956) has been especially influential in this regard. He once argued that the structure of a culture's language determines the behavior and habits of thinking in that culture, observing that:

> Human beings do not live in the objective world alone, nor alone in the world of social activity as ordinarily understood, but are very much at the mercy of the particular language which has become the medium of expression for their society. It is quite an illusion to imagine that one adjusts to reality essentially without the use of language and that language is merely an incidental means of solving specific problems of communication or reflection. The fact of the matter is that the "real world" is to a large extent unconsciously built up on the language habits of the group. (134)

Political scientist Murray Edelman also expounded upon the impact of symbols in a political system, particularly in a polity that must make decisions. He argued that (1971, 65) "political events are largely creations of the language used to describe them," and that our understandings of political institutions rest on our beliefs or perceptions of them, whether or not those cognitions are accurate. In his work on poverty, for example, Edelman (1977) showed how "naming" can contribute to, or prevent, the creation of public policy by giving choices to politicians and the public. Specifically, when governmental elites introduce a phrase such as "the deserving poor" into a policy debate, new choices emerge. Should we help the "deserving" poor? What should be done with the "undeserving" poor (a concomitant rhetorical by-product)? Do both groups deserve our help? (Remember, of course, that assistance to the poor was not even a real political choice until the symbol of "deserving poor" entered the policy debate.) The very creation of a symbol for the *deserving* poor, concluded Edelman, encouraged (1) government to do nothing for millions of poor people (after verbally categorizing them as undeserving) and (2) impoverished citizens to regard other poor people as "undeserving" (thereby siding with governmental elites rather than identifying with those who shared their economic conditions).

Michel Foucault (1970) is another scholar who noted the controlling forces of language. For Foucault, each era has a distinct worldview or conceptual structure that determines the nature of knowledge in that period. He called the character of knowledge in a given epoch an *episteme* or *discursive formation*. In reviewing these concepts, Stephen Littlejohn (1989, 60) states that "the episteme, or way of thinking, is determined not by people, but by the predominant discursive structures of the day, and the vision of each age is exclusive and incompatible with those of other ages so that it becomes impossible for people in one period to think like those of another." While it would be difficult to empirically test this approach (indeed how might one operationalize something as nettlesome as a discursive formation?), Foucault raised a provocative question. If language systems are culturally determined, and if these systems predict our ways of thinking, the power elites helping to craft these systems have untold power over people's thoughts and actions.

Richard Merritt also underscores the importance of systematic attention to the conscious and subconscious treatment of political words. In his content analysis of community terms in colonial America, Merritt (1966, xiii) wrote that:

> the unconscious or latent structure of a message may even outweigh its manifest content. If, for instance, with the passage of time a Tory newspaper in colonial America such as the *Massachusetts Gazette*, devoted an increasing share of its space to news of the American colonies, or if it increasingly identified its readers as "Americans" rather than as "His Majesty's subjects" or even "colonists," we might say that, despite its pro-British point of view, the latent

content of the *Gazette* encouraged its readers to think of themselves as members of a distinctly American community and to turn their thoughts inward toward that American community.

Taken together, then, language is important because it helps individuals frame their thoughts, enables them to share ideas, encourages them to prefer certain understandings over others, and is often beyond their conscious control. Language, too, is more likely to touch American voters than other aspects of partisanship. For these reasons, it is a prime way to uncover meanings of party in the polity.

Traditionally, however, scholars in political science have hesitated to conduct such research, possibly because of a number of methodological objections: this work is largely descriptive, and therefore, nonfalsifiable; this research offers more research questions than hypotheses, and is therefore difficult to test; this research captures broad meanings and therefore cannot be neatly generalized to the individual citizen; and this research accepts ambiguity and multiple interpretations of symbols in the body politic and therefore violates positivistic assumptions about a measurable, objective reality. While these limitations might be viewed as a shortcoming of this project, a constructionist approach can lead to rich understandings and theoretical advancement that would escape conventional quantitative analyses because it invites attention to how meanings are mediated, constituted, interpreted, and challenged in the polity (Bennett 1993; Shapiro 1993). This perspective recognizes that even subtle linguistic cues can draw attention to some topics and displace other ways of thinking about issues and problems. Listening to how parties are discussed can reveal that the meanings of partisanship are unfolding, complex, and managed by an interplay of voices.

To employ a social scientific metaphor, this chapter encourages viewing language as an intervening variable in politics, one that introduces complexity into a design that objective scientists would prefer straightforward. Indeed, in the year 2000, a constructionist approach to political parties seems to be a good fit for a series of puzzles in the literature and in the polity, including: If parties are really weak, why have they not disappeared? If the party is really over, why do scholars and journalists revisit them in their analyses and news reports? Or, if party loyalty has disappeared, what can explain the limited number of Independent or third-party public officials? Listening to the meanings of party in discourse may shed new light on these questions.

This chapter now turns to provide an example of what a constructionist approach to the meaning of parties would look like, and presents a set of findings from an extensive content analysis conducted on partisan discourse between 1948 and 1996. This research was guided by three questions: (1) Why do American elites speak of political parties as they do? (2) What specific meanings have they assigned to parties across time and circumstance? (3) What are the consequences of those assignments?

This study utilizes the method of content analysis to examine how four sets of political elites (presidential candidates, print journalists, civics textbook authors, and U.S. congressional representatives) constituted parties over the past fifty years in discourse.[1] As Bennett (1993, 113) notes, several methodologies fit the constructionist approach, so long as they "search for general patterns" instead of lawlike relations among variables. To answer the study's research questions, I draw on data from the Campaign Mapping Project (CMP) directed by Roderick Hart of the University of Texas and Kathleen Hall Jamieson of the University of Pennsylvania.[2]

Six keywords have been chosen for the current analysis. They are *Democrat, Republican, Independent, Liberal, Conservative,* and *Party* (and their derivatives). The terms *Democrat, Republican,* and *Party* were obvious choices. As scholar Richard Weaver (1953) might say, these are the "ultimate" terms of partisanship. The terms *Liberal* and *Conservative* have been added to provide a broader understanding of the shifts in meaning surrounding partisanship. Clearly, there are important denotative and connotative distinctions between the terms *Liberal* and *Democrat* and between *Conservative* and *Republican*; the former word in each pairing refers to an ideological position while the latter regards a formal, organized political group. Because the terms *Liberal* and *Conservative* have come to be used as proxies for the parties (that is, the word *Liberal* was used regularly by Vice President George H. W. Bush in the 1988 presidential campaign), they have been included here to enrich the project. Additionally, the term *Independent* has been included in an attempt to measure support for third-party candidates as well as to be sensitive to patterns of "dealignment" in the American system (Burnham 1970).

Many party scholars agree that the two key jobs of the parties are to facilitate elections and to organize government (Sorauf and Beck 1988). Thus, I chose to analyze the discourse of partisanship in two moments: a *campaigning condition* (focusing on presidential campaign speeches and news coverage of those speeches) and a *governing condition* (focusing on debates on civil rights issues in the U.S. House of Representatives and civics textbooks).[3] Please see appendix A for a discussion of the sampling procedure and coding scheme.

MEANINGS OF PARTY

Given the size of the database and the nature of my questions, it makes sense to present this project's findings propositionally. After analyzing quantitative and qualitative patterns in the data, I found (with few exceptions) three predominant ways in which partisanship has been constituted: (1) parties have not disappeared, (2) parties have been constituted by elites *as elites*, and

(3) parties have not been interpreted in depth. Although these claims may appear modest, they invite critical inspection because they tell a hegemonic story of party in the U.S. political system, the uniform and stubborn ways in which four different sets of actors have discussed partisanship. Indeed, because of their constancy, these themes are central to an informed understanding of the meanings of parties in the United States.

Parties Have Not Disappeared

Simple frequencies from the Campaign Mapping Project data reveal that elites have not stopped talking about parties. Prior to sampling this data, I found that the word *Democrat* appeared more often in campaign speeches in 1996 than in earlier years (see figure 8.1), and that newspapers used the terms *Democrat, Republican,* and *Party* as frequently in 1996 as in the 1950s (see figure 8.2). Moreover, simple frequencies from the debates also show that legislators used more tokens per total words in the 1995 congressional debate than in any other year examined in this study.[4] Given concern about the vitality of parties at the close of the twentieth century, what accounts for the persistence of such tokens? I advance a simple answer: parties may be far more important than is commonly realized.

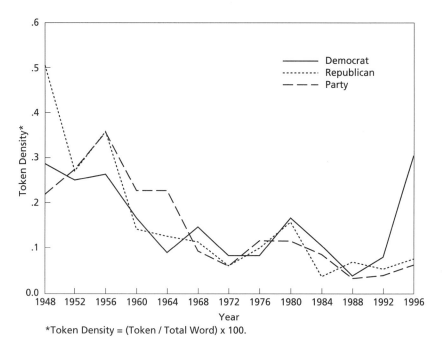

*Token Density = (Token / Total Word) x 100.

Figure 8.1.   Tokens over Time—Speeches

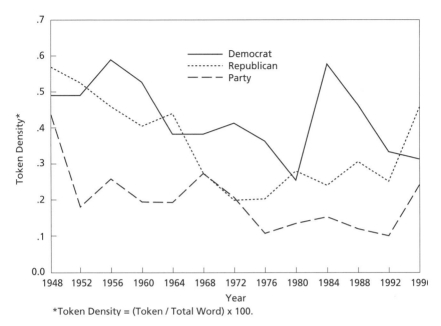

*Token Density = (Token / Total Word) x 100.

Figure 8.2.   Tokens over Time—News Coverage

In examining the qualitative aspects of these trends, one reason why elites continue to discuss parties is that they are consequential, as illustrated by the variables *Potency* and *Role*. *Potency* was created to measure whether parties were portrayed as "actors" or "recipients of action" in a given sentence. As table 8.1 illustrates, they were considered to be "actors" 47.2 percent of the time and "recipients" 30.1 percent of the time.[5] The variable *Role* was created to assess the social or political job performed by the parties, and as displayed in table 8.2, we see that party tokens were more commonly found to be "part of the solution" (31.4 percent) than "part of the problem" (20 percent). Although elites did not always editorialize about parties in these ways, they did portray parties as having a generally positive impact on the political environment. In both of these instances, then, parties were discussed as powerful and beneficial, as helpful agents on the political scene.

Textual examples illustrate the patterns found in these figures. Take the following statement made by Representative Bill Richardson (Dem.–N.M.)

Table 8.1.   Party Tokens by Potency Variable

	n	*(%)*
Unclear	610	21.0
As actor	1370	47.2
As recipient	874	30.1
Balanced	50	1.7

Table 8.2.   Party Tokens by Role

	n	(%)
Part of the solution	912	31.4
Part of the problem	582	20.0
Unclear/as conflicted	1410	48.6

on March 21, 1995, whereby Democrats are portrayed as working to improve the lives of welfare recipients, children, and parents. Notice how Democrats are constituted here as active (tied to such comforting verbs as "require," "provide," "support," and "maintain") and empathic (concerned with resources, the safety net, and self-sufficiency). In both obvious and subtle ways, Richardson constitutes Democrats as confident and dynamic, up to the task of governance. "Democrats are strong on work. The Democratic proposal actually requires that recipients prepare for and engage in work; provides resources for the assistance needed to become self-sufficient, such as education, training, child care, and transportation. Democrats support children. Democrats maintain the national commitment to providing a safety net for kids, while requiring their parents to become self-sufficient."

Textbook authors also stress the potency and positive role of parties, and do so far more unapologetically than either legislators or candidates. The authors commonly go so far as to equate democracy with the two-party system, repeating (if not always quoting) E. E. Schattschneider's (1942, 1) seminal phrase, "political parties created democracy, and . . . democracy in the United States is unworkable save in terms of parties." In the following examples, note how authors suggest that the two-party system is emblematic of democracy, encouraging impressionable students to believe that parties are indeed central to the U.S. system:

- Today's political parties are so much a part of government that it would be hard to imagine government without them (Lewinsky 1987, 174).
- Nearly everyone who gets elected to the House belongs to either the Democratic or the Republican Party. Legislators of other parties run for election, but seldom win (Gross 1979, 436).
- Today, Democrats and Republicans similarly dominate the contests for elective office (Ladd 1985, 437).

As table 8.2 also shows, however, parties were not always portrayed positively. Indeed, all four voices sometimes placed parties in a negative context (20 percent of the time) and in a conflicted context (48.6 percent of the time). Negativity was injected into statements in both direct and obscure ways. First, consider the direct route as evidenced in these passages from presidential candidates Michael Dukakis in 1988 and George H. W. Bush in 1992, respectively. Note how Dukakis accuses the Republicans of mismanagement, while Bush blames Bill Clinton (along with the liberal wing of Clinton's party) for making the wrong choices:

- after another $25 billion and eight years of Republican mismanagement, our ICBM's are more vulnerable than they were in 1980 (Dukakis 1988, September 14);
- the liberal McGovern wing of the other party, including my opponent, consistently made the wrong choices (Bush 1992, August 20).

While negative statements like these advanced by Dukakis and Bush appeared in the data, they were not the most common portrayals of political parties. Instead, elites—a politically savvy group—were often cautious and measured when critiquing parties, often resorting to "conflicted" statements (ones which featured both positive and negative features of partisanship).

Frustrations with political parties are not unique to this data set. Revisiting the party decline/resurgence literature is something of a cottage industry in political science, with a considerable number of books, hundreds of published articles, and myriad conference and seminar papers exploring how parties have or have not lived up to their potential. But even though academics often lambaste parties in their research, they rarely ignore them, thereby ensuring that the construct of party continues to wield influence over their thoughts, conversations, and careers. Although some doubters worry that the breakdown of the party system could lead to "government by the NRA and professional wrestlers" (also known as interest groups and outsiders), my data suggest that this will probably not be the case if legislators, journalists, presidential candidates, and textbook authors have a say in the matter.

Party Tokens Are Used Hierarchically

Political scholars heretofore have conceived of parties in physical, as well as conceptual, space. One effort to do so, credited first to V. O. Key (1964), and then picked up in political scientist Frank Sorauf's (1988) textbooks (coauthored with P. A. Beck), locates party in three places: in government, in organizations, and in the electorate. If repetition and widespread use can serve as a guide, this trilogy has been found useful in describing the activities of parties, often appearing, for example, in most of the civics textbooks examined here. In the 1990s, however, Gerald Pomper (1992) and John Aldrich (1995) challenged this schema, preferring to think of parties as groups of elites, as entities distinctly separate from the voters.

My data reveal a similar preference. Over time and circumstance, the voices in this study have constituted parties as elite actors whose paths do not intersect with the people. This finding is not controversial, but its implications may well be. When journalists and textbook authors, as well as candidates and legislators, adhere to a consistent discourse about parties, no official voice exists to challenge the party system.[6] Even though these elites do not always celebrate parties, my data reveal that even when they do critique them, they do so deferentially. According to Kenneth Burke, citizens are sentenced to the sentence, committed to the realities created when people describe their worlds. Rhetorical treatments, then, suggest that the privileged position of parties is constantly being upheld—at least by the elites in this study—in the body politic.

The elite nature of party tokens can be viewed in several ways. The variable *Position* was created to trace the party's place in the governmental process as implied by the speaker. As table 8.3 shows, party tokens were almost four times more likely to be constituted at the elite than at the mass level.

Of the four genres, congressional debates saw the highest percentage of elite statements (89.5 percent), often making their discourse sound inclusive, at times self-congratulatory. Conceptually, the job of Congress is to represent the public, and theorists have advanced various paradigms of representation ranging from delegate models (in which representatives voice the desires of their constituencies) to trustee models (in which representatives exercise greater personal judgment in governance). When using party tokens, legislators seem to prefer the latter, and so prevalent is this construction that the following sentence by Representative Jaime Whitten (Dem.–Miss.) instantly sounds familiar: "Mr. Chairman, I can see the coalition of northern Democrats and Republican leaders on the Judiciary Committee have the votes to defeat us" (1964, February 3). Behind this familiarity, though, lurk structural markers. Whitten refers to a Chairman, a coalition, Democrats and Republicans, leaders, and the Judiciary Committee. All are *elite* instantiations of party, a common pattern in congressional debates.

The variable *Associations* adds to the rhetorical construction of parties as elites. This variable, which measured the entities with which parties must interact, reveals that parties most commonly interacted with their "own or another party" (38.5 percent), followed by "named politicians" (20.1 percent), "voters" (18.1 percent), "international entities" (3.0 percent), "interest groups" (1.1 percent), "the media" (.8 percent), or "other" (5.1 percent). Collapsing these coding categories into two categories ("associations with citizens"

Table 8.3.   Party Tokens by Position

	n	*(%)*
Elite	2073	71.4
Mass	526	18.1
Global/undifferentiated	305	10.5

and "associations with other entities"), parties were portrayed as interacting just 18.1 percent with "the voters" and 81.9 percent with "other entities." To be sure, there is an inevitable correlation between the *Position* and the *Associations* variables, for if a political party is seen to be interacting with citizens, chances are that the statement places party at the mass level, as well. This correlation does not detract from the overall pattern though: elites constitute parties as interacting with ordinary citizens less than one-fifth of the time.

Of the four genres, candidates (26.4 percent) and journalists (25 percent) were more likely to associate parties with citizens than were legislators (12.9 percent) or authors (7.6 percent). These distinctions make sense, considering how the data were drawn (that is, the speeches and news reports came from campaign periods; debates and textbooks came, largely, from noncampaign periods). Ronald Reagan, as a candidate and then as president, was particularly known to mention citizens in his speeches. A qualitative read of the data suggests that he also associated parties with citizens more convincingly than did other politicians. Consider how the "Great Communicator" did so in the following speech delivered on July 17, 1980:

> You know, as the first Republican President once said, "while the people retain their virtue and vigilance, no Administration of any extreme of wickedness or folly can seriously injure the Government in the short space of four years." . . . These visitors to that city on the Potomac do not come as white or black, red or yellow; they are not Jews or Christians; conservatives or liberals; or Democrats or Republicans. They are Americans awed by what has gone before; proud of what for them is still a shining city on a Hill.

Kathleen Hall Jamieson (1988, 170) has written how Reagan's rhetoric comfortably singled out special groups and individuals for direct address without sounding self-serving. Whether Mr. Reagan was speaking directly to the families who lost astronauts in the explosion of the space shuttle *Challenger*, thanking a physician or nurse who had written him a thank-you note following his hospitalization for colon cancer, or referring to his wife as "Nancy" (Jamieson notes that most prior presidents often referred to their wives as "Mrs."), he placed people in his speeches more intimately than had his predecessors, most likely inviting "affection that prevented him from attack" (189). Probably so, but more important for the current purpose is that Reagan also brought attention to a powerful contraindication: political rhetoric in the United States rarely salutes its subjects.

Kenneth Burke would find the treatment of parties as elites to be quite natural. In his writings, Burke contends that humans are "goaded by the spirit of hierarchy (or moved to a sense of order)" (1989, 69). This passion for order, wrote Burke, encouraged the creation of rules for organizing sentences (grammar), organizing arguments (logic), and cooperation based on identification of speakers with audiences through symbols (rhetoric) as the foundation of human activities; in all of these ways, people craved order so much that they enforced it in places where it did not otherwise exist. This need to categorize—to understand life in terms of hierarchies—offers a helpful perspective in interpreting why parties continue to be seen in an elite frame. That is, for at least the past fifty years, party tokens have efficiently reduced uncertainty by rhetorically identifying those in charge, thereby contributing to a narrative of power in the United States. As long as parties are regarded as elites, their role in government is, in a semantic sense, secure even when they are occasionally vilified.

Parties Have Not Been Interpreted in Depth

In the American context, parties have a strong tradition of both loose and decentralized ties, the observation of which prompted E. E. Schattschneider (1942) to write, "Decentralization of power is by all odds the most important single characteristic of the American major party; more than anything else this trait distinguishes it from all others. Indeed, once this truth is understood, nearly everything else about American parties is greatly illuminated. . . . The American major party is, to repeat the definition, a loose confederation of state and local bosses for limited purposes" (132–133).

The disjointed nature of political parties creates special tensions for the elites who must describe them. Specifically: How do elites go about depicting historically loose coalitions? Do they prefer an aggressive approach (one which interrogates deep conflict, exposes tensions, and publicizes disagreement)? Or do they favor a more moderate approach, one that glosses over the conflict, works to prevent future tensions, and ensures requisite room for bargaining and cooperation in the future? In a sense, the question becomes: how partisan are the portrayals of parties in the American political system?

According to my data, they are not terribly partisan at all. Rather than offering pointed opinions and judgments about parties, my findings suggest that elites often described parties in "unclear" or "mixed" ways. Qualitative researchers who stress the connection between "thick description" and cultural meanings might be disturbed by elites' reluctance to offer clearly delineated portrayals of parties. Indeed, seminal work in ethnography suggests that "thick description leads to thick understanding" (Geertz 1973); and that "thick description allows for thick interpretation" (Denzin 1989). Elites in this study seemed to prefer a less detailed route; instead of offering "thick meanings" filled with attributions and judgments, they advanced a much more skeletal narrative which merely glossed the history, qualities, and activities of partisan institutions. While this rhetoric may be inspired by the best intentions (that is, as a way of protecting a loose, decentralized party system), it is likely that these skeletal portrayals prevented citizens from understanding the party system in complex and sympathetic ways.

And this is ironic since political parties have one of the richest histories of any institution in the United States. According to Aldrich (1995, 70), they began to form as early as 1790 in response to the problems of "majority instability" (that is, the unsteadiness of temporary majority coalitions which dealt with problems on an issue-by-issue basis). Because problem solving was both difficult and unpredictable when new majorities had to be built on an issue-by-issue basis, several founders (for example, Alexander Hamilton, James Madison, Thomas Jefferson) found it beneficial to "organize their supporters" into teams. Gradually, Aldrich continues, these teams strengthened over time, widened their scope with respect to members and issues, and became "the first political parties of modern democratic form in this or any nation" (69). Given their longevity and the passions surrounding them, one might think that parties would inspire fulsome description from elites. My data, however, suggest the opposite.

The variable *Time* examined the extent to which elites place tokens in the present, past, and future. As table 8.4 shows, overall party tokens were placed in the present 80.4 percent of the time, in the past 18.6 percent of the time, and in the future just 1.1 percent of the time. These data become more descriptive when broken down by genre. Textbook authors—as one would imagine—are most likely to mention the past (45.3 percent) followed by candidates (15.5 percent), legislators (12.2 percent), and journalists (6.3 percent). Candidates—also as one would expect—are most likely to feature the future (3.7 percent), followed by legislators (.4 percent), authors (.3 percent), and journalists (.1 percent). What is interesting here, though, is that if textbooks are ignored, parties are placed in the past just 8.7 percent of the time; and, speeches aside, tokens are placed in the future just 0.2 percent of the time. Why do political parties have no past? No future?

From a strategic perspective, there are several reasons why elites (at least those supportive of parties) treat party tokens presentistically. An obvious one is that parties therefore cannot be held accountable for their pasts. Mistakes, blunders, corruption, graft, and scandals—all connected with party lineage—remain left out of the conversation (not to mention voters' political memories) when the past goes unmentioned.

Table 8.4. Time Overall and by Genre

Time	Overall		Speeches		News		Debates		Textbooks	
	n	(%)	n	(%)	n	(%)	n	(%)	n	(%)
In Present	2334	(80.4)	544	(80.8)	730	(93.6)	716	(87.4)	344	(54.4)
In Past	539	(18.6)	104	(15.5)	49	(6.3)	100	(12.2)	286	(45.3)
As Potential	31	(1.1)	25	(3.7)	1	(.1)	3	(.4)	2	(.3)

Another benefit of ignoring the past is that a rhetoric of the moment is highly efficient for intraparty communication. As V. O. Key noted, there are often as many disagreements within a party as between parties. Thus, conversations rooted in the moment can be more careful and grounded, as well as less likely to offend various factions of the party. Similarly, ignoring the past could also be beneficial in public communication. While parties know that their best chance of electing their candidates is to mobilize loyal voters, they also know that swing votes often decide elections. In this way, rhetorically sidestepping the past may open up space for new or independent voters to feel comfortable with the party's candidate.

While party strategists and candidates might find presentistic politics advantageous, scholars are typically troubled by it. Aldrich (1995), for one, has written that three forces shape a political party: ambitious politicians, governmental institutions, and political history. History matters because it describes the ideas, values, and technological possibilities available at any given moment, says Aldrich, making a more meaningful understanding of these institutions possible.

To abandon history, then, is to deny the successes of parties in the past. Eschewing history encourages citizens to forget that parties socialized, organized, instructed, and provided for massive numbers of Americans in an earlier place and time. Scholar Michael Nelson (1995, 72) recalls how parties helped his family directly by offering them the opportunity to go to college. He writes, "I know that politics was the vehicle that integrated generations of our immigrant ancestors into the main-stream of American society—the job on the city road crew that my German grandfather got from the Frank Hague machine in Jersey City is the reason that my father and then I were later able to build careers of our own in the private sector." Touching as such narratives are, they are rarely heard among professional politicians themselves.

Thus, presentism exacts a price, since an understanding of the past inevitably informs our understanding of the present. When political tokens are stripped of their history, Americans ultimately develop a shallow understanding of parties. As social influence researchers attest, individuals who are only casually involved in an issue are more likely to be persuaded by contrary messages. From this perspective, the finding that parties are stripped of their histories suggests that their meanings are thereby rendered more open to manipulation by partisan actors of all sorts.

Another important trend over time is that parties are portrayed largely as campaign organizations. The variable *Task* examined the jobs that parties are said to perform in political life (see table 8.5). I found that 43.2 percent of the tokens were placed in the *campaign* condition, followed by 32.9 percent of the time in the *governing* condition, 9 percent of the time in the *mobilizing* condition, and 14.9 percent in the *mixed* condition.

Table 8.5. **Party Task Overall and by Genre**

Task	Overall		Speeches		News		Debates		Textbooks	
	n	(%)	n	(%)	n	(%)	n	(%)	n	(%)
Not Applicable	292	(10.1)	92	(13.7)	41	(5.2)	87	(10.6)	72	(11.4)
Mobilization	260	(9.0)	30	(4.5)	78	(10.0)	37	(4.5)	115	(18.2)
Campaign	1254	(43.2)	351	(52.2)	560	(71.8)	62	(7.6)	281	(44.5)
Governing	956	(32.9)	187	(27.8)	69	(8.8)	585	(71.4)	115	(18.2)
Mixed	142	(4.9)	13	(1.9)	32	(4.1)	48	(5.9)	49	(7.8)

Admittedly, these percentages are somewhat skewed due to the texts sampled: both the speeches and news articles were drawn during campaign periods. Nonetheless, it is clear that some partisan tasks are featured far more than others. For instance, candidates—despite their presence in a campaign—were more likely to mention governing and mobilizing than was the news, a finding that resembles Hart's (2000) assertion that politicians attempt to broaden political discussions while the media try to narrow them. For their part, journalists were more likely to mention the mobilizing function of parties (reporting on events, discussing the efforts of parties to increase turnout, etc.) than were the candidates.

These data suggest that the media cover parties to satisfy journalistic needs for drama, conflict, and newsworthiness. What slips out of their coverage, however, is governance. As we see above, the tokens were associated with governing only 8 percent of the time. This pattern would no doubt disturb political scientist Nelson Polsby (1983, 3) who has argued that "no newly elected President in the entire history of the republic was less prepared to take office than Jimmy Carter, unless it was Ronald Reagan." Polsby's point was not personal but institutional. In his book *Consequences of Party Reform*, he notes that when the public is allowed to select presidential nominees, they do not often attend to the issues of prior preparation or political experience. This finding that journalists rarely link parties to governance (especially during campaign periods) underscores Polsby's concern. If the public is not primed by the media to think of parties as governing (as well as campaigning) bodies, then voters are likely to be attracted to ersatz candidates possessing limited governing experience. Indeed, the success of candidates like Ross Perot, Jesse Ventura, and Sonny Bono may indicate that such "priming failures" have already exacted their tolls.

E. J. Dionne (1991) has noted that Americans are cynical because they believe that Democrats and Republicans offer them false choices. This study suggests that an underemphasis on the governing role of parties in elite discourse may put forward another type of false choice. Although political scientists are mixed as to whether parties are campaign or governing institutions, most would agree that parties are interested primarily in attaining power and that they emerge organically to organize the disparate interests of a legislature. Yet when parties are constituted largely as campaign entities, citizens are unlikely to view them in a more multidimensional way. Such a view has political consequences.

CONCLUSION

Traditionally, scholars have examined what parties *are* and what they *do* (Finer 1980). This chapter has attempted something different: an analysis of what parties *mean*. A first set of conclusions is that elites have used party tokens continuously, hierarchically, and skeletally over the past fifty years in the United States. These trends tell us both about the meanings of parties and a bit about the preferences and latent assumptions of political elites who—despite their very different job descriptions—constituted parties in similar ways.

Political and historical perspectives help inform the "cultural collusions" found in these data. From a political perspective, Sorauf and Beck's (1988) work notes that it is very difficult for Americans to think "outside of the two-party system"; indeed, because of its political dominance and resilience, the two-party system may simply pattern elites' understandings of parties as well as determine how they discuss them. From a political development perspective, Samuel Huntington (1968) has claimed that Americans possess a "traditional" mindset that encourages them to accept their political world as predetermined. Here, because Americans have accepted the system as given (and laws to be preestablished), it stands to reason that they may, too, see parties as an inevitable element of the system. Similarly, Daniel Boorstin (1953) argued that a characteristic of American political thought is the axiom of "givenness"—that politics and ideas are a gift from the past. From his perspective (as well as that of Huntington), the finding that four different sets of elites articulated the same version of partisanship makes sense; having been raised in the American climate, these elites instinctively felt pressured to look to tradition (indeed all the way back to the late 1700s) to understand the present moment.

In addition to these specific findings, this chapter also concludes that when one takes a step back to critically examine how parties have been constituted via discourse, broader patterns emerge than were previously available, one of which is that partisan institutions are hard to resist. The first finding noted how parties continue to be discussed, frequently positively, sometimes in a more critical way. An entire volume could be devoted to this finding (and the ways in which scholars have inadvertently praised parties while trying to tear them down), but perhaps the following statement captures these tensions best. Witness the "inevitability" of party institutions as described by James MacGregor Burns et al. (1981):

> Why this pattern of failure? Why do we stick to a "two-party" system when most democracies have multiparty systems? In part because the American people, despite their many divisions over religion, race, and the like, have been united enough that the two big parties could adequately represent them. In part it is also because of the nature of our election system. Most of our election districts have a single incumbent and the candidate with the most votes wins. Because only one candidate can win, the largest and second-largest parties have a near monopoly of office. The system of the election of the president operates in this way on a national scale. The presidency is the supreme prize in American politics: a party that cannot attain it, or show promise of attaining it, simply does not operate in the major leagues.

Attending to the ways in which elites have constituted parties reveals that they are more important than has been previously acknowledged. Listening to the sounds of partisanship brought this finding to light, and it follows that much can be learned by applying this method to other modes of party discourse, including party convention rhetoric, advertisements, portrayals in popular films, television programming, and political cartoons, as well as the presence of parties on the Internet, in other nations, in burgeoning democratic systems, and in the everyday conversations of citizens and other nonelites. Attention to each of these venues would add to our understanding of the concept, enriching what is known about how citizens make sense of these institutions. Furthermore, focusing on individual tokens of party might clarify key questions at the dawn of the new millennium. For instance, how, when, and why did *liberal* become a dirty word? And conversely, how, when, and why did *Independent* become such a cherished entity in politics?

Analyzing how parties are constructed in language reveals something important: parties matter because they are still talked about. That elites continue to use party tokens, portray them in a hierarchical manner, and discuss them skeletally are somewhat modest findings. Their modesty, however, fades when we consider their consistency and when we reckon with the underlying myths their consistencies reveal. While political scientists have produced a wealth of knowledge about parties, they have yet to take a step back to analyze the rhetoric surrounding them and the assumptions undergirding this rhetoric. As long as elites continue to discuss parties, it stands to reason that parties will continue to hold a type of power over the public imagination. Because language ultimately makes action possible, this is a finding of considerable intellectual and political significance.

NOTES

1. These four voices were selected because they help to manage the meanings of party in the United States. Of course, other voices could be selected to answer the current research questions, and it is not my intent to argue that these voices can be generalized to other types of political actors.

2. With support from the Ford and Carnegie Foundations, Hart and Jamieson have built an impressive database of presidential campaign discourse which (1) contains five genres of political communication (campaign speeches, political advertisements, campaign debates, newspaper and broadcast coverage and letters to the editor written by average citizens during election seasons), (2) covers thirteen presidential campaigns (1948–1996), and (3) houses the voices of twenty-one different presidential candidates (see Hart 2000).Two sets of texts were drawn from the Campaign Mapping Project database: presidential campaign speeches and print news coverage of presidential campaigns.

3. With regard to the *campaign condition,* presidential campaign speeches delivered over the past thirteen campaigns as well as the newspaper coverage accompanying these speeches were examined. Presidential speeches were selected primarily because the president is the focus of government for millions of Americans. Moreover, presidential speeches are appropriate for this study because presidents are often regarded as the spokespersons for their parties, and these speeches, for the most part, receive more popular press attention than would speeches delivered by regional or local candidates. I also examined how newspapers treated these party tokens. To draw time comparisons, I analyzed campaign coverage during the same period as the speeches (both texts have been collected from the convention to election day for the campaigns 1948 through 1996). The newspaper articles came from the *New York Times, Washington Post, Chicago Tribune, Los Angeles Times, Christian Science Monitor, Atlanta Constitution* and AP-Wire stories.

For the *governing condition,* two additional sources will be examined: congressional debates (in the U.S. House of Representatives) and civics textbooks. Many scholars note that partisanship is more pronounced in the House than in the Senate, largely due to the increased number of members, the committee structure and rules on floor debate, and the amending process. Thus, to capture how partisanship is treated by a governmental institution that depends on it, tokens were traced during four debates (two raised by Democrats: one successful, one not successful; and two raised by Republicans: one successful, one not successful) focusing on one issue (Civil Rights—roughly defined). These debates include discussion of: (1) the Civil Rights Act of 1957 (encouraged and signed by President Dwight Eisenhower), (2) the Civil Rights Act of 1964 (encouraged and signed by President Lyndon Johnson), (3) the busing debate of 1979 (introduced by Democrats, did not pass the House), and (4) the welfare reform debate of 1995 (introduced by Republicans, passed the House but was not signed by President Clinton). Transcripts of the U.S. House debates were drawn from the *Congressional Record.*

With regard to civics books, political scientist Thomas Cronin writes that most textbook authors see their work as having two preeminent functions: to instruct students and to train citizens. As he puts it, these authors see themselves as primary agents in the political socialization of the next generation of citizens. Therefore, it stands to reason that an analysis of civics textbooks should provide a glimpse into what the educational system is teaching Americans to think about parties.

4. The ratios are as follows: 1957 = 0.000391623; 1964 = 0.000198643; 1979 = 0.000165904; 1995 = 0.00151489.

5. Tokens were also considered to be "unclear/balanced" 22.7 percent of the time for this variable (*Potency*).

6. Bartels (2000a, 44) writes that one account for the revival of partisan voting in the 1990s may be that "increasing partisanship in the electorate represents a response at the mass level to increasing partisanship at the elite level. . . . In an era in which parties in government seem increasingly consequential, the public may increasingly come to develop and apply partisan predispositions of exactly the sort described by the authors of *The American Voter.*"

7. The KeyWords program locates a requested word in a batch of texts and yields a forty-one-word text-snippet of each instance of that word in the sample; these forty-one-word clusters feature twenty words preceding and twenty words following the requested term, as well as the requested term highlighted in bold.

8. Specifically, 1,240 instances of *Democrat, Democrats,* and *Democratic;* 1,373 instances of *Republican* and *Republicans;* 136 instances of *Independent* and *Independents;* 140 instances of *Liberal* and *Liberals;* 66 instances of *Conservative* and *Conservatives;* and 1,355 instances of *Party, Parties,* and *Partisan.*

9. Specifically, 22,858 instances of *Democrat, Democrats,* and *Democratic;* 18,924 instances of *Republican* and *Republicans;* 1,627 instances of *Independent* and *Independents;* 1,679 instances of *Liberal* and *Liberals;* 1,482 instances of *Conservative* and *Conservatives;* and 10,103 instances of *Party, Parties,* and *Partisan.* There were a total of 1,051,277 words in the speeches and 5,363,587 words in the news. Thus, there was one party token per 0.0004099 words in the speeches in one token per 0.0010566 words in the news. This study presents qualitative findings from my stratified random sample of these tokens as well as some trends from the larger data set found in the Campaign Mapping Project. For more detail on the texts in the Campaign Mapping Project, see Hart (2000).

10. The desired 780 tokens were drawn from the news data in the CMP. In some instances in the campaign speeches, however, there were not enough tokens to meet this sampling approach. Thus, the tokens analyzed for the speeches are as follows: *Democrat* (n = 130), *Republican* (n = 125), *Independent* (n = 104), *Liberal* (n = 124), *Conservative* (n = 62), and *Party* (n = 128).

11. Specifically, the tokens for these genres are as follows: 848 tokens in the congressional debates (228 instances of *Democrat, Democrats,* and *Democratic;* 357 instances of *Republican* and *Republicans;* 5 instances of *Independent* and *Independents;* 44 instances of *Liberal* and *Liberals;* 10 instances of *Conservative* and *Conservatives;* and 204 instances of *Party, Parties,* and *Partisan*), and 632 tokens in

the textbooks (160 instances of *Democrat, Democrats,* and *Democratic;* 155 instances of *Republican* and *Republicans;* 54 instances of *Independent* and *Independents;* 52 instances of *Liberal* and *Liberals;* 44 instances of *Conservative* and *Conservatives;* and 167 instances of *Party, Parties,* and *Partisan*).

APPENDIX A

Texts

The texts in this study were scanned and introduced to a Keyword-in-Context program. The KeyWords program locates any "key terms" (party tokens, in this study) of interest and reproduces them, preceding and following each with twenty words of verbal context. These forty-one word clusters served as the coding units for this project.[7] In my case, the KeyWords program located 4,310 party tokens in the database's *speeches*[8] and 56,673 party tokens in the *news coverage*.[9] To reduce this count to a manageable size, I drew a stratified random sample of the tokens, selecting ten tokens per year in each of these genres, collecting 780 tokens from the news coverage and 679 tokens from the speeches.[10] Additionally, 848 tokens were located in the congressional debates, and 632 were collected from the civics textbooks using a similar stratified sampling procedure.[11]

Coding Scheme

The content-analytic scheme employed in this study was created to measure the rhetorical and political nuances of party tokens in political discourse. All coding decisions were designed to be mutually exclusive for each variable. There are two parts to the following coding scheme. First, it features a series of descriptive measures. These include text number, year of token, specific token (*Democrat, Republican, Independents, Liberal, Conservatives,* or *Party*), the token's era (Era 1 = 1948-1960; Era 2 = 1964-1980; Era 3 = 1984–1996), speaker or newspaper, and party task (mobilization, campaigning, governing, mixed).

The coding scheme was also inspired by theoretical approaches to parties. These variables were coded as follows:

Role: Social or political job being performed by the party (see Broder, 1972; Schlesinger, 1985)

   0 unclear ("Rep. John Anderson is the *Republican* nominee from Illinois.")
   1 part of the solution ("Our aims have been drawn from the finest of *Republican* traditions.")
   2 part of the problem ("The Whip complained, again, about the *Democratic* leadership.")

Potency: The speaker's calculation of the force exerted by, or upon, the party

0 unclear ("What are the goals of our *party?*")

1 as actor ("As *Republican* leader, I've always wanted to do that.")

2 as recipient ("I am not too concerned with *partisan* denunciation.")

Time: The party's moment in history as implied by the speaker (Not a simple measure of a predicate's "tense"; see Burnham 1970)

0 in present ("Bush is in-line with his *party.*")

1 in past ("The *Republicans* have always wanted to do that.")

2 as potential ("Our *party* shall always remain committed to a secure future.")

Context: The speaker's attribution of the social scene affecting the collective

0 unclear ("The *Republicans* want to put that bill on the president's desk.")

1 identity condition ("Anderson, a *Republican* from IL, expressed that sentiment.")

2 positive ("A *party* that can unite itself will unite America.")

3 negative ("Humphrey rejected the advice of his own *party.*")

4 balanced ("The *Democratic* party, in good times and bad.")

Associations: A reference to some social entity with which the party interacts (for good or ill; see Key 1949; Lowi 1979; Ostrogorski 1902/1964)

0 no other entity mentioned ("The *party's* platform calls for balancing the budget.")

1 same party ("as well as some in his own *party*")

2 different party ("The Taxpayer *party* threw its support to the Republican party.")

3 politician of same party ("fellow *Democrats*—Gene McCarthy and George McGovern")

4 politician of other party ("Texas *Democrats* disagreed with Nixon.")

5 voters ("Suburban voters will offer the *Republican* party.")

6 political interest group (" 'Project 500' attacked the *party.*")

7 the media ("newspaper editors agree that the *Democrats*")

Position: The party's position in the governmental process as implied by the speaker (see Aldrich 1995; Eldersveld 1982; Key 1949; Sorauf and Beck 1988)

0 elite—organization, bureaucracy, candidates ("*Democrats* will vote to override the President's veto.")

1 mass—voters, media ("third-*party* supporter, Mr. Hagelin, said"; "Reform *party* supporters")

2 global/undifferentiated ("I accept the nomination of our *party.*")

Goals: The party's goals for the American body politic, as implied by the speaker (see Pomper 1992)

0 no goal mentioned—("the *Democratic* candidate from New York")

1 a broad (collective) goal—ideological, theoretical or community focus, lofty promises for the public good (*"Democrats* stand for liberty, the protection of all.")

2 a narrow (coalitional) goal—utility maximizers, narrow interests, specific platforms (*"Conservatives* demand Capital Gains Tax cuts today.")

Behavior: How does the speaker conceptualize the party as measured by party-linked verbs (see Hart, Smith-Howell & Llewellyn, 1991)?

0 unclear ("third *party* appeal is growing")

1 party as intellectual body (rational choice theorists—opine, think) (*"Republicans* questioned")

2 party as acting body (policy making construct—funded, voted) ("the *party* would restore"; "the *party* has labored")

3 party as feeling body (psychological/affective construct—believed, felt) (*"Democrats* care deeply")

9

The Mass Media and Group Priming in American Elections

Nicholas A. Valentino

The evening news leads off with dramatic video of a drive-by shooting, a holdup, a drug bust, a car-jacking, or a home-invasion robbery.[1] The story involves crime, the crime is usually violent, and the suspects are usually non-white (Gilliam, Iyengar, Simon, and Wright 1996; Entman 1990). In another story, welfare is the topic and again the recipients are nonwhite. Although they comprise a minority of the poor and those on welfare, nonwhites play the leading role in a majority of TV's depictions of these social policies (Gilens 1999). When the anchorperson cuts to a commercial break, a political advertisement appears. Grainy footage of men and women streaming across the U.S.–Mexican border allegedly documents an incumbent's inability to control illegal immigration. The incumbent responds with a spot insisting that he has done a great deal to prevent illegal immigrants from taking *our* jobs, and threatening *our* values. In another political advertisement, the narrator suggests that while the opponent supports wasteful government spending on programs like midnight basketball or alpine slides in Puerto Rico, the sponsoring candidate supports tax cuts for hard-working Americans.

The issues raised during these common broadcast occurrences differ from one another. They focus on crime, welfare, illegal immigration, and balancing the budget. They use different sources, stem from disparate motivations, and employ different presentational styles—but they well may exert a common effect. In each case, the message highlights a group stereotype in the mind of the viewer. When attitudes about such groups are activated, the political world is viewed somewhat differently than before. This effect is called group priming.

The priming of group attachments, animosities, and conflicts is likely to occur during political campaigns as candidates attempt to build winning

145

coalitions. Coalition-building efforts take place in every campaign as candidates and their handlers try to achieve short-term electoral goals. However, the impact of group priming may reach far beyond any particular electoral struggle. If candidates and the news media return in each election cycle to the tried-and-true strategies of the past, then people may be consistently reminded of the political relevance of particular groups in society and that may well affect subsequent political decisions.

The earliest fears about the impact of mass-mediated propaganda campaigns were concerned with the direct impact of media exposure on group attitudes. Theories of mob psychology proposed by Lebon and Freud suggested that individuals in large groups would lose many of their inhibitions and transfer their blind allegiance to charismatic group leaders. At the beginning of the twentieth century, radio (and then television) became available tools for expanding political elites' access to large populations. Furthermore, the catastrophic human toll of several political movements during this same historical period led many to fear that mass-mediated propaganda campaigns were in part responsible because they allowed totalitarian leaders to create strong resentments toward a common enemy, in many cases a minority group (Doob 1935). Figure 9.1 displays this simple linear relationship.

However, empirical support for this causal linkage was scarce (Hovland, Lumsdaine, and Sheffield 1949). The consensus view soon developed that the media had no such massive effect on attitudes or behavior, and that exposure did more to reinforce existing beliefs (Klapper 1960). Attitudes about groups, such as racial beliefs in the United States, were to be learned at an early age and were quite resistant to change during adulthood (Sears 1983; Miller and Sears 1986).[2]

Thus, despite early concerns about the massive impact of the media, the direct influence of mass media exposure on attitudes about groups is likely to be small and cumulative over time, serving as only one of many socialization agents. However, another route of media influence exists. My research agenda adopts and extends a somewhat recent shift in thinking about the relationship between mass-mediated campaigns and election outcomes. Instead of exploring the direct impact of mass media on the choices people make in the voting booth, I explore the impact of mass media on *how* people make those choices (Cohen 1963) and in particular on how the media environment can alter the criteria citizens use when making political decisions. Even more specifically, my research explores the possibility that

Figure 9.1.   Long-Term Media Exposure

exposure to mass media can activate attitudes about certain groups, while leaving others inactive, during election campaigns.

I begin by accepting the well-worn notion that, for the average citizen, attitudes about groups play a central role in organizing information about politics (Converse 1964; Conover 1984, 1988). Early scholarship on voting behavior identified group memberships and attachments as important determinants of individual electoral choices (Lazarsfeld, Berelson, and Gaudet 1944). The Columbia scholars argued that certain social group dimensions, especially class, would have a consistent impact on individual political behavior across elections. The media during any given election campaign would serve more to remind people of their existing group interests than to persuade or manipulate them (Berelson, Lazarsfeld, and McPhee 1954). Finally, these scholars argued that every individual maintained a constellation of group memberships that might present consistent or conflicting pressures toward any given political choice (Lazarsfeld, Berelson, and Gaudet 1948; Kriesberg 1949; Kelley 1955).

Subsequent research suggested that the impact of group memberships might not derive simply from similar life circumstances, but from a more active process of politicization via strategic communication of group norms, interests, and political standards (Converse and Campbell 1960). This was followed by the realization that the salience of these group concerns might not be constant. The presence of vivid reminders of group membership raised the likelihood of behaving in accordance with the group's norms (Charters and Newcomb 1958). Conover (1984, 765) clearly stated the phenomenon: "[B]y shaping the political environment so that it has more relevance for some groups than for others, political officeholders, candidates, and the media may play an important role in activating group identifications." Figure 9.2 depicts this interactive relationship between group attitudes, mass media exposure, and political decision making. This model suggests that the media can affect political outcomes in the short term by strengthening the causal linkages between particular group attitudes and evaluations of the candidates.

Although several decades have passed since the pioneering work in this area appeared, several aspects of the group-priming process and its consequences

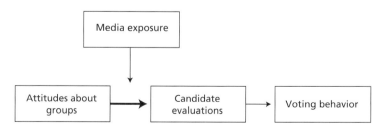

Figure 9.2. Group Priming: Short-Term Effects

remain unclear. Studies have demonstrated that the news media can prime issue opinions during political decision making (Iyengar and Kinder 1987; Krosnick and Kinder 1990; Krosnick and Brannon 1993). However, much less is known about when and how the media might prime attachments to, and opinions about, social groups.

In this chapter I have three specific goals. First, I set out several hypotheses for how the media might activate various attitudes about groups during election campaigns. These hypotheses involve a conceptual specification of the theory identified in the above figure: (1) What sorts of group attitudes matter in the political arena? (2) Which messages activate those attitudes? (3) What types of political decisions are affected? The answers to these questions are certainly interdependent, and all three are likely to change as a function of time and locale. As with many models of political behavior, the dynamic nature of these relationships makes theoretical generalizations and empirical tests difficult. The object here is to establish a general framework for understanding how the media can activate group attitudes during mass political decision making, not for making predictions about which particular attitudes will be activated at a particular point in time in any particular social system.[3]

Next, I present results from my own research testing some of these hypotheses. The first group domain to receive some attention has been race, in part because of continuing debate over the government's proper role in addressing persistent racial inequality in American society.[4] I have found that exposure to common, local news coverage of crime boosts the impact of particular racial attitudes on evaluations of the president. In one experiment I conducted, those subjects who viewed crime stories with African American suspects were more likely to evaluate President Clinton based on his performance on crime and welfare, two racialized issues, compared to those who saw the same crime story with nonblack suspects. The news did not affect how important nonracialized issues like taxation or balancing the national budget were regarded when subjects were asked to evaluate the president.

Further, racially stereotypic coverage also seems to boost the impact of racial identification in attributions made about the causes of crime in society, and therefore might alter the policy solutions people support. In another experiment, subjects who viewed crime news involving black crime suspects were more likely to link their thinking about the causes for crime with their attitudes about their own racial group: Highly identified whites were more likely to support crime explanations that focused on groups and individuals, not society, while highly identified blacks were likely to cite societal explanations after exposure to stereotypical crime news. Subjects who saw no black suspects were not likely to make the linkage between their group identity and the causes for crime in society.

Last, I find some evidence that exposure to political advertisements focusing on "racialized" issues, such as illegal immigration or drug use, primes racial sentiments during presidential evaluations. In a third experiment, subjects who viewed 1996 presidential advertisements focusing on these racialized issues were more likely to apply their racial attitudes in evaluating the candidates. In general, then, my results suggest that there is a wide variety of mass-mediated content that can "trigger" group attitudes and therefore affect political decision making.

The last section of this chapter attempts to identify some productive paths that scholars of political communication might take to advance research agendas like mine. The findings collected thus far suggest that candidates have an incentive to struggle over which group identities are salient during campaigns. Therefore, we must broaden our understanding of campaign effects beyond the outcome of a given contest. Short-term strategies may have long-term implications for how citizens view their government's role. In particular, the implications for group polarization and the viability of redistributive economic policies are discussed.

A PLAN FOR STUDYING GROUP PRIMING

According to cognitive psychologists, priming effects are driven by two fundamental realities of human information processing. First, people are not able to inventory all relevant information stored in memory when making a given decision. Instead, they use whatever limited information is readily available to them at the time to arrive at a satisfactory, or reasonable, preference (Simon 1979). Second, accessibility theory suggests that recently activated constructs are more readily invoked in current judgments (Srull and Wyer 1978). The group-priming approach suggests that since attitudes about groups help people to organize the political world, cues about groups embedded in political communication, as well as in news coverage of important issues, should be powerful priming agents.

Some issues explicitly revolve around group interests. Attitudes about racial groups, for example, drive opinions about affirmative action policies (Kinder and Sanders 1996; Sears, Hensler, and Speer 1979). Other issues are less explicitly group relevant but have become symbolic of social group cleavages. Opinions about welfare (Gilens 1999) or crime (Entman 1995), for example, are said to be "race-coded." This observation leads to the key proposition that mass media coverage of such issues might not simply prime opinions about them, but could also prime underlying group attitudes as well.

How Might the Media Prime Group Attitudes?

One possibility is that the salience of a group attitude rises and falls in accordance with the attention paid to specific group-relevant issues in the news. For example, coverage of violent crime might raise the salience of racial attitudes, since such news frequently contains stereotype-reinforcing cues about violence committed by blacks. Political campaigns are another likely source for group priming. Candidates may hope to intentionally manipulate the salience of various group dimensions in order to build winning coalitions. The campaign's goal is to encourage the viewer to evaluate the contest through the lens of a particular set of group interests. In this sense, attention to a particular group, without any direct mention of conflict between groups, might be enough to prime relevant attitudes.

Depictions of group conflict might be a particularly potent subset of all group-relevant stimuli. The mass media provide a fertile hunting ground for cues that pit groups in society against each other. Price (1989, 199) argues that one of the most "basic roles of mass communication lies in its representation of *who the sides are*" in a given social conflict. He writes: "A principal way in which mass communication may contextualize public issues, then, is in representing the issue socially, in depicting how various groups of people within the public are crystallizing into opinion factions." Political advertisements may also provide a potent source of group conflict cues. Racial priming effects via political advertising are suggested by vivid historical examples. For example, the now infamous "Willie Horton" ad and the Bush campaign's turnstile ad that followed were widely criticized after the election as race-baiting, and research suggested that this ad did make racial attitudes salient among whites (Mendleberg, 1997). Thus, one question we must address is whether simple exposure to images of group members in the media will be enough to prime attitudes about the group, or if exposure to group conflicts over rights and resources is necessary for activating these attitudes.

Which Groups and Which Group Attitudes Can Be Primed?

One could argue that the media's ability to prime attitudes about particular groups will vary across social systems, according to the baseline levels of those attachments in the general public and the politicization of each group (Converse and Campbell 1960). In the United States, race might be consistently salient, while gender, ethnicity, nationality, religion, age, and other demographic matters may have a lower profile. In other political systems, other social cleavages may play a more important role in structuring politics, and consequently figure more centrally in political decision making. Religious and ethnic distinctions in the Balkans and the Middle East are obvious examples.

But which attitudes about groups are likely to be activated by any given media environment? Politics is about balancing the interests of competing groups in society, and parties must build coalitions out of these broad-based interests. Thus, the nation's various social coalitions and policy beneficiaries are most frequently emphasized in the news, and especially in political news coverage or candidate advertising. Therefore, the focus here is on the activation of such social categories as race, ethnicity, gender, age, and religion. Several attitudinal dimensions are worthy of consideration, including ingroup identifications, group self-interest, and out-group animosity. Of course, these various attitudes are undoubtedly linked both in terms of their antecedents and their effects. Here, I merely speculate about the circumstances under which one type of attitude might become more active than another, and the political outcomes related to that difference.

What exactly does it mean to have a "group identity"? Research on reference group theory has relied primarily on the feelings respondents have for other group members (Kelley and Volkart 1952; Miller, Wlezien, and Hildreth 1991). On the other hand, social identity theory (Tajfel 1981; Turner 1984, 1987) argues that affective attachments to groups, by themselves, are not sufficient to produce meaningful effects on attitudes or behavior. According to this approach, group identity must contain a cognitive component because identifying *as* a group member, with all the shared values, cultural histories, material interests, and ideological beliefs that go along with membership, is necessary if it is to influence behavior. When the media focus on positive outcomes for a particular group, therefore, identification with that group alone might become more powerful as a determinant of vote choices and policy opinions.

Group identification potentially confuses a group member's material interests with more symbolically driven psychological attachments to groups. Perhaps it is simply the case that membership in a group carries material implications for the individual. If so, then reminding the individual of his or her membership would activate very practical concerns that would then shape political behavior. The basic premise of the self-interest thesis is drawn from Downs' (1957) argument that voters are rational actors who attempt to maximize personal benefits when choosing among competing policy stands or candidates. However, support for this hypothesis has been quite scarce, especially with regard to public opinion about racial policies such as busing to achieve school desegregation (Kinder and Sears 1981; Sears et al. 1980).

Some have argued that individual self-interest may not sufficiently explain racial attitudes because it does not consider the material or economic interdependence among group members. Realistic group conflict theory suggests that perceived competition for resources between groups will lead to negative attitudes about out-groups and positive identification with the in-group (Blumer 1958). This approach suggests that group identifications will have little impact unless citizens appreciate the threats that other groups pose. Evidence for group-based evaluations of self-interest has been found where explanations based on individual interests fail. For example, black Americans of a given income strata tend to support race-targeted social welfare policies more than whites in that same strata, and whites are more strongly opposed to policies that target blacks than they are to policies that target the poor of all races (Bobo

1991; Kluegal and Smith 1986; Bobo and Kleugal 1993; Bobo and Hutchings 1996). The implication here is that material, in-group interests might be primed by political communication that highlights material threat from out-groups.

Another relevant perspective focuses on the impact of out-group animosities, such as prejudice and stereotyping, or policy attitudes and electoral choice. Symbolic racism theory (Kinder and Sears 1981; Sears 1988; Sears, van Laar, Carrillo, and Kosterman 1997) suggests that subtle forms of racial animus persist even though few Americans believe in the biological inferiority of blacks. Symbolic racism and its relatives—modern racism (McConahay 1986), aversive racism (Gaertner and Dovidio 1986), racial resentment (Kinder and Sanders 1996)—stem from antiblack affect combined with a sense that blacks violate basic American values such as the work ethic, respect for traditional authority, and common moral values. The implication of this perspective is that issues containing symbolic racial cues should primarily stimulate racial animus among whites toward nonwhites (Jessor 1988). In-group attitudes might be unaffected by these same cues.

Of course, some types of group attitudes may be chronically salient, such that they do not require explicit repetition in order to become active in political decision-making situations. For example, given the history of racial conflict in American society, the salience of racial identities and interests may be chronically active among African Americans, especially when evaluating candidates associated with the major parties with long-standing reputations on racial issues. The influence of racial attitudes on certain public policy stands, however, might vary according to the degree to which race is emphasized in the message. Racial identity is less chronically salient among whites because whites are less often reminded of the political implications of their group membership (Lau 1989). Among those with multiple and conflicting attachments to groups, priming one identity or another might have significant effects on opinions and behavior. Sears and Huddy (1990), for example, argue that women are deeply divided on many "women's issues" because they hold a variety of other group memberships—including religious, class, and ethnic attachments—which conflict with their interests as women. When crosscutting cleavages are present, priming one or the other identity might have significant implications for political decisions.

These points lead to a somewhat complicated set of predictions about when group attitudes will be primed for various individuals. Media portrayals that focus on the conflicts between groups might activate group interests as well as identifications, especially for oppressed minorities. A media portrayal that reinforces negative stereotypes about a group might also activate animosity among nonmembers. Positive depictions of a given group, without implications of threat or conflict for other groups, might simply activate in-group identification among members while leaving nonmembers unaffected. Furthermore, for certain political choices, identifications among oppressed groups might be chronically salient, such that attempts to boost the importance of these attachments via the media become difficult. Out-group animosities, however, might exhibit a wider range of priming effects because concerns about various out-groups might be relevant to a particular policy or election outcome.

Which Political Outcomes Are Affected?

How broadly will priming a group attitude influence political opinions and behaviors? Previous work on priming suggests that media cues only narrowly activate concerns directly related to the message itself. For example, Iyengar and Kinder (1987) found that coverage of the Camp David peace accords or the Iran hostage crisis boosted the impact of the president's performance in dealing with foreign countries, but did not affect the predictive power of a seemingly related issue: the decline in American power and prestige. One explanation for this narrow finding is that the particular stories used in Iyengar and Kinder's experiments did not strongly implicate groups. If group attitudes are helpful to people in organizing and responding to the political world, and if two political issues are related through their common significance for a given group, then concerns about both issues might be affected simply by activating concerns about the group.

In general, then, we might consider several possible political implications of group priming. First, activating group attitudes during deliberation about specific policies might affect how people think about those policies, leading them toward different solutions. For example, attributions of responsibility for social problems might be altered because the implications of the policy for a particular group are made most salient. When racial identities are activated, whites who feel closest to their group might be more likely to attribute group-level responsibility to blacks who commit crimes, while highly identified blacks might attribute societal responsibility for those same acts. Second, at election time, perceived responsiveness to salient groups may powerfully drive support for particular candidates. Activating group concerns might also be an obvious way to mobilize group members to participate in politics in the first place. Finally, members of groups made salient in the political arena might be motivated to learn more about the candidates running for office at the time, especially on issues that are relevant to the group.

TESTING THE GROUP PRIMING HYPOTHESES

Crime News and the Activation of Group Identities

This first set of studies involves news coverage of crime that reinforces negative stereotypes about blacks as violent criminals. Research has demonstrated a growing tendency among local news networks to feature crime coverage, especially that involving violence (Gilliam et al. 1996). This increase comes in spite of the fact that violent crime rates have been declining steadily in the United States for over a decade. This increase in crime coverage has been accompanied by another disturbing trend: In contrast to actual crime statistics, a disproportionate share of the suspects in these stories is African American (Peffley, Shields, and Williams 1996; Dixon and Linz 2000). This is especially true when the crime is violent (Gilliam et al. 1996). In addition, when whites are depicted as suspects, they are less likely than blacks to be shown in handcuffs or lying prone (Entman 1992). Local crime coverage also tends to be primarily episodic in nature, focusing on single events, suspects, and victims. In separate content analyses, Iyengar (1991) and Graber (1980) found that at least 75 percent of crime news on ABC, CBS, and NBC was of the episodic type. Local news is even more likely to focus on individual incidents of crime (Entman 1990). One might expect that exposure to this type of coverage would lead to individual or group-based (as opposed to societal-level) explanations for crime. Political elites aid in this process by using episodic frames when they take a public stand on this issue. For example, Beckett (1995) found that when official sources are used in stories about drug use, they frame the issue primarily in terms of "law and order." This frame leads the audience to place blame for the problem on drug dealers and users, and bolsters support for policy solutions that call for stricter punishments.

These patterns paint a disturbing and unrealistic picture of crime in general, and of the criminality of African Americans in particular. Still, researchers are only beginning to study the effects of exposure to racially stereotypic news coverage on various public opinion domains. One particularly important set of public opinions involves explanations for crime in America. In order to develop effective policy solutions for crime, we need to understand how news coverage leads the public to place blame for the problem where it does. Increased public concern about crime has been accompanied by the rising popularity of punitive crime policies, such as mandatory minimum sentencing for drug felonies and "three strikes" legislation mandating life sentences for repeat offenders that, in turn, have led to burgeoning prison populations. The cycle is a dangerous one, since vast amounts of resources are required to maintain America's huge prison population, straining resources that could be spent to prevent crime in the first place.

Crime coverage could indirectly pit groups against each other because it overemphasizes crimes committed by blacks. Stereotypic crime news might serve as a "vivid reminder" of group membership, to use Charters and Newcomb's (1958) phrase. For whites, stereotypic crime stories may raise fears about the threat they face from "aggressive" and "violent" blacks. For blacks, the stories reinforce the belief that they are treated unfairly by law enforcement and the criminal justice system. News about crime committed by whites would not explicitly reinforce the stereotype, and would therefore be less likely to lead to attributions based on race. African Americans would also be unlikely to feel that white crime suspects negatively implicate their group.

This first study tests the hypothesis that crime news reinforces negative stereotypes of blacks, subsequently bringing opinions about crime into line with the norms and interests of the group. Stereotypic crime news, for example, could prompt highly identified blacks to cite societal forces that contribute to the crime problem, while less identified blacks might be less likely to shift blame away from the group. These same stories might reduce agreement with explanations that have been linked to blacks as a group. Similarly, highly identified whites might be more likely to adopt explanations for crime that are linked to African Americans as a group after seeing the stereotypic portrayal, while less identified whites might be less likely to do so. In addition, more highly identified whites might express less support for societal explanations for crime than less identified whites.

An experiment was designed to test these hypotheses. The experimental setting was in a shopping mall in west Los Angeles, and was constructed to look like a living room replete with couches, houseplants, coffee tables, etc. A convenience sample of adults was drawn that was roughly representative of the Los Angeles metropolitan area in terms of gender, education, income, and partisanship. Blacks were oversampled and cells were stratified by race so that equal numbers of each racial group were spread evenly throughout the design. Lastly, the news stories used in these experiments were drawn directly from local news broadcasts and were minimally edited to produce the desired stimuli. The total sample size used in these analyses is 498 (308 whites and 190 blacks).

Respondents were randomly assigned to one of four groups and told we were interested in their opinions about "issues in the local news." Each group viewed a twelve-minute selection of news. Each story was manipulated in one simple way: the race of the suspect identified in a head shot during the story was altered. One group of subjects saw a crime story with no suspects present. Another group of subjects viewed the same story, but with a picture of white suspects inserted for approximately five seconds. The third condition involved a crime story with white suspects present, and the final group viewed stories with a picture of a black suspect in place of the white suspect. A global control group viewed a selection of stories that had nothing to do with crime. Each respondent, in other words, viewed either one, or no, crime story. Three of these conditions, the control, the crime story without a suspect, and the crime story with a white suspect all had one thing in common: they did not explicitly reinforce the stereotype that African Americans are prone to commit crime. These conditions produced quite comparable results, and were therefore pooled in these analyses and compared to the conditions containing an explicit reminder of the stereotype: black crime suspects.

Figures 9.3 and 9.4 display the results of a test of the hypothesis outlined above. In each panel, respondents are separated according to their exposure to the stereotype (circles) versus nonstereotypic (squares) news. The degree of identification with one's own racial group (measured with a question about how "close" the respondent feels to the interests, values, and feelings of members of the group) is plotted along the x-axis. Agreement with each explanation for the crime problem in America is plotted along the y-axis. The hypotheses posit that the slope of a given line will become steeper (either more positive or negative, depending on the group and the explanation for crime) when racial cues are present in the crime story.

"Societal" explanations for crime

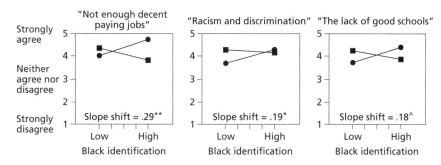

"Group" explanations for crime

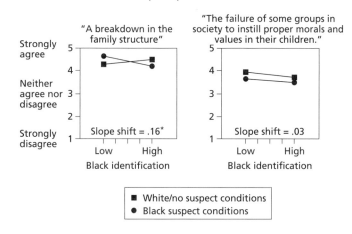

Note: Entries are partial effects of group identification on explanations for crime shown at the top of each panel. Coefficients were drawn from an OLS regression model containing the main effects for identification with the group, a dummy variable for suspect type, and the interaction between the two.^ = p < .10, * = p < .05, ** = p < .01, by a two-tailed test.

Figure 9.3.   African American Explanations for Crime

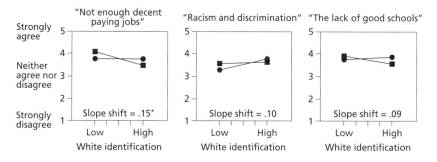

"Societal" explanations for crime

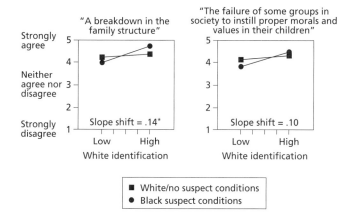

"Group" explanations for crime

■ White/no suspect conditions
● Black suspect conditions

Note: Entries are partial effects of group identification on explanations for crime shown at the top of each panel. Coefficients were drawn from an OLS regression model containing the main effects for identification with the group, a dummy variable for suspect type, and the interaction between the two.^ = p < .10, * = p < .05, ** = p < .01, by a two-tailed test.

Figure 9.4. White American Explanations for Crime

Causal attributions for crime were measured with a battery of Likert scale items indicating levels of agreement with a list of reasons for the crime problem in America. The battery began with the following statement: "Now, here is a list of potential reasons for crime. For each, tell us whether you strongly agree, agree, neither agree nor disagree, disagree, or strongly disagree with the proposed reason." Explanations for crime were divided into two groups: those placing blame on societal-level factors and those emphasizing group-level factors. Societal explanations included "the lack of good schools," "not enough decent paying jobs," and "racism and discrimination." Group-based explanations included the "failure of some groups in society to instill proper morals and values in their children" and "a breakdown in the family structure." Although this last item does not mention groups explicitly, it invokes the problem of broken homes, a problem that the media and political elites have placed squarely on the doorstep of the black community.[5]

In the top row of panels in figure 9.3, the relationship between identification and agreement with each explanation for crime is close to zero among those African Americans who were not exposed to the stereotypic crime stimulus. For example, among those who did not see a stereotypic crime story, higher levels of black identification are associated with small declines in agreement that crime in America is caused by "not enough decent paying jobs." However, the relationship between racial identification and agreement with that same statement is quite positive among those blacks exposed to the stereotypic stimulus: More closely identified blacks were much more likely to agree with societal explanations for crime after exposure to the black suspect.[6] Similar positive slope shifts occur for agreement with the two other "societal" explanations for crime: poor schools, and racism and discrimination. In general, the stereotypic crime story produces a positive relationship between group identification and agreement with societal explanations for crime among African Americans.

A different pattern of results emerges for group-based explanations of crime among blacks exposed to a stereotypic stimulus, as displayed in the bottom row of figure 9.3. Among blacks who saw nonstereotypic crime stories, racial identification was not associated with agreement with the statement that crime is caused by "a breakdown in the family structure." Among blacks who saw the racially stereotypic depiction, however, group identification is negatively associated with this explanation for crime.[7] The association between group identification and the other group-based explanation—that crime is caused by "the failure of some groups to instill moral values in their children"—is not affected by the stimulus. The evidence, therefore, is somewhat mixed but, in general, stereotypic stories lead highly identified blacks to reject group-based explanations for crime and endorse societal explanations for this problem.

The second hypothesis predicted that racial identification among whites should be more negatively related to societal explanations for crime, and more positively related to group-based explanations, among those exposed to a stereotypic crime story. In the top row of figure 9.4, we see that, contrary to expectations, increasing racial identification did not lead whites to reject societal explanations for crime when they were exposed to a stereotypic news story.

In the bottom row of panels in figure 9.4, the same analysis is presented for group-based explanations for crime. This time, the results do support the hypothesis. Among whites who saw a nonstereotypical crime story, the relationship between racial identification and the statement that crime is caused by "a breakdown in the family structure" is a flat line. Among whites exposed to the stereotypic stimulus, however, this relationship is much more positive. The other group-based measure, that some groups "do not instill moral values in their children," is also more positively linked to group identification among whites exposed to the stereotypic news.

Crime News and Priming Group Interests

So far, we have seen that crime news that reinforces negative stereotypes about blacks can prime racial attachments with regard to explanations of crime itself. But if racial attitudes are indeed activated by these stories, then other attitudes should be affected as well. In another experimental study, I focused on exactly how these patterns of crime coverage affect evaluations of the president.[8] Using a design very similar to the one described above, I attempted to determine whether stereotypic crime coverage activated citizens' concerns about the performance of incumbent President Clinton on racialized issues such as crime and welfare, as well as his concern for the interests of whites and blacks in society. I predicted that racially stereotypic crime coverage would prime Clinton's performance on racialized issues like crime and welfare, but would not boost the impact of his performance on nonracial issues such as taxation and balancing the budget on his overall evaluation. Furthermore, I predicted that Clinton's perceived concern for the interests of whites and blacks would become a more important predictor of his overall support when race was made salient.

I found strong support for these predictions. Clinton's performance on crime and welfare became important predictors of his overall support when subjects viewed a black crime suspect than when they saw a white suspect or none at all. Furthermore, the importance of Clinton's performance on economic issues such as taxation and balancing the budget were not enhanced as predictors. These issue-performance items were enhanced as predictors of Clinton's support among both white and black respondents. In terms of Clinton's perceived concern for whites and blacks, the results were different for whites and blacks. Figure 9.5 presents these findings.

In the top panel of the figure, we see that the stereotypic portrayal of blacks as suspects primes whites' in-group concerns. When subjects viewed a crime story with white suspects, Clinton's concern for the interests of whites is virtually unrelated to his overall approval. Among whites who viewed a black crime suspect, however, this same measure is highly predictive of Clinton's overall evaluation. In the bottom panel of the figure, we see a different result for black respondents. For them, Clinton's concern for their group is always a very important predictor of his overall support. Regardless of the presence or absence of a stereotypical cue, therefore, black respondents evaluated Clinton according to how well they thought he represented their interests.

Political Advertising and Out-Group Animosities

Evidence that common, local crime coverage can activate racial identities and interests is intriguing and carries important implications for the production of news, the maintenance of negative stereotypes of blacks, and the impact of the general media context on political decision making. A persuasive empirical demonstration of group-priming effects via political advertising is

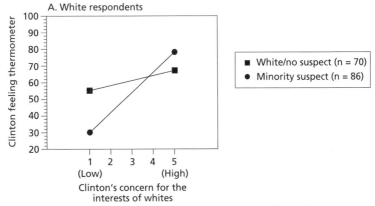

Slope shift from nonminority to minority condition = 7.36 (p < .01).

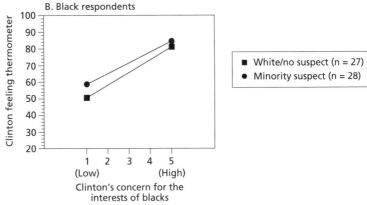

Slope shift from nonminority to minority condition = –.94 (p = n.s.).

Note: A version of figure 9.5 originally appeared in Valentino (1999), and the findings are reprinted here with permission of University of Chicago Press. Entries are partial effects of Clinton's performance with regard to each racial group on Clinton's overall feeling thermometer rating. Coefficients were drawn from an OLS regression model containing controls for education, party identification, ideology, racial attitudes, and gender. The slope shift was calculated with an interaction between suspect type (1 = minority suspect, 0 = white or no suspect) and Clinton's performance rating with regard to each group.

Figure 9.5. Racially Stereotypic Crime News

presented by Mendelberg (1997). Exposure to news about the Willie Horton advertisement aired by a conservative political action committee on behalf of George H. W. Bush in 1988 primed racial prejudice in opinions about affirmative action and other racially explicit policies. The group-priming effect also spread to issues that were only implicitly racial: prejudice against blacks became a more important predictor of whites' attitudes about welfare policy after seeing the Horton story. Given that this particular advertisement received so much attention after the 1988 campaign, and given that the study was not performed until 1992, we need to test the hypothesis across a broader set of appeals to determine how pervasive the group-priming effect really is. The final step in this series of investigations focuses on direct attempts by candidates to raise the salience of these group concerns.

A third experiment explored whether certain political advertisements primed racial attitudes during evaluations of the candidates. Randomly assigned groups of adults in the Los Angeles area viewed political ads that were actually airing during the 1996 presidential campaign. Each subject viewed only one political ad embedded in a series of common product advertisements. A control group viewed only a series of product advertisements with no political ads present. Some of these political ads by Dole and Clinton focused on economic issues, such as balancing the budget or cutting taxes, while others involved racialized issues such as drug use and illegal immigration. Drug use has been repeatedly linked to the African American community in the past (Beckett 1995; Reeves and Campbell 1994). The drug-use appeal was sponsored by Dole, and argued that under Clinton's leadership drug use among teens had doubled. During the ad, a white child is seen smoking a crack pipe. Illegal immigration has also become infused with racial symbolism. In ads by both Dole and Clinton in 1996, Hispanics were featured prominently as the greatest threat among all immigrant groups. Both advertisements used video and narrative techniques to pit the interests of white Americans against those of Mexican immigrants. These appeals tied American identity and white racial identity together by suggesting that immigrants were threatening "our jobs" and "our values" while white faces were shown on the screen. Evaluations of the candidates by subjects who viewed the racialized ads were compared to those who had seen standard economic appeals or no political ads at all.

The results were mixed. Dole's drug-use ad did not seem to boost racial attitudes as a predictor of support for the candidates among whites or blacks. The illegal immigration spots, however, did strongly boost the impact of racial animus toward blacks as a predictor of white support for the presidential candidates. The explanation for these findings with regard to the two race-coded issue appeals may lie in the apparent cues in the ads themselves. While the drug ad contained only images of white adolescents, the illegal immigration ads both used stark juxtapositions of whites and nonwhites as the narrator described the conflict between the groups. As predicted, appeals involving taxes and balancing the budget produced no racial priming effects.

WHAT ELSE MUST WE LEARN?

The evidence presented here for the media-based activation of group attitudes is tantalizing. Common, local crime news that reinforces negative stereotypes about blacks tends to boost the significance of racial identities among both whites and blacks during deliberations about explanations for the crime problem. Such depictions also boost concerns about race as a predictor of support for the presidential incumbent, although this effect was restricted to whites because racial concerns were chronically salient among African Americans. This difference in findings is intriguing, because it suggests that racial attitudes might be chronically active in evaluations of certain political objects but not others. When it comes to evaluating candidates for president, the salience of race is consistently high for blacks. The racial implications of voting for president might be obvious to blacks, who overwhelmingly support the Democratic candidate. For whites, presidential vote choice can become racialized given the presence of certain media cues but is otherwise a decision made on other grounds. The impact of identity on explanations for crime policies, however, is more variable for both groups based on the cues present in the information environment.

In the political advertising experiment, only a few ads were studied, and the results were not terribly strong or consistent. The experiments employed real presidential advertisements, ones that necessarily contained a good many cues besides purely racial ones. In real life, that is, ads often differ in terms of the characteristics of the sponsoring candidate, background music, the gender of the narrator, the presence of attacks on the opponent, etc. A more rigorous experimental test of the group-priming hypothesis with regard to political advertising is therefore needed, one that would pit two ads against each other that were similar in every way except for the presence of racial or other group cues. Then, if these same differences were discovered, we could more strongly conclude that group priming was at work.

Another avenue of pursuit would be to leave the experimental laboratory entirely. Previous evidence bearing on the political implications of group priming has been, for the most part, based on evaluations of survey evidence collected during periods when certain group-based issues were receiving unusually large amounts of coverage in the news media (Koch 1994; Paolino 1995). A more precise survey-based test of group-priming theory would involve continuous tracking of the effects of group attachments on political attitudes and behavior before, during, and after a critical event occurs. For example, by anticipating a clash over affirmative action policy, one might measure the effects of racial identities before the rise of elite discussion and consequent news coverage, then measure these relationships again at the peak of coverage, and a third time when the issue had fallen off the agenda. Extended periods of intense group conflict can not only temporarily raise the salience of particular attachments but might also permanently affect the degree of attachment to those groups in society. The suggested design would be unique in its ability to map out the dynamics of the priming process, the degree to which fundamental attachments were being altered, and would also fulfill the demands of external validity that the current research may lack.

The evidence presented here has focused primarily on the media's ability to prime racial attitudes. However, the priming approach may help us understand when many different group dimensions will affect political outcomes of interest. Gender, religion, ethnicity, class, age, and even region can rise and fall in the political arena as a result of news trends and the strategies of political elites. Furthermore, the implications of group priming during political campaigns become much more interesting when multiple social group identities, animosities, and interests are explored. Many issues can be framed several ways, emphasizing the impact on one of several groups. Citizens often hold conflicting attitudes that might be activated differentially during any given campaign. On affirmative action, for example, white women might be torn between their racial and gender identities. The ways in which elites frame these issues might prime concerns about one or the other group, leading to significant shifts in public opinion and political behavior.

In addition, these analyses leave out more intimate attachments that are quite significant influences on political behavior. Friendship and workplace networks have been shown to play an important role in political decision making, and it is quite possible that contextual factors can affect the salience of these groups as well. A significant amount of research indicates that smaller group interactions form critical mediating influences in the transfer of messages from elites to mass publics (McGuire 1985). Such attachments condition the flow of political information (Huckfeldt and Sprague 1987), stabilize partisanship and voting behavior over time, and are critically involved in the process of attitude change (Knoke 1990). It is possible, therefore, that the media can prime primary group attachments as well.

The consequences of group priming may reach far beyond the actual vote decision. More research is required to better understand the ability of media campaigns to boost electoral turnout among groups via the activation of relevant concerns. Furthermore, more research is needed on the impact of media-based group priming on domain-specific learning about politics, and monitoring candidates on relevant issues. Finally, the implications of group priming for support for various redistributive policies must be more adequately explored. Edsall and Edsall (1992) have argued that during the 1980s the national debate about fiscal priorities was infused with racial significance. Thus, one would assume that exposure to elite debates about where tax dollars should be spent may periodically become a prime for various group attitudes. Gilens (1999) has shown convincing evidence that this might be taking place with regard to social welfare policy, as a result of the racialized coverage of welfare since the 1960s. Current policy debates involving school vouchers, the death penalty, drug prevention, immigration, AIDS research, health care, child care, and many other issues carry group cues that can be manipulated by candidates and elected officials. If the group framing of policies narrows the public's attention to only a few group-relevant criteria, ineffective and perhaps inegalitarian legislative outcomes may result.

CONCLUSION

Group-priming effects should be of great interest to anyone hoping to understand the impact of political communication on attitudes and behavior. The news media and those who have the resources to acquire airtime can alter the bases upon which citizens make political decisions. The implications of this form of influence are serious. Viewing the world through the lens of a particular group identity may be completely appropriate in certain circumstances. During the Civil Rights movement, for example, individual African Americans might not have been mobilized effectively if group identities other than race were salient. The question that arises, however, is *who determines the salience of various group identities in our society?* If candidates are able to manipulate the degree to which certain group identities are salient during political decision making, we must understand how appeals reinforce racial cleavages in a society already rife with such divisions. Is the tendency to structure political choices around the interests of racial groups a healthy and appropriate characteristic of the modern, media-driven electoral system?

This question is not new. Gunnar Myrdal (1944) noted years ago that the racial divide stimulated the most fundamental dilemma in American politics. Some might argue that we have come a long way toward reducing the tendency for politics to be structured around racial conflict. Others, however, insist that the problem of racial group priming is becoming more important in a political environment that favors independently funded, independently managed, and media-savvy candidates. We now find ourselves in an era when the news media unwittingly reinforce racial stereotypes by adhering to an "if it bleeds, it leads" strategy of crime coverage. At the same time, the need to purchase advertising space in mass media outlets drives campaign budgets to exorbitant levels. The messages politicians use in attempting to persuade voters are uncensored, and political consultants are becoming more adept at pressing the "hot button" issues of the day. In many cases, these "hot button" issues are actually thinly veiled attempts to cleave the electorate along group fault lines. We must therefore pay close attention to how these appeals affect attitudes and behavior.

The evidence discovered here is troubling. The mass media can raise the specter of race in the minds of voters, and can therefore structure how they view the political arena and their role in it. In repeated experiments using different stimuli, exposure to racially stereotypic or race-coded communication powerfully affected the priorities of respondents during political decision making. Judgments were increasingly determined by how strongly people held various racial attachments and sentiments. These concerns might lead voters to overlook important, nonracial criteria that could both maximize their individual interest as well as that of society at large. We already knew that the mass media helped us to define what is important about our political choices. This new agenda suggests that they also help us define what is important about each other and ourselves when making those choices.

NOTES

1. The research described here was supported via grants from the Markle Foundation and the Ford Foundation to Shanto Iyengar and Frank Gilliam while the author was a graduate student at UCLA. The author is grateful to these individuals for providing financial support and invaluable substantive feedback with regard to the analyses herein. Errors are solely the author's.

2. Some more recent work has suggested that the contextual factors, including those delivered via the mass media, may have some modest impact on levels of group identification (Lau 1989), but other individual factors are at least as important.

3. It is probably the case, however, that in a given social system the particular group attitudes, effective media messages, or affected behaviors are not likely to change rapidly.

4. Nonracial groups and nonracial attitudes will be considered by the theory.

5. The results for this item strongly conform to the theory, providing post hoc evidence that the classification of this item as "group" relevant is appropriate.

6. The difference in slopes associated with exposure to the stereotypic stimulus is + 0.29 points per unit change on the group closeness scale, a statistically significant shift ($p < 0.05$).

7. This difference in slopes is statistically significant ($p < 0.05$).

8. Due to space contraints, I will only summarize the findings of this study here. A full explication of the data and results can be found in Valentino (1999).

10

The Outside Game: Congressional Communication and Party Strategy

Daniel Lipinski

On August 5, 1999, congressional Republicans held a press conference to applaud final passage of the Taxpayer Refund and Relief Act of 1999. On the same day, President Clinton joined congressional Democrats at a rally to denounce this $792 billion Republican tax cut bill. Six weeks later, on September 15, the legislation was formally signed by Republican congressional leaders and sent to the White House; this enrollment ceremony was conducted for the news media on the East Front of the Capitol. Minutes later and a few hundred feet away, congressional Democrats, along with Vice President Gore, held their own press conference to once again criticize the legislation. Finally, on September 23, President Clinton invited the news media to the White House to witness his veto of the bill. Congressional Republicans quickly responded that day with a press conference chastising the president for this action. Although each of these points in the policymaking process was accompanied by attempts by both parties to communicate their messages on tax cut policy, they were but the tip of the iceberg. In this chapter, I discuss the communication efforts of both congressional parties regarding tax cut proposals in 1999 to show just how extensive and intensive these activities are. In doing so, I demonstrate why the study of such congressional strategies should constitute a new agenda in political communication research.

The ability to develop and implement communication strategies has been recognized as a key power employed by political elites. For example, Kernell (1997) addresses presidential use of such strategies, Cook (1989) examines strategic communication by individual members of Congress, and Manheim (1991) presents a general overview of communication strategies used by politicians and government officials. However, how political parties in Congress use the modern means of communication has not been studied in depth. Congressional party strength is often gauged by the formal powers that can be wielded by party leaders within the institution. Some scholars argue that these leaders play a crucial role in shaping processes and outcomes in Congress (Rohde 1991; Cox and McCubbins 1993; Sinclair 1995, 1999; Aldrich and Rohde 1998), while others question their influence (Krehbiel 1991, 1998). Most of this work (Sinclair being the one exception) has a common focus on the "inside game"—that is, direct influence by party leaders within the institution. Because of this focus, scholars have largely missed the important role played by the "outside game" of public communication.

The use of communication strategies to shape public opinion cannot be overlooked if we are to fully understand the importance of communication to congressional parties, the significance of parties in Congress, the operations of the institution, the behavior of its members, and the public policies that result. The study of communication by congressional parties is important, however, not only to those who are interested in internal and external congressional processes. Scholars of the policymaking process, of campaigns and elections, of political parties, and even of presidential policymaking can also gather important insights by examining such forms of communication.

WHY AN OUTSIDE COMMUNICATION STRATEGY?

In order to understand why congressional parties would use "outside" strategies, it is helpful to begin by examining inside strategies. Cox and McCubbins (1993) and Rohde (1991) argue that congressional parties have developed a solution to the problem of getting their members to work together to further party goals. The answer, they say, is to grant party leaders powers to induce party discipline and control procedures in order to facilitate passage of items on the party's policy agenda. Rohde claims that legislators value passage of this agenda because of the policy outcomes thereby produced. Cox and McCubbins maintain that legislative victories build the party's record of achievement, which generates favorable electoral results for party members. In these ways and more, inside strategies are being used by leaders to achieve policy and electoral goals.

Leaders advance party-favored policies in other ways as well. Kernell describes "going public" as a "strategy whereby a president promotes himself and his policies in Washington by appealing to the American public for support" (1997, 1). The keystone of this strategy is "the ability to rally national public opinion" (145), but presidents are not the only politicians who have the ability to affect public opinion. Although the use of communication strategies by individual members of Congress has received some attention (Cook 1989; Kedrowski 1996), little focus has been placed on congressional *parties* as a whole. Party leaders, especially those in the majority, have the greatest ability among members of Congress to procure media coverage. Therefore, much as presidents have been said to utilize the strategy of "going public" to promote their agenda by influencing public preferences, congressional leaders have a similar (though less obvious) ability to employ this outside strategy as well.

The electoral goals of congressional parties also can be promoted through public communication. Cox and McCubbins (1993) argue that parties build their records of achievement through legislative victories, which makes the public more likely to vote for their candidates in future elections. However, the American people must be made aware of a party's activities for that effect to occur. Also, members of Congress do not passively accept how the media portray their activities. They realize that it does not really matter what a party does unless it communicates its actions and beliefs effectively to the public. Therefore, successful communication becomes essential if the party wants to build a record of electoral success.

The activities engaged in by both congressional parties in 1999 to promote their positions regarding tax cuts serve as excellent examples of the use of party communication strategies.[1] Although attempts to garner public attention increased during the crucial period in which Congress and the president were acting on the tax cut bill, they were only part of the action. Tax cuts, for example, were the subject of numerous messages sent out by the parties from the beginning of the year. Both the Democrats and the Republicans began their tax cut strategies during the first weeks of the year as each put forward a proposal.[2] Although the exact content of the messages went through some alterations (as did the proposed policies), the persuasive efforts continued throughout the year; many of them were part of an overall, planned strategy to affect public opinion.

CONTENT OF TAX CUT MESSAGES

A communication strategy requires a message, and both Democrats and Republicans clearly had specific messages to share regarding tax cuts. Knowing that tax cuts are an issue on which Republicans are usually viewed more favorably than Democrats, the majority party sought to emphasize this issue as an important part of their legislative agenda for 1999. At the beginning of the year, both parties put together a list of policies that they intended to get passed in the House during the session.[3] In 1999, the House Republicans promoted the "BEST Agenda for All Americans" which included "Tax Relief for Working Americans."[4] In the Democrats' agenda, one of their top four priorities was "Targeted Tax Cuts for Retirement Savings, Child Care, and Long-Term Care."[5] These agendas are an important part of the strategies designed to promote the party's goals. The fact that tax cuts appear on both parties' agendas shows that this issue was a top priority for them—right from the beginning of the year.

In January, the Republicans announced a proposal to cut income tax rates by 10 percent. Talking points published by the House Republican Conference proclaimed, "Common sense tax relief will accomplish three essential objectives: Control the growth of government. Stimulate economic growth. Provide relief to *all* taxpayers" (House Republican Conference 1999a). The Democrats' targeted tax cut plan was presaged by the president's State of the Union address on January 19, was contained in Clinton's budget released in early February, and was included in the Unified Democratic Agenda unveiled in early March. The Democrats' targeted tax cuts were much smaller than those the Republicans proposed.

The Democratic rhetoric against the Republican tax "scheme" included claims that their tax cut was for the wealthy and that it was harmful to Social Security, Medicare, paying down the debt, and the economy. The most common message sent by House Democrats regarding the Republican plan was that instead of "strengthening Medicare and Social Security," the Republicans wanted to "siphon off the surplus" for "tax cuts for the wealthy" (Gephardt 1999). The Democrats strengthened their attacks by proposing, and widely publicizing, a plan for setting aside part of the budget surplus for Social Security and Medicare. This allowed Democrats to turn the Republican tax cut plan into an issue of protecting these programs. It was a "risky Republican tax scheme" to help the wealthy and special interests versus the sound, targeted tax relief the Democrats promoted to help the middle class and protect the economy. In order to counter this message, especially with senior citizens, the Republicans introduced legislation creating a "lockbox" for the Social Security surplus. The Republican leadership went on its own offensive to promote this plan in the spring and the legislation was eventually passed.

The contents of the Republican tax cut plan were altered before it finally came to the floor as the Financial Freedom Act of 1999. Talking points published by the Conference in July stated, "Tax relief is about freedom. Freedom to save, spend or invest as you see fit. It's about returning dollars and decisions back home to you and your families" (House Republican Conference 1999b). The three main points the Republican Conference encouraged its members to focus upon were:

- It's your money, not Washington's.
- This debate is not about money. It's about time.
- Republicans trust you—the American people—to spend your hard-earned dollars (House Republican Conference 1996b).

The Republicans argued that their plan was not only designed to aid "everyone" but also that it would provide specific tax relief for education, marriage, retirement, death, and medical expenses, and would create jobs and growth. Although the Republicans focused most of their attention on their own tax cuts, when they addressed the opposition's plans they usually spoke in terms of the "Clinton–Gore" proposals (instead of referring to congressional Democrats). Although the Republican plan was altered, the Democratic message remained fairly constant throughout the year.

METHODS OF COMMUNICATING THE PARTY MESSAGE

In both parties, the responsibility for the communication strategy resides in an elected leader who is in charge of an office endowed with significant resources for carrying out this job. On the Democratic side, the House Democratic Policy Committee (DPC), chaired by Democratic Leader Dick Gephardt (Mo.) is the organization responsible for producing the party message.[6] The Republicans set up their leadership responsibilities differently, putting the chairman of the conference (in the 106th Congress, Rep. J. C. Watts [Okla.]) in charge of the communication operations.[7] The general resources (that is, staff, facilities, and equipment) that leaders are given to conduct message operations dwarf those of any other member. The communication efforts led by these party leaders can be divided into three categories of activities—the remarks of individual leaders, coordination of communication through special events and group outreach, and coordination of individual members' messages.

INDIVIDUAL LEADERS AND THEIR MESSAGES

Members in leadership positions, especially majority party leaders, have better opportunities to publicize the party message because journalists consider them to be more newsworthy than other members. One way leaders promoted tax cut messages was through personal appearances on Sunday morning news programs and other television news venues. For example, Fennis Hastert appeared on *CNN's Late Edition* (September 19), Dick Armey on *Fox News Sunday* (August 8), Watts on *Fox Morning News* (July 2), Richard Gephardt on CBS' *Face the Nation* (September 26), and David Bonior on C-SPAN's *Washington Journal* (July 14). Floor speeches also provide an opportunity to send out a clear message on issues; party leaders usually only give these on major issues. With regard to the tax cut, members of Congress Gephardt, Bonior, Frost, Hastert, Armey, DeLay, and Watts all made speeches during the legislative debate.

House Democratic Leader Gephardt held at least one (televised) press conference each week to make a statement and to take questions from reporters. The Speaker of the House did not hold regular press conferences, but the majority leader frequently had "pen-and-paper" conferences (no recording devices) with reporters. In addition, leaders produced a large number of press releases with statements regarding hot issues such as tax cuts.

Another way in which leaders help get out the party message is through web sites. These sites contain written material, including in-depth partisan analyses, talking points, and transcripts of messages communicated by party leaders. Also included on these sites are audio and video clips of some of the speeches and other public events. Both the Democrats and Republicans made extensive use of their sites to communicate party messages on tax cuts.

Special Events and Group Outreach

Congressional party leaders helped to coordinate all of the press conferences cited at the beginning of this chapter. Special events such as these are planned to bring members together to share the party message in ways that will maximize news coverage. These events feature people considered newsworthy (such as the president or vice president), they bring in large numbers of members to show widespread support for the issue, they include speeches by "average Americans" to produce a wide appeal, and they provide good visuals. An event that was carefully planned for weeks and that contained all of these features was the announcement of the Unified Democratic Agenda on March 4, 1999.

There was significant cooperation between congressional Democrats and the White House on tax cut messages. Having the ability to use the presidential bully pulpit to communicate party messages is a distinct advantage for a congressional party. Even when congressional Democrats and the president did not appear on the same stage together, they were often working to communicate the same message. The president used his weekly national radio address to discuss tax cuts at least six times from July through September. This is not surprising considering that the White House has continual contact with Democratic leaders in Congress and that members of the president's staff participate in meetings with the congressional party leadership staff at least once a week. The White House also had a representative at the weekly meeting of House Democratic press secretaries.

Because interest groups are playing an increasingly important role in congressional policymaking, parties work closely with friendly groups when planning not only legislation but message events. Parties take advantage of the resources, established networks, and grassroots organizations that interest groups possess. For example, the National Committee to Preserve Social

Security and Medicare served as an ally of the Democrats in attacking the Republican tax bill in September. This seniors' group claimed that their ads were developed to "counter a multi-million dollar advertising campaign being run by Americans for Tax Reform" which praised the tax cut bill (National Committee to Preserve Social Security and Medicare 1999). In addition, in March the AFL–CIO launched a "grassroots education and mobilization program" in which they promised to "educate working families about Social Security" and "thank members of Congress who vote to support President Clinton's proposal, and hold accountable those who choose tax cuts over Social Security and Medicare" (American Federation of Labor and Congress of Industrial Organizations 1999). These are just a few examples of the cooperation between interest groups and parties, much of which remains behind the scenes.

Coordinating Members' Messages

Although these first two activities involve party leaders directly, leaders also put significant effort into encouraging their members to communicate the party message on their own. How they did this on the tax cut issue nicely reflects the variety of methods employed. Both parties held weekly meetings for press secretaries to apprise them of the current party message and the events being held to promote that message, in addition to providing suggestions on how to garner local press coverage. Staff briefings were held to keep party members "on the same page" when taking positions and explaining them. Weekly Democratic caucus and Republican conference meetings focused members on current issues (such as the tax cut) and laid out communication strategies. In addition to these meetings, the leadership message operations disseminated a number of different publications that highlighted issues, actions, or events that the party wanted to promote. For example, the Democratic leader sent out a one-page email message to members' offices every legislative day, proclaiming a "Daily Message" that members were encouraged to communicate. In 1999, there were more than a dozen such messages sent to House Democrats addressing the tax cut issue.

The House floor is one particularly important place where communication must be coordinated by party leaders. The introduction of C-SPAN in 1979 greatly expanded opportunities to get messages to the public from the chamber floor. These tailor-made message opportunities took place outside of legislative business and included "one minutes," "morning hour," and "special orders."[8] All provided opportunities for members to speak on any topic of their choosing and all were used extensively by both parties to promote their tax cut messages. The Democrats, for example, had an organization called the Message Group that met every legislative day to talk about the party's message, to encourage one-minute speeches, and to organize groups of members to speak on a party issue during the one-hour special order at the end of the day. The Republicans had a group called the Theme Team that served similar functions and also enlisted the aid of a speechwriter to compose floor statements for members. Throughout 1999, but especially when the tax cut legislation began to move toward consideration, both of these groups encouraged and organized their members to share the party message on the floor.

When the tax cut legislation was up for consideration, the leadership put out a great deal of partisan information to let members know exactly what the party's position was on various issues (for example, on the rule for consideration, amendments, the Democratic substitute, and the underlying legislation) and the arguments supporting those positions. This information had two purposes: to convince members of the party's position and to help members articulate that position when talking on the floor during debate, speaking to the news media during and after floor consideration, and communicating with constituents.

Since most Americans do not watch C-SPAN and get their news from local sources, communication in congressional districts is extremely important not just for individual members but for the party. In order to help Democratic members communicate the party message, the Democratic Policy Committee provided them with a packet of information to take home every weekend. This publication, called the *Weekender*, contains not only materials explaining the party message on various current issues but also suggestions on how to get press coverage in the district. During the tax cut debate, the *Weekender* included statistics showing the effects of the Republican tax cut on different income groups, along with the Democratic tax cut message in the form of sample op-ed pieces for local papers, sample press releases for local news outlets, sample letters which could be sent to local editorial boards, ideas for mailings to constituents, and suggestions for local events packaged to get maximum media attention. All of these techniques helped the leadership encourage their members to promote the party message on the issue at hand.

The Republican conference publishes a much less extensive packet for their members to take home on the weekend, called the *Boarding Pass*. Traditionally, Republicans put more emphasis on communication during extended recesses. On August 10, 1999, for example, the Republicans kicked off a month-long recess campaign dubbed "Takin' It to the Streets." This was a coordinated effort by House and Senate Republicans to communicate their tax message directly to constituents in their districts. On August 4, it was reported that Whip Tom DeLay (Tex.) had distributed an information package to Republican members for the upcoming recess which included "a communication 'check-list' of press releases, town halls, op-eds, and the like for members to complete and return to the whip's office" (Dealey 1999, 1). The purpose of the dictum was to encourage members to complete all the communication tasks on the list.[9]

Although to a large extent all of this material is intended for use by members in their districts, it also helps members who go on national news programs to have the same "talking points." It is no accident that different members often say exactly the same thing when they appear on the news.

NEW AGENDA, MANY QUESTIONS

The extensive communication efforts by both parties on the tax cut issue in 1999 demonstrate the significance of these strategies and the importance of initiating a new research agenda to study them. In this section, I outline a few of the important questions that should be addressed as part of the agenda and offer some preliminary answers as well. As with any communication issue, the critical questions relate to the content, methods of communication, and effects of the messages being sent. These are separated into four main categories: (1) issue and language choices for messages, (2) partisan cooperation on communication, (3) the success of communication strategies in helping to achieve party goals, and (4) the impact of party communication strategies on congressional policymaking.

Issue and Language Choices for Party Messages

The first step for leaders in constructing an outside public communication strategy is choosing policies for inclusion in the party message. From the large number of issues that Congress addresses (or could address), leaders determine which subset they want to incorporate into party-organized communication. Although the aims of leaders are clear—furthering the electoral and policy goals of the party—choosing the issues and the policy solutions that promote these goals is often difficult.

When discussing how Democratic leaders create a party agenda, Sinclair states, "Leaders try to include some legislation that is really important to every member, avoid to the extent possible any that will seriously hurt an appreciable segment of the membership, and assemble a package of bills that reflects favorably on the Democratic party" (1995, 273).

Leaders choose policies that most of their members will solidly favor and few will oppose because this will produce broad and enthusiastic support for the message. Thus, party leaders must consider their members' preferences when choosing these items. This may be accomplished through formal consultation with members in caucuses or smaller meetings, or leaders may rely on their daily interactions with members to understand what they are willing to support.

The other major objective in creating a party message is to include policies that will attract significant support from the public. One way parties do this is by using opinion polls to make choices favored by large segments of the public. Commissioning such polls is one way in which party campaign organizations work with leadership to further party goals. Just because parties use polls does not mean that they will determine issue positions based solely on this information. One major use of polls is that of telling leaders about which policies will best define the party in the eyes of the public. As might be expected, this desire to garner wide public support pushes party messages toward the ideological center of the American public (as Downs might predict [1957]). In addition, when creating messages, parties pay special attention to the marginal districts where they are trying to protect or unseat vulnerable incumbents. Not surprisingly, leaders will choose policies that are especially salient to people in these districts. Since moderate voters usually tilt the electoral balance in such districts, this is another reason why party message agendas move toward the middle of the political spectrum. However, it is important to note that Democratic and Republican policy messages still retain their distinctiveness, with Democrats remaining to the left of the Republicans.

There was a significant difference between House Democrats and Republicans in the creation of their agendas in the 106th Congress, with the Democrats putting forth a Unified Democratic Agenda negotiated by House leaders, Senate leaders, and the White House. This agenda was promoted in a rally that featured Bill Clinton, Al Gore, Dick Gephardt, and Tom Daschle, and included over one hundred House members and over twenty senators on the dais. The Senate and House Republican conferences did not coordinate their agendas and listed different—albeit similar—policies. Part of the reason for these different approaches has to do with majority versus minority status. Since the minority does not have the power to enact its policies, it is easier for minority parties to agree on an agenda than for majority parties. Even if the House minority leader and Senate minority leader were to disagree somewhat on the details, it is much easier to ignore these disagreements when neither has the ability to set the legislative agenda. Having the president as the clear party leader also makes it easier for the (minority) Democrats to settle on a list of priorities.

One theory of issue agendas that needs testing is Petrocik's (1996) claim that each party "owns" certain policy topics (that is, that one party has a better record of handling the issue). For example, it is typically assumed that Democrats "own" health care, education, and the environment, while Republicans are viewed as being better on defense and taxes. Although Petrocik focused on presidential campaigns in his studies, it seems reasonable to test the issue ownership theory in a congressional context. The 1999 tax cut issue provides an excellent opportunity for such an analysis.

Since Republicans are presumed to own the tax cut issue, we would expect their congressional leaders to emphasize this issue in order to keep public attention focused on something on which their party is usually viewed more favorably. In addition, tax cuts are an issue that generally unites the social conservatives and the libertarians in the Republican Party but does not necessarily unite Democrats. However, a look at the data shows that from the beginning of 1999, both Republican and Democratic congressional leaders made tax cuts an issue. Although at first glance this may seem to violate the issue ownership theory, the key is the *content* and *message strategy* behind the Democratic tax cut proposals. As stated earlier, the Democratic tax cuts were much smaller in size than those proposed by the Republicans and they were targeted for retirement, child care, and long-term care. All of these collateral issues are usually viewed as Democratic issues because of their appeal for Democratic constituencies.[10] The strategic purpose of this proposal was to take away the Republican advantage by letting Democrats claim that they were in favor of tax cuts for specific, especially deserving groups.

The attacks the Democrats made on the Republican tax cut plan demonstrate how parties use issues they own. As described earlier, the Democratic messages included claims that the Republican tax cut was for the wealthy and that it was harmful to Social Security, Medicare, paying down the debt, and the economy. This allowed Democrats to transform the discussion into one featuring Social Security and Medicare (which are owned by Democrats) along with the economy, which was a Democratic strong point under President Clinton. This battle over the framing of the issue is a particularly interesting aspect of party message design. Further study of such messages can help us learn how issue ownership affects communication choices not only by congressional parties but by political actors in a variety of circumstances.

Of great interest for communication scholars is the specific language used in party messages. The strategic choices of language by congressional parties became front-page news in 1997 when Frank Luntz prepared and distributed a book to House Republicans entitled "The Language of the 21st Century" (Connolly 1997). Luntz called his book "the most serious effort ever made by either party to put together an effective, comprehensive national communication strategy" (Luntz 1997, 3). He gave suggestions regarding how best to speak on more than twenty specific issues, ranging from taxes to health care to the gender gap. His suggestions for communication included using specific words and phrases designed to appeal to certain groups and to the general public. Of course, it is not only Republicans who carefully choose their language. In 1999, Democrats did not use the phrase "gun control" but instead spoke of "gun safety" when discussing proposals to curb the availability of firearms. When talking about their plans for Social Security and Medicare, Democrats stayed away from the word "reform" because its connotations frightened many. Instead, Democrats said their plans would "save" and "strengthen" these programs.

We can learn more about language choices by examining the parties' messages, noting how, when, and why specific decisions about language were made. For example, the Republicans decided to call their tax cut bill the "Financial Freedom Act of 1999" and to emphasize that the tax cuts directly encouraged freedom. By opening up party communication to this type of examination, we may be able to develop entirely new, rhetorically based theories of congressional politics and, indeed, of politics in general.

Partisan Cooperation on Communication

Having discussed leaders' choices for party messages, the next step is to examine why members cooperate in these communication campaigns.[11] Each member, after all, knows that she is most responsible for her own electoral destiny, so she must make her own communication decisions to further this goal. That is why party leaders attempt to choose messages that most members will find politically useful. In addition to appealing to members' own electoral goals, party leaders will place some pressure on their members to communicate party messages. The degree to which leaders do so seems to depend on the individual and the issue, but leaders do not possess coercive powers and hence can ensure full cooperation only rarely. Just as party discipline on floor votes is not uniform, achieving rhetorical coordination is also difficult.

Party leaders understand that their first priority is to get their incumbents reelected; therefore, if casting a vote or communicating a message will harm a member's chances of reelection, it is best for that person not to follow the party line. At times, it is even electorally beneficial for members to oppose a few proposals supported by their party in order to demonstrate their independence. Thus, cooperation in communicating party messages is shaped foremost by constituents and only secondly by leaders. An issue works particularly well for a party when constituents' preferences encourage, or at least permit, members' cooperation with leadership. Otherwise, members go their own way. If not enough members cooperate, a party message cannot succeed despite the best efforts of party leaders.

Both Republicans and Democrats demonstrated a high degree of unity on the 1999 Republican tax cut proposal. This unity developed because Republicans made the tax cut a keystone of their agenda. For Democrats, this meant that defeating the tax cut would rob Republicans of an accomplishment they were hoping would crown their record for the year. Because of the importance of the tax cut issue, party leaders exerted unusually strong pressure on their members to cooperate. These activities, along with compromises made by leaders with some of their members regarding details of the legislation, helped to maintain Republican unity. Democratic unity was easier to maintain because all they needed to do was agree to block the Republican proposal while offering an alternative tax cut, which would undoubtedly fail.

There has been little study of the messages that members send to their constituents regarding policy matters, much less any work specifically exploring the effect of partisanship on such communications. One piece of research that has explored these matters is my (forthcoming) examination of the official franked mass mailings members send to constituents. This unique data source facilitated a systematic analysis of the messages disseminated by representatives in one hundred congressional districts over a five-year period in the early 1990s. In addition to exploring other questions, this study investigated why members communicate positive and negative judgments of congressional policymaking.

In that study, I found that when members made remarks about how Congress handled policymaking, they were actually commenting on the performance of the majority party. For example, when a member of the majority sends a message *praising* a policy initiative passed by Congress, his main job is communicating support for his party. When a member of the minority *criticizes* the congressional policymaking process, on the other hand, she is actually denigrating the majority party and praising her own party in contrast. My study found that almost three-quarters of the members communicate such global messages to constituents.

This study reveals some of the important factors determining when members support the party when communicating with constituents. The most significant variable was a member's support for the party on House floor votes. The more often a member voted with her party (on party unity votes), the more likely she was to send messages home that were favorable toward the party. Another factor found to predict party endorsements was the relative partisanship of voters in the member's district. The more contentious the district, the more likely a member of Congress was to soft-pedal praise for the party as a whole. In addition, a member's rhetorical support for her party likely depends on a number of other factors including personal ideology, constituents' beliefs, and current or potential service in the leadership. Further study will hopefully better explain communication strategies vis-à-vis party discipline.

There are also important questions to be explored concerning partisan cooperation outside the House. Although Democrats in the House, Senate, and White House all agreed to an agenda in 1999, the House and Senate Republicans offered different agendas and sometimes failed to coordinate their communications. Republicans in the two chambers often espoused different messages about the specifics of tax cut policies right up until compromise legislation was passed; only then did Republicans cooperate on message making. The reasons for partisan cooperation (or lack thereof) between the House and Senate are important to analyze. It is easier for a party in the minority in both chambers to remain united in message strategy because neither is responsible for writing or passing legislation. This could account for the greater ability of Democrats to communicate a unified message in 1999, but these dynamics require further study.

The communication cooperation of most import is that between the president and his party in Congress, since the chief executive is greatly advantaged over any individual or group in Congress in garnering publicity (Grossman and Kumar 1981; Kernell 1997). In the late 1990s, for example, House Democrats attempted to coordinate their messages as much as possible with the White House in order to take advantage of the Clinton presidency, but cooperation between the president and his congressional party has received little systematic study.[12] By studying such matters, we can determine where congressional communication strategies fit into the presidential "going public" strategies described by Kernell (1997).

Communication and Party Goals

It is not easy to test whether communication strategies have the intended effects of furthering parties' policy and electoral goals, although one study has tried to measure the impact partisan messages have on reelection (Bianco and Lipinski 1999). Just as in the Lipinski (forthcoming) study cited above, members' messages were measured in this second study by examining official franked mass mailings. Bianco and Lipinski showed that Democratic House members who communicated messages to their constituents indicating support for the actions of their (then) majority party were more likely to lose in 1994 than those who did not. This finding held even when controlling for the incumbents' prior vote margin, their support for Clinton, Perot's 1992 vote in the district, and the effects of redistricting. These results suggest that the partisan messages that members communicate to their constituents can have a significant impact on electoral fortunes. Congress in general and the Democratic Party in particular were perceived negatively by a large number of voters. By sending partisan messages, Democratic incumbents succeeded in tying themselves to people's poor perceptions of the institution, thereby turning voters against them. Of course, the purpose of party messages is to increase the likelihood of reelection and the expectation is that members are going to communicate messages that they believe will be helpful to them. However, just the opposite occurred in 1994; Democratic members who communicated partisan messages hurt their chances of reelection.

Measuring the impact that party messages have on policymaking is complicated by the many factors influencing these outcomes, but it is possible to get a rough measure of whether a party is able to rally national public opinion on the issues it chooses to promote. Anecdotal evidence regarding the 1999 tax cut suggests that the communication efforts of the Republicans did not succeed in building public support for the bill that Congress passed. A formal analysis of this case would require systematic measurement of what messages were disseminated by party leaders and individual members. With the addition of survey data measuring public beliefs about the content and effects of the tax proposal, it would be possible to examine levels of support and the extent to which public beliefs reflected Republican and Democratic framing of the issue. Public opinion polls taken before and after the parties began their communication efforts would be the best way to gauge the full impact of the parties' message strategies, thereby allowing us to analyze which messages the public receives and which, if any, they accept.

Communication and Congressional Policymaking

The use of communication strategies by parties may even affect the *content* of policies and the overall conduct of congressional policymaking. Much of what we can learn about this impact will occur in case studies of particular issues. Focusing on the tax cut issue, two potential consequences for process and policy are considered. Exploring these and other effects of party communication strategies will increase our understanding of contemporary congressional policymaking.

Excessive concentration on communication strategy may hinder the compromises that are essential to the legislative process. In his examination of presidential communication strategies, Kernell argues that, "posturing makes subsequent compromise with other politicians more difficult" (1997, 4). When positions are publicly proclaimed, they become fixed and cause intransigence in leaders. Evans and Oleszek (1999) have noted effects on congressional policymaking similar to those discussed by Kernell. They dub the use of communication strategies by congressional parties "message politics." In their examination of unanimous consent agreements in the Senate, Evans and Oleszek claim that message politics has had a serious impact on Congress. They argue, "Bargaining that centers on legislative outcomes usually is a positive-sum game, which allows for a degree of cooperation, as well as conflict. However, the national electoral game between the two political parties is strictly zero-sum. When issues touch on the agenda of one or both parties, it becomes extremely difficult to devise an acceptable procedure for floor action, with gridlock the likely result (18–19)."

If communication strategies not only get the party leadership staked to particular positions nationally but also do the same for members in their districts, little room may be left for compromise. This effect on policymaking has been recently noted by reporters who cover Congress. An article in the *Washington Post* on August 1, 1999, for example, claimed that "Republicans and Democrats on Capitol Hill seem eager to draw sharp distinctions between the parties, making compromise elusive" (Grunwald and Dewar 1999).

By studying party messages, it may be possible to determine whether parties are tying themselves to particular positions or to wider principles. If messages do not stake out hard policy positions, they do not directly rule out compromise. This will require measuring the messages that party leaders and their members publicly disseminate to see how specific the policy proposals are in these messages. In addition, it is important to examine whether these commitments remained in force later in the policymaking process.

Another research question is whether the choice of legislation for the congressional calendar and the content of these policy proposals are significantly shaped by a party's strategic goal of having a good message to communicate. When governing becomes campaigning, policy may work to serve rhetoric. During the debate on the tax bill, for example, Democrats suggested that both policy and process had become nothing more than message instruments. One claim by Democrats was that "the risky GOP tax scheme is nothing but a fundraising gimmick" (U.S. House Democratic Policy Committee 1999). They repeated a quotation from National Republican Campaign Committee Chairman Tom Davis who said the tax cut "has been a big money-raiser for us."

Since the president had declared that he would veto the Republican tax cut, it was apparent to some that the legislative exercise was futile. One could argue, however, that if public opinion had changed and support for the policy grew, the president would have changed his mind or at least decided to take the legislation as a point from which to compromise. After all, the Republicans went on a communication campaign to try to rally support for the plan after it was passed and the Democrats had indeed worked against it. Although the claim that this legislation was only a "message vehicle" and not a sincere policy proposal is difficult to sustain, this does not mean that we should ignore the quite tangible effects of communication strategies on the policymaking process.

CONCLUSION

The tax cut issue in 1999 provided an excellent demonstration of how congressional parties put significant effort into utilizing communication strategies to pursue their goals. Despite their importance, however, scholars have largely ignored these activities. By creating a new research agenda in this area we can address a number of significant questions regarding not only the import of communication to congressional parties but also the role of parties in Congress, the operations of the institution, the behavior of its members, and resulting public policies. I have briefly addressed some of these questions here, but many more need to be explored by scholars who study Congress, the policymaking process, campaigns and elections, political parties, and presidential policymaking strategies. This is an especially fertile area for communication scholars and also for anyone interested in political processes writ large.

NOTES

1. For an extensive analysis of every aspect of congressional party communication strategies, see Lipinski (2000).

2. It could be argued that the communication of messages about tax cuts began long before the beginning of 1999. Although this argument probably can be supported, I begin at the beginning of 1999 when specific legislative proposals for the new Congress were first communicated. The fact that messages about tax cuts go back even further serves to support my claim that message communication is a strategy that is often engaged in over long time periods.

3. It is important to be clear about what these agenda are. They are not platforms from a party convention or a statement of policy that all members are expected to agree to support as in a parliamentary system. They are devised primarily as message tools. This is not to say that the leadership and members of the party are promoting an agenda in a Machiavellian manner without any intention or desire to support the policies. Quite the contrary, these are policies that large numbers of partisans can agree to. However, these items are put on the agenda because the party believes promotion of these policies will further their electoral goals.

4. BEST is an acronym coming from the four key points on the agenda—*B*olstering National Defense, *E*xcellence in Education, *S*trengthening Retirement Security, and *T*ax Relief for Working Americans.

5. The Democratic agenda was a "unified" agenda that was agreed to and promoted not only by members in the House but also Senate Democrats and the White House. The other three top agenda items were (1) invest the surplus to save Social Security and Medicare and pay down the debt, (2) modernize public schools, and (3) establish a patients' bill of rights.

6. Many of the insights and much of the data contained in this paper were gathered during my year as an American Political Science Association Congressional Fellow working on the policy communication staff in the House Democratic Policy Committee.

7. This means that Watts is in charge of coordinated Republican communication efforts, but the other party leaders (Speaker Hastert, Majority Leader Armey, Whip DeLay) have roles in communicating party messages on their own. The chair of the party conference or caucus is usually considered to be behind the leader and whip (and Speaker on the majority side) in terms of power and prestige, but he has significant responsibilities on the Republican side because he is in charge of coordinating communication.

8. "One-minute" speeches occur immediately after the House goes into session almost every day. Members are allowed to speak for one minute on any topic. "Morning

hour" is usually the hour before the House goes into session on Mondays and Tuesdays. Democrats and Republicans have one half hour each. Members can speak for up to five minutes. Special Orders occur after the day's legislative business is completed. "Special Orders" are divided into two sections. The first section is unlimited and is for any member who wants to speak for up to five minutes. The second section is comprised of two two-hour blocks, one for each party.

9. Reportedly, when Whip Tom DeLay did this, a "signature prize" was offered to the first member to complete all of these tasks. The prize was a skybox at a Washington Redskins game (VandeHei and Bresnahan 1999, 1).

10. Seniors who had been counted as strong Democratic voters have been lost to the Republicans in recent elections and are now seen as a pivotal group that both parties battle for.

11. Sellers (1999) has done some work on this question in regard to the Senate. He found that party members are much more likely to cooperate in communicating the party message on issues owned by the party.

12. In addition to aiding communication, agreeing with the president on an agenda also places congressional Democrats in a better position of power. Minority parties don't have a lot of power in Congress, but if they can work with a president of their own party they can gain significant leverage.

11

Internet Politics: A Survey of Practices

Robert Klotz

> As ever in politics, you have to restate a message a thousand times before even a small fraction of the people hear it.
>
> —Tony Blair, prime minister of Britain, 1997

> He [a great orator] saw that the public ear was formed to a new matter; and eloquence, he knew, was to find new approaches to the heart.
>
> —Tacitus, Roman rhetorician, A.D. 81

Like any decision maker, citizens in a democracy rely on information. Better decisions arise from better information, yet frequently the available information seems limited. Citizens and decision makers may desire information novelty; they may seek information that has previously been unavailable. Information novelty might be made possible by enhancements in technology. It can lead to new ideas and new solutions.

Political communicators, however, may not benefit from providing new information. They may be torn between the contrasting sentiments of Tony Blair and Tacitus. Information novelty may conflict with the desire of a politician to stay close to familiar territory. This is captured by the recommendation of Tony Blair "to restate a message a thousand times" (Jones 1997, 16). On the other hand, information novelty may help a politician reach new people. Tacitus (1830, 19) suggests that a political communicator may want to "find new approaches to the heart." In other words, it is often necessary in politics to make an ongoing calculation of the costs and benefits of providing new information.

One occurrence that may significantly alter the calculation is the development of a new forum or medium. Practical politicians may see the new forum as an opportunity to provide new information to new people. They may also feel compelled to act in unprecedented ways if a new forum raises expectations of information novelty. Alternatively, a new forum may simply provide an additional opportunity to convey the same information to the same established constituencies.

THE INTERNET

The Internet is a new forum that has implications for politics generally and for information novelty specifically. Although its beginnings can be traced to the ARPANET of the Defense Department originating in 1969, the Internet as a mass political forum is a new phenomenon. The first major innovation that allowed the Internet to move beyond a technologically elite environment was the development of email in 1972. The World Wide Web was not introduced until 1991 and did not have the potential to be a mass political forum until the development of a tool that made the information widely accessible. Thus, the second major innovation that secured the Internet as a mass forum was the development of the Mosaic browser in 1993 and the subsequent Netscape browser in 1994, both of which enabled data and images to be read in a user-friendly manner.

Scarcely visible in 1995, the Internet began the twenty-first century as a bona fide mass forum. The number of Americans going on-line increased from 14 percent in 1995 to 42 percent in 1998 (Pew Research Center 1999) and surpassed 50 percent by the summer of 1999 (Strategis Group 1999). Although the on-line population remains better educated and wealthier than the population at large, the gap is declining significantly. Another common measure of the magnitude of the Internet forum is the percentage of people with an Internet connection at home. The century began with about two in five American homes connected to the Internet (NBC 2000). Of course, this conventional measure of Internet connectivity severely understates the number of people who have access to the Web. After all, one would never say that a person lacks access to health care just because that individual's doctor does not routinely make house calls. A better measure of Internet access would include those who can obtain access at their public libraries. As early as May 1998, three-fourths of libraries in the United States provided public Internet access and the most likely to do so were those serving high poverty populations (Bertot and McClure 1999). As public access moves toward universality, so has the presence of political actors on the World Wide Web. By early 1999, every U.S. Senator and over 95 percent of Representatives in the House had established a Web site (Barkham 1999).

This new forum of communication has tremendous potential for transmitting information. All forums increase information flow, but the Internet seems particularly well suited to doing so. In fact, the Internet is frequently referred to as the "Information Highway," if not the "Information Superhighway." The technology of the Internet imposes few limits on political communicators: they have virtually unlimited space available to transmit text, audio, and video. Also, people increasingly expect to receive political information on the Internet. A study by the Democracy Online Project (1999) showed that 74 percent of the on-line public would like to receive information about presidential candidates via this medium.

THE RESEARCH AGENDA

With almost all federal and many state-level political actors on the Internet, it is not too early to embark on research that addresses information novelty through the Internet. In the years ahead, researchers will be asking an important question: Are political communicators using the Internet to restate a message heard elsewhere or to bring new substance to political discourse? The answers will provide an indication of whether on-line political discourse will be able to fundamentally change American politics as we know it.

More needs to be known about how the Internet is contributing to the content of political discourse and that research should strive to be systematic. It is important to move beyond the anecdotal evidence that has characterized Web content as "repurposed," "billboards," or "brochures." Broad assertions that the Internet is returning power to the people (Morris 1999) or is "just one more crass instrument of hard-sell consumer capitalism" (Barber 1999) are unlikely to capture the complex and competing influences on Internet content.

Assessing information novelty may not be easy but it is important. New information can improve decision making and cause new solutions to emerge in connection with pressing social problems. New information may energize different people as well. As public opinion polls reveal a declining interest in politics and an increasing sense of alienation, information novelty has the potential to connect new people to the political system.

In some nondemocratic countries, there are early hints about the impetus of the Internet for information novelty. Some governments have found it difficult to prevent unfavorable information from being distributed through computer systems that can remain anonymous. Dramatically increased chat room participation and on-line broadcasting helped provide information about bombing raids and missing persons when the Yugoslavian government shut down an independent radio station in 1999 (MacFarquhar 1999). Amnesty International credits the Internet with advancing the cause of human rights worldwide by allowing information about violations to elude government censors (CNN 1999). Nondemocratic countries have also used the Internet to receive information from the people, such as an unusual—if half sincere—call by China in 1998 for its citizens to provide input on-line (AP 1998). Of course, evidence of information novelty is likely to be far less dramatic in democratic nations.

As scholars pursue this area of investigation, the research agenda should try to be as true to the technology as possible. The characteristics of the Internet present a unique set of constraints and opportunities for the researcher. The Internet is a dynamic international forum and, therefore, the research agenda should strive to be both longitudinal and comparative. Since the Internet is in its early stages, the research agenda will necessarily be preliminary.

A research agenda that reflects the technology should be longitudinal since the Internet is always changing. Researchers must be precise in establishing the time frame for their analysis. Until this point, the approach has been to assess rigorously the nature of Internet communication at a particular point in time; systematic research of this type is useful in establishing a historical record of the technology. A better approach, however, is to analyze the Internet over time using a similar framework, thereby enabling the researcher to identify trends and to make realistic forecasts.

A research agenda that reflects the technology will also be comparative across institutions and countries. Studying Internet politics comparatively will allow the researcher to contemplate what communication is motivated by the institutional context and what may result from the impetus of the technology. Across American institutions, information novelty through the Internet has manifested itself in a variety of ways. For instance, the pursuit of information novelty through the Internet has clearly resonated with traditional media organizations. It is important for both symbolic and practical reasons that many have established their Web operations as independent entities. The commitment to information novelty by the media is seen in the regular use of original content such as discussion boards, in-depth studies, and news updates.

On the other hand, in the context of federal agencies and the judiciary, Internet communication is seldom framed in terms of information novelty, but rather in terms of getting documents that already exist on-line. The editorial board of the *Washington Post* on July 30, 1999, made this very clear: "While the Supreme Court of Mongolia has its own official Web site, the U.S. Supreme Court doesn't, forcing Americans to search through unofficial Web sites in hope of finding its briefs and opinions." In fact, it was not until April 2000 that the U.S. Supreme Court launched a Web site. Getting existing documents from federal agencies on-line also has been challenging. Use of technology has been central to recent reforms to increase the openness and efficiency of government. The Electronic Freedom of Information Act of 1996 requires agencies to provide data in either paper or electronic form where possible, and Executive Order 13011 binds the use of information technology to the basic mission of agencies. As articulated by Ari Schwartz of the Center for Democracy and Technology, the Internet provides an avenue for restating content in a more accessible way. "Information should be available by the means most accessible to the average citizen and right now we think [that means] the Web" (Dean 1999).

Even if the goal is to understand the American context specifically, the research will be more illuminating if it includes examples from other countries. The Internet presents a unique opportunity to study comparative political communication. Not only is communication around the world easily accessible but it is also undertaken within a similar framework. This provides a sharp contrast to broadcasting in which political communicators around the globe utilize strikingly different templates of communication as a result of complex and varied regulatory environments. The template used by Internet communicators is almost entirely a product of the technology since content regulation has been minimal in democratic countries. In terms of campaign communication, differences in the communication template based on the intricacies of a nation's campaign finance system are also largely sidestepped by the inexpensive nature of Internet communication.

A research agenda that reflects the technology will be preliminary since we are at an early stage in its development. Political communicators want to take advantage of the new technology but are often betrayed by a lack of understanding. The desire to become associated with a technology that one does not understand well can lead to some awkward moments. One particularly amusing misstep occurred in a 1998 U.S. Senate debate in Alaska when Senator Murkowski tried to show that he was up to speed on the Web: "I have also been quite a fan of it [the Web page] . . . I think I have been . . . ah . . . reviewed as the 7th friendliest Web page user and so forth of the 535 members of Congress" (KAKM 1998). Over time, communicators of political information will learn and adjust to the technology. They will not be the first or best at utilizing its potential but they will become more efficient users of technology. The investigation of whether substance is new or restated is ongoing.

INSIGHTS FROM PREVIOUS MEDIA

The research agenda on Internet communication benefits from the insights gained through the study of previous political media. Scholars must resist the temptation to ascribe too much that is new to the Internet since it is, at root, a personal and mass medium open to communication in any format—print, audio, or video. As a computer-enabled integration of previous media, the Internet constitutes a rhetorical situation sharing many elements with other communication techniques throughout time. For instance, several assumptions about the rhetorical situation made in Aristotle's classic treatise, *The Rhetoric*, are more relevant to the Internet than to the television forum from which most Americans receive their political information: potential for interaction, lack of accidental exposure, unfiltered content, and extensive space for communication.

Studies of previous media encourage researchers to look at a new medium as simply one more strategy available to communicators (for example, Trent and Friedenberg 1991). Expectations that new media will displace old techniques have not come to fruition (Patterson 1982). Further, a new medium does not compel a certain type of communication, nor does it change the institutional context of political interaction. As described by Kenneth Burke (1966, 416), the medium is not the message but "expert practitioners of a given medium may resort to the kind of contents that the given medium is best equipped to exploit." Thus, the task of the researcher is to discover what content is being favored by practitioners adopting a new Internet strategy.

Although certain types of content will be favored over others, previous studies suggest that it is unrealistic to expect the content of a new medium to continue to be aimed at the well-educated population that first uses it. As the user base of a medium expands, diversity will no doubt be reflected in its content. For example, entertainment programs squeezed out public affairs programming on television over time (Dominick and Pearce 1976). Some scholars have already seen signs of the "massification" of the Internet. Napoli (1998) has argued that an expanding user base and economies of scale in content production are increasingly favoring the production of mass appeals by established organizations.

THE INTERNET AND CAMPAIGNS

My research focuses on the implications of the Internet for discourse in political campaigns. To some extent, the quality of decisions in a democracy is based on the information made available to voters. Although some political entities routinely generate volumes of material, political candidates have an incentive to stay on message and to be defensive. Thus, the amount of information novelty provided by political campaigners can be expected to be much lower than that provided by the media, interest groups, citizens, and other communicators not subject to the same pressures to stay on message. Campaigns, therefore, provide a particularly difficult test for determining if technology may provide the impetus for information novelty.

My examination of information novelty strives to be longitudinal, comparative, and preliminary, with my main evidence coming from 1996 and 1998. Although my work focuses on U.S. senatorial candidates, I gain additional insight by looking at the Web campaigning of political parties in other democracies. Ultimately, though, my study illustrates an early example of the emerging research agenda on information novelty through the Internet. Consistent with its preliminary nature, I do not strive to consider all possible sources of information novelty here. Instead, four potential manifestations of information novelty will be explored: (1) new information from financially disadvantaged candidates, (2) new positive information, (3) new candid information about issue positions, and (4) Web-enabled content.

New Information from Financially Disadvantaged Candidates

New information may result from a forum being open to new sources. A potentially new source of information for citizens might be financially disadvantaged candidates who have found it prohibitively expensive to share information in other media. It has been widely assumed that the inexpensive nature of Internet space evens the playing field for third-party candidates and those with limited funding (for example, Kern 1997). Many of these assumptions, however, have been based on anecdotal evidence observing the presence of poorly funded candidates on the Internet. Although the existence of candidates with limited funding on the Web does show that having limited financial resources is not an absolute barrier to an Internet campaign, it does not speak to the relative frequency of such candidates. Measuring how common Web sites are among candidates and what factors may or may not contribute to having a Web site require selecting a population independent of the Internet. Although studies with Internet-derived populations (for example, Yahoo listings) might employ very good content-analytic procedures, their generalizations are limited since they have restricted themselves to candidates having Web sites. With this in mind, *all* Democratic, Republican, and Libertarian candidates have been studied here.

My approach to gauging the strength of new sources is straightforward. The existence of a campaign site was determined by a rigorous search of the four most popular search engines and various election sites. Consistent with the priority of voters to discover issue positions, a home page was considered to be "substantive" if it contained at least two pages (500 words) of text devoted to discussion of issues. Data on whether a home page or substantive home page existed were broken down in terms of the financial resources of the candidate. For major party candidates, a financially disadvantaged candidate was defined to be one who raised less than half the funds of the opponent. The Libertarian Party was selected for study because it is the third party that fields the greatest number of local candidates and because its ideology has been historically well represented on the Internet. The methodology for the 1996 and 1998 analyses was identical except that a measure of referring links was added in 1998. Referring links were determined by using

Alta Vista Discovery software, which provided an indication of the relative
prominence of a Web site by determining the number of external Web sites
that reference it.

The evidence presented in table 11.1 suggests that although some new information from new sources is being communicated, the Internet as a political forum is not a level playing field for all political aspirants. This is most
clearly seen for Libertarian candidates. Although the difference between Libertarian and major party candidates having a home page in 1996 was almost
gone by 1998, there remained a substantial gap in terms of providing a *substantive* page—that is, providing issue positions. There is also a significant
gap between Libertarians and major party candidates in the number of other
Web sites that provide links to them. The disadvantage in a smaller number
of referring links means that there are fewer ways for people to find the Libertarian information. Considering the comparative lack of substance on Libertarian sites, the rest of the analysis will include only the major party candidates.

Among major party candidates, those who are financially disadvantaged
are less likely to have a strong Internet presence. The difference between
the Internet presence of major party candidates who are financially disadvantaged and those who are not, however, did decline significantly from

Table 11.1. U.S. Senate Campaign Web Site Characteristics, by Party and Resourses

Characteristic	1996	1998
Home Page Existence		
Financially disadvantaged major party candidates	56%	76%
Not disadvantaged major party candidates	79%	86%
Total major party candidates	74%	82%
Libertarian Party candidates	45%	75%
Substantive Home Page Existence		
Financially disadvantaged major party candidates	25%	52%
Not disadvantaged major party candidates	56%	63%
Total major party candidates	49%	59%
Libertarian Party candidates	10%	31%
Prominent Home Page Existence		
Financially disadvantaged major party candidates		24%
Not disadvantaged major party candidates		42%
Total major party candidates		35%
Libertarian Party candidates		6%

Notes: A substantive home page is defined by the existence of over 500 words of issue discussion. Prominent home pages have 10 or more referring links. A candidate raising less than half the funds of the opponent is classified as disadvantaged.
For 1996, n = 16 financially disadvantaged, 52 not disadvantaged, and 20 Libertarian.
For 1998, n = 25 financially disadvantaged, 43 not disadvantaged, and 16 Libertarian.

1996 to 1998. The greatest reduction occurred in the likelihood of having a substantive home page. A 29 percent gap in 1996 had closed to 11 percent by 1998. The significance of the declining gap in having a substantive home page is reduced somewhat by the low prominence of the sites of financially disadvantaged candidates. Using at least ten referring links as a proxy for prominence, only six of twenty-five (24 percent) financially disadvantaged candidates had a prominent Web site. In contrast, 43 percent of all candidates who were not financially disadvantaged had at least ten referring links.

New Positive Information

Depending on the forum, the incentives for positive or negative campaigning may be different. It has been suggested that there is something about Internet technology that encourages the use of positive campaigning (Campaign Web Review 1998). New positive information may be facilitated by features of the Internet forum, especially by low accidental exposure. If true, the Internet would provide a sharp contrast to television advertising, whose thirty-second format has been widely criticized as contributing to negativity. Almost half of all television ads involve negative campaigning, which has been found to contribute to decreased voting and increased alienation (Ansolabehere and Iyengar 1995/1996).

The methodology for assessing whether the Internet provides an incentive for new positive campaigning includes an analysis of all major party candidates' Web sites. The three most common aspects of home pages—main page, biography, issues—and any immediate links referencing the opponent were scrutinized for discussion of the opponent for the purpose of putting that person in an unfavorable light. The first goal was to determine if negative campaigning had occurred at all. In addition, the prominence of negative campaigning was assessed by determining if negative campaigning could be found on the main home page and if so, if over four pages (1,000 words) were devoted to negative campaigning.

The evidence suggests that despite an increase in negativity, Internet campaigning continues to highlight positive information. As shown in table 11.2, only 34 percent of 1996 candidates with a campaign Web site had any negative campaigning, and in many of these cases it was a minimal amount. In 1998, negative campaigning continued to be underemphasized, although negative material is becoming a small but significant aspect of campaign sites. The number of candidates with at least some negative campaigning grew from 34 percent in 1996 to 48 percent in 1998. Perhaps more importantly, the *prominence* of negative campaigning increased. The percentage of candidates who had extensive negative campaigning or included it on their main page more than doubled.

Table 11.2. Frequency of Negative Campaigning

Characteristic of Negative Campaigning	1996	1998
Some negative campaigning	34%	48%
Negative campaigning on main home page	16%	38%
Extensive negative campaigning (over 100 words)	8%	18%

Note: Includes only candidates with Web sites. For 1996, n = 50; for 1998, n = 56.

New Candor in Issue Discussion

It is possible that the Internet's unlimited space and capacity for linking to supporting evidence may encourage candidates to be more candid in their issue discussions. Perhaps more subtle and challenging positions might be offered. Since budgetary and economic matters received the most issue discussion on Web sites, a good indicator of issue candor would be whether or not candidates used the new forum to make a case for the politically tough options of cutting spending or increasing taxes. The test for issue candor, therefore, was operationalized by documenting all instances in which a spending cut or tax increase was proposed in the budget-economic sections of the site.

The study reveals little evidence that candidates are using the Internet to develop support for these politically tough decisions. In both 1996 and 1998, nearly all proposed spending reductions or tax increases were nebulous statements about waste. As shown in table 11.3, besides "waste" and "corporate welfare," few subjects were mentioned more than once. The only significant finding other than the overall lack of proposed spending cuts or tax increases is the pronounced decline in proposals from 1996 to 1998, which may be caused by a decreased salience of the budget issue following significant deficit reduction in the intervening period.

Although the tougher standard of candor was not met, it is important to acknowledge that Internet campaigning is disproportionately focused on issues. The amount of attention devoted to issue discussion has been shown to vary considerably by medium (Kingdon 1966), and so it is not insignificant that approximately 90 percent of the text on campaign Web sites was devoted

Table 11.3. Spending Cuts and Tax Increases with Multiple Mentions

	1996	1998
Unspecified waste	9	6
Corporate welfare	9	4
Welfare	5	—
Defense	4	—
Tobacco tax	—	3

Note: Indicates how many candidates took the position in budget-economics section.

to issue discussion. Although the statements made in favor of fiscal responsibility are not particularly candid, the relative emphasis on a particular subject can be very helpful to voters trying to distinguish among candidates (Patterson 1982).

Web-Enabled Content

The most dramatic example of information novelty occurs when candidates use a new forum to do something that simply cannot be done elsewhere. Not only is new information being communicated but it is also unique to the forum. There are already numerous ways in which Internet technology can be applied to video, audio, and text materials. The Web also offers a unique potential for perpetual updating. To what extent are candidates taking advantage of such possibilities?

The methodology for studying Web-enabled content is multifaceted. Here, I scrutinized Web sites in order to assemble a comprehensive inventory of original applications. In addition, Web sites were examined forty, twenty, and two days before the election to determine if any modifications were made to the site. Finally, the most common elements of Web sites were tabulated to give a sense of the relative frequency of original material. In order to add breadth to the study, the sites of U.S. Senate candidates were supplemented with the campaign sites of major political parties in Britain (Labour, Conservative), Canada (Liberal, PC, Reform, NDP), and Ireland (Fianna Fáil, Fine Gael, Labour), three countries that had elections within forty days of each other in 1997. In each country, the minimum number of parties that *collectively* captured 80 percent of the vote share in pre-election polling were selected for further scrutiny.

The content analysis indicates that U.S. Senate campaigns have generally undertaken few experiments with content original to the Web. The only frequently used types of Web-enabled content were standard email and, to a much lesser extent, on-line credit card donations. The unique capacity for perpetually updating material was truly utilized by only a handful of candidates. Although changes were observed on thirty-five of fifty-six sites in 1998, they often involved little more than a routine updating of press releases. The 63 percent of sites updated in 1998 represents only a modest increase from 54 percent in 1996. An otherwise impressive increase in the use of audio or video from 4 percent in 1996 to 21 percent in 1998 is mitigated by the fact that the video involved almost always consisted of replaying a thirty-second television advertisement.

Perhaps the Web-enabled feature most helpful to citizens seeking information is the site-specific search engine. Although that technology is not difficult to incorporate, only four of fifty-six candidates included a search mechanism for exploring their site. Few candidates took advantage of the opportunity to support issue positions with documentation from nonpartisan sources, and in the few cases where it was attempted, the link was usually to a brief newspaper article. Attempts to receive information from citizens were made almost exclusively through email. No candidate utilized an open discussion board and only three conducted an on-line poll.

The comparative data lend additional support to the assessment of low Web-specific content. As shown in table 11.4, the vast majority of the contents of party Web sites also existed outside of the Web. The campaign Web site was just another forum to restate the party manifesto, candidate list, and press releases. As with U.S. Senate candidates, outside of standard email and on-line donations, Web-specific applications were uncommon. Five of the parties, however, did take advantage of the capacity for updating by providing a daily commentary. Perhaps the most original application was an on-line contest by the Irish party Fianna Fáil in which the visitor could win a Michael Collins video if they answered ten questions whose solutions were located somewhere on the Web site. There were only isolated instances of other Web-enabled content: (1) A Conservative contest in which visitors marked the location of a cricket ball batted by John Major, (2) Fianna Fáil's approximation of what is done on election day through virtual voting, (3) an NDP ticker of escalating untaxed corporate profits in Canada, and (4) a Progressive Conservative hookup to a live interview.

A noticeably uncommon example of Web-enabled content was the message board. Of all the parties and candidates, only the Progressive Conservatives established an open discussion forum. Some credit is probably due to them for allowing this interactive element to remain spontaneous by including all messages. Some communicators have been unable to resist editing out negative messages as, for example, with the 1996 Clinton campaign (Nielsen 1996). A more typical response is the decision of New Zealand First to simply eliminate its open bulletin board midway through the 1996 campaign (Roper 1997).

Table 11.4. Number of Parties Having the Component on Their Campaign Site

Universal (9): Electronic version of campaign manifesto, invitation to contribute money/time, complete list of legislative candidates, press releases, email contact

Majority: Biographies of legislative candidates (7), compilation of issue positions besides manifesto (6), daily itinerary of party leader (6), full text of at least one speech (5), daily commentary on the campaign (5)

Minority: Television commercials online (3), excerpts from media outlets (3), contest (2), quote of the day/week (2), interactive television to join live events (1), uncensored message board (1), search engine for policy subjects (1), separate section for opponent weakness (1)

The data gathered here paint a mixed portrait of information novelty on the Internet in political campaigns. Although the burden is on voters to call up the information, voters can access substantial amounts of previously unavailable information from financially disadvantaged candidates. From 1996 to 1998, most of the gap in content between financially advantaged and disadvantaged candidates evaporated. In contrast, other potential manifestations of information novelty on the Internet have scarcely materialized. Generally speaking, communicators have been slow to adopt Web-enabled content. Most of the material found consisted of old content in a new setting. This finding is not surprising in light of the work done on previous media. The Internet is currently being used as simply one additional strategy available to campaigners. New technologies do not, it seems clear, compel a certain type of campaigning independent of the institutional context, although they may favor some content over others. Based on existing data, it appears that the Internet is a medium that favors broad discussion of issues with a predominantly positive tone. As the audience base expands, political communicators may well increasingly frame their presentations for a mass audience. To some extent, this is already occurring and may help explain the increase in negativity reported here.

Examining allied scholarship in this area suggests that my findings can be generalized. Studying a convenience sample of federal, state, and local candidates across the three branches of government, Sadow and James (1999) found that communicators have been slow to take advantage of the Web's potential for information novelty: "If the unique added value to the Internet lies in its interactive potential, a large portion of the campaigns did not exploit its capacities nearly enough nor were entirely convinced that they should." Their work also confirms that Web advocacy is more important to financially disadvantaged candidates. Following one hundred gubernatorial campaign sites from the primary to the general election, Greer and LaPointe (1999) observe that Web sites are dominated by content that exists in other media and that candidates have a tendency to abandon interactive elements. Harpham's (1999) study of Senate and House candidates in 1998 confirms the finding of positive, issue-focused material, with 94 percent of sites discussing at least three major issues and only 13 percent launching an ideological attack on the opponent.

Typical of a new, unproven strategy, the Internet has not assumed a high priority for candidates. Its use remains at the periphery of political campaigns, accounting for only 6 percent of 1998 budgets (Sadow and James 1999). This is symbolized by the official campaign Web site of Mark Neumann (1998), which was among the most sophisticated sites. The acknowledgment section of the site provides a hint that the Internet was not a high priority for the candidate: "I am currently going to UW–Milwaukee. Even though I will still update this site regularly, it will probably be only on weekends and homework-free holidays."

QUESTIONS RAISED

Clearly, scholars have much to learn about information novelty on the Internet, yet even as findings about the substance of Web politics are only preliminary, the agenda will be pushed further and additional questions will be asked. In particular, two questions motivated by my research agenda have already surfaced and will become more compelling in the future. One of the questions is for the legal system and the other is for the research community.

The question for the legal system is a practical one: How will the law treat new substance? This is a question that must be addressed regardless of how much is known at the time. Cases will arise that have to be resolved. Legislators will want to be seen as addressing whatever problems arise. By one estimate, over 350 Internet bills were introduced in Congress in 1999 (Miller 1999), but the answers provided by the legal system may turn out to be unsatisfactory. After all, technology is fast and the law is slow. Wrestling openly with this fact during the oral argument of the landmark case *Reno v. ACLU* (1997), Justice Anton Scalia contemplates the dilemma of assessing the constitutionality of a constantly moving subject: "You know, I throw away my computer every 5 years. I think most people do. This is an area where change is enormously rapid. Is it possible that this statute is unconstitutional today, or was unconstitutional 2 years ago when it was examined on the basis of a record done about 2 years ago, but will be constitutional next week?"

In spite of the challenges, the legal system does make decisions and the ruling in *Reno v. ACLU* is arguably the only true landmark Internet case. Emphasizing the limited bandwidth and unlikely accidental exposure of the Internet, the Supreme Court ruled that the Communications Decency Act was an unconstitutional violation of free speech. Beyond the specific ruling invalidating one technique for restricting indecent speech on the Internet, the larger message of the case was that the legal system is prepared to afford broad protection to original content on the Internet. Despite the general protections set by the Court, legal questions about new content will continue to arise and the legal system must address them.

Perhaps the best starting point for thinking about the myriad questions that will arise is to consider how the legal system has approached early examples of original content. One example of original content receiving at least a partial answer from the legal system is that dealing with how on-line credit card donations to political campaigns will be treated. Before the Internet, credit card donations were excluded from matching funds, in part because of the lack of a paper trail for reporting purposes. Not wanting to thwart the emerging use of on-line donations, the FEC in June 1999 made a ruling that allows matching funds to be applied to on-line credit card donations.

There are numerous other legal questions whose resolution will not be as straightforward. Legal issues have emerged when citizens unwittingly encounter new information ranging from parody to pornography as a result of misleading domain names. Although Congress passed a 1999 law making it a crime to purchase a domain name in bad faith, stronger protection is afforded to trademark holders than to political communicators, and the new century saw visitors to *www.whitehouse.com* greeted with pornographic images. Although the incentive for political communicators to sponsor unsolicited mass emailings, or "spam," is low (after those who have tried it found themselves awkwardly apologizing for doing so), there may be a time when the legal system is forced to deal with what mass mailings are appropriate for political figures. Other legal questions will arise from the fact that political communicators are able to discover new information about voters through their Internet behavior, thereby making issues of privacy highly important. These and other legal issues will be raised in the context of rapid technological change.

A second major question raised about information novelty on the Internet will invariably attract the attention of researchers and political practitioners: What is the *impact* of novelty? Has the decision-making process been improved? Is the Internet leading to a more active polity? In 1996, political practitioners seemed content with using the Internet for little more than showing that they were up-to-date. Increasingly, they will want to know how the Internet is affecting voters. Typically, practitioners have been collecting information about the practical concerns of raising money and volunteers. By these measures, the impact of the Internet has proved modest. One study of 1998 campaign Web sites found that requests to mail a check greatly outnumbered on-line credit card capabilities and that the sites did a poor job of screening out the "spurious information" the authors inputted into on-line donation forms (Dulio, Goff, and Thurber 1999). In the early stages of the 2000 presidential primary season, the most effective on-line fundraising efforts accounted for substantially less than 5 percent of candidate funds (Kelley 1999). One possible sign of things to come may be the ability of John McCain to raise approximately $3 million on-line in the two weeks following his victory in the Republican New Hampshire primary (Drinkard 2000).

The impact of the Internet at an individual level has been slowly drawing attention from the research community. The first prominent study was conducted by a multidisciplinary team of scholars and published in *American Psychologist* in 1998. Implementing an elaborate, well-funded design that included buying computers and Internet access for 169 people and watching their behavior for at least a year, the researchers from Carnegie Mellon found that "using the Internet adversely affects social involvement and psychological well-being" (Kraut et al. 1998, 1028). By early 2000, insight into a potentially paradoxical social impact of the Internet had emerged from national random samples of over 1500 Internet users. While the Stanford Institute for the Quantitative Study of Society found that 26 percent of people using the Internet over five hours per week reported that their Internet use decreased the amount of time spent with their family (Nie and Erbring 2000), the Pew Internet and American Life Project found that 55 percent of Internet users felt that email had improved their connection to family members (Raney 2000). In trying to gauge a mass political impact, the low actual use of the Internet for obtaining political information has posed nearly insurmountable difficulties. As the year 2000 began, even when the population was limited to regular on-line users, only 22 percent of those surveyed had used the Internet for political information (Democracy Online Project 1999).

CONCLUSION

Looking into the future, researchers must be willing to adjust their research to changes in technology. The scope of their research will no doubt expand beyond that which is envisioned here. Even as technology changes in unanticipated ways, the basic question of information novelty will remain compelling. Researchers will want to know whether the Internet is adding original content to politics. They will be able to solidify or dismiss the findings of early research. With wider use of the Internet by the public and an improved understanding of the content of Internet politics, researchers will be ready to gauge the impact of the Internet as a mass political forum. Without the luxury of waiting for more data, the legal system will use existing evidence to shape the legal context of new Internet content.

As for the present, political communicators remain subject to the tension between the urging of Tacitus to find new approaches to the heart and the practical concern of Tony Blair of wanting to restate the message a thousand times. On balance, the content of the communication has been more "new medium" than "new approach." Most campaign material on the Web has had its origin elsewhere. Looking at information novelty on the Internet, the image of Tony Blair is clearer than the image of Tacitus: the incentive to forego new approaches to the heart in favor of restating the message is strong. The impetus of technology is also strong, and advocates will get better at utilizing the strengths of the Internet as part of their overall communication strategy. This change may occur in small steps.

One of these steps is documented by Lucy Ward (1998), who reported on a landmark Internet event. A year after his election, noted Internet novice Tony Blair took part in the first Internet interview of a sitting British prime minister. Questions emailed by the public prior to the interview were read to Blair by journalist David Frost. There is obviously some distance to travel before the web truly constitutes a new approach to the heart. Over time, however, looking at information novelty on the Internet should produce a weaker image of Tony Blair. There are already signs that that is happening: In the first Downing Street cyber-interview, technical difficulties made it appear that the face of Tony Blair was melting on the screen.

12

Political Advertising and Popular Culture in the Televisual Age

Glenn W. Richardson Jr.

The thirty-second advertisements that mark modern political campaigns have been linked to a decline in the deliberative ethos in Congress (Clinger 1987, 731–732; Diamond and Bates 1988, 385), lower voter turnout (Ansolabehere, Iyengar, Simon, and Valentino 1994; Ansolabehere, Iyengar, and Simon 1999), and even the bombing of the Alfred P. Murrah Federal Building in Oklahoma City (Greenfield 1995). Candidates for major offices typically spend most of the money they raise on television commercials; this combination of acquisitiveness and "negative" campaigning fuels the conflagration of cynicism that pervades the public mind about the political process these days (see for example, Bennett 1996; Capella and Jamieson 1997; Hart 1999).

Academic investigation of political advertising and its effects has tracked a similar path, focusing extensively on "negative" ads and their potential consequences. Indeed, the positive/negative and issue/image continua provide the bedrock underpinnings of much of the standing literature on campaign spots. They also bear relevance to raging public policy debates on the nature of political campaigns (see for example, Thurber, Nelson, and Dulio 2000; Johnson, Hays, and Hays 1998; Ansolabehere and Iyengar 1995; West 1992).

Given the accumulated weight resting upon the concept of negativity, probing the meaning and usefulness of the term is an endeavor of some urgency. So too is consideration of promising alternative approaches to understanding political advertising. It is possible that in some ways the very product of academic and journalistic attention to negative campaign tactics may have served to increase citizen cynicism with politics. If this is so, and if we can develop new ways of thinking about ads that do not so readily and unnecessarily lead to apathy or disdain, the quest for a new agenda in political advertising research is clearly warranted.

We can advance our understanding of political advertising, political communication, and ultimately American politics itself in two ways. First, we can unpack the component elements of negativity and extend our attention beyond the tone of advertising toward the complex yet familiar forms of audiovisual narratives found on our televisions and in our minds. Second, we can sharpen our focus on the emotional aspects of viewer reaction to political advertising. Both of these tasks are facilitated by considering the holistic functioning of the audiovisual and narrative elements of campaign spots in information processing. In particular, the evocation of popular cultural elements provide useful forms for understanding the stories and images in which political communication traffics. Indeed, they often allow viewers to "fill in the details" of a message to fit an overarching form even if they miss some of the details. Using both open-ended responses and fixed-item data drawn from small group quasi-experimental research, it is possible to understand how viewers respond to the "packages" of information embedded in political advertising with greater depth and precision than has been the case with surveys or experiments. Such an approach also allows us to probe how viewers actually respond to ads on their own terms, rather than viewing such responses exclusively through the prism of preexisting academic constructs.

The discussion below begins with negativity, the epicenter of the political advertising debate. I then suggest that we broaden our gaze to include emotion and cognition, and more closely examine the holistic audiovisual and narrative conventions of storytelling in the televisual age. Exploratory data are presented that illustrate both the limits of existing approaches and the possibilities for useful alternative efforts. I conclude by suggesting potentially profitable directions for future research and practice.

NEGATIVE INFORMATION AND INCIVILITY

Today, "going negative" is marked with the stain of opprobrium. It is seen as not only a self-serving tactic but as deleterious to democracy as well. During the 2000 presidential primaries, both John McCain and Bill Bradley positioned themselves as harbingers of a new kind of politics, one specifically devoid of attack campaigning. Perhaps unsurprisingly, both soon found themselves engaged in a bitter battle with their opponents about who went negative first.

Serious reformers have considered relieving voters of the contagion through legislation, spurred in part by supporting studies from academic quarters. A careful canvass of this terrain reveals that negative advertising may be a far more elusive phenomenon than scholars have allowed.

It is hard not to draw such a conclusion upon examining a four-article forum on negative advertising recently published in the *American Political*

Science Review (93: 851–909). Alternatively, negative ads decrease turnout (Ansolabehere, Iyengar, and Simon 1999), increase turnout—or at least did so in 1992—(Wattenberg and Brians 1999), or increase or decrease turnout depending on the nature of the attack (Kahn and Kenney 1999a). Further ambiguity is suggested by a metanalysis of fifty-two studies of negative advertising that failed to support *any* of the major consequences attributed to negative political spots (Lau, Sigelman, Heldman, and Babbitt 1999).

Perhaps some of the problem is the fuzziness inherent in our notions of negativity. Each of three original studies in the *APSR* forum defined negativity in a different way. Ansolabehere, Iyengar, and Simon held the audiovisual elements of their experimental ads constant, operationalizing negativity essentially as criticisms of one's opponent. Kahn and Kenney distinguish harsh, irrelevant attacks from legitimate criticisms. Wattenberg and Brians allow survey respondents to define negativity in their own minds, revealed through the recall probes of the American National Election Study. Yet other approaches exist. Bruce Gronbeck (1994) offers a tripartite typology of argumentatively structured negative ads: *implicative* (attacks on the opponent are not explicit; the ad focuses on the candidate), *comparative* (explicit comparison between the candidate and their opponent), and *assault* (the ad's single focus is an explicit attack on their opponent's character, motives, associates, or actions). Others have adopted essentially this same demarcation (Newhagen and Reeves 1991; Lang 1991; Johnson-Cartee and Copeland 1991).

Attempts to distinguish between injurious and benign negativity rest on the useful recognition that free and vigorous debate is an essential element of electoral democracy, yet they are also positioned to condemn some forms of political attack as pathological. The difficulty is in determining whether that line can be drawn without eroding broad protections for free expression and, if so, where objectionable conduct lies. Both the validity of this line of research and much of the policy debate surrounding campaign communications turn upon being able to sustain such distinctions in practice.

Kahn and Kenney rely upon political consultants to identify the main themes of their opponent's campaigns, coding certain responses as indicative of races characterized by "mudslinging." Campaign managers' depictions of their opponents' campaigns as "harsh," "strident," or "relentless attacks" point to races that have gone beyond the boundaries of democratic civility. Still, while it is sometimes easy to tell that some campaigns have "crossed the line," it is harder to tell exactly what they did to create that impression.

One plausible point of demarcation distinguishes policy attacks from personal ones. The former are seen as legitimate and relevant but not the latter, yet candidates often make personal character a key element of their campaign appeals. Should their opponents be denied the opportunity to challenge such claims without fear of being attacked for engaging in negative tactics? Even when candidates don't explicitly emphasize "character," it may be a readily accessible heuristic or cognitive shortcut for many potential voters (Popkin 1991). Even exceptionally well-informed voters might wish to weigh aspects of character in their evaluations of presidential contenders (Barber 1972). Should office seekers be prohibited from anticipating such developments and then responding to them?

Even if one answers in the affirmative, the complex ways advertising communicates carries the potential for subterranean pathologies lurking beneath the radarscopes of current formulations of negativity. In short, political ads consist of more than claims and counterclaims. They are textured audiovisual packages, rich with evocative associations that can affect the emotional impact of all campaign communications.

Most pointedly, political advertising is an audiovisual medium, yet audio and visual elements do not factor into the three *APSR* pieces presenting original research. Ansolabehere, Iyengar, and Simon (1999) hold audiovisual elements constant. The others do not explicitly consider them at all. Yet it is precisely the combination of audio and video elements into complex yet familiar packages that can be so effective in conveying emotion in ads, both positive and negative.

EMOTIONAL POLITICS

Far from being uniformly carcinogenic, negative emotions may play a positive role in the political process. Finkel and Geer (1998, 577) challenge Ansolabehere and Iyengar's (1995/1996) demobilization hypothesis, suggesting three reasons why negative ads might actually *increase* voter turnout. First, negative advertising conveys a significant amount of information (Joslyn 1986; Brians and Wattenberg 1996), and informed citizens are more likely to vote (Erickson and Tedin 1995). Second, negative information may really be quite helpful to citizens in distinguishing among the candidates (Lau 1985; Garramone et al. 1990). Third, negative advertisements may produce stronger emotional effects than positive ones, stimulating learning in ways "positive" spots do not (Marcus and MacKuen 1993).

Despite their insight, however, Finkel and Geer (1998) do not explicitly examine the evocation of emotion in political advertising, nor do the other *APSR* researchers. A substantial literature does, however, indicate the salience of emotion in viewer response to political advertising (Kern 1989; Lang 1991; Jamieson 1992; Morris, Roberts, and Baker 1999).

A broad and deep literature addresses the role of narratives in social and political discourse (see for example, van Dijk 1988; Carey 1988; Jamieson 1992b; West and Loomis 1998, especially 75–108), and emotions provide important punctuation to the narratives or stories that citizens use to understand and communicate about politics. Popkin's (1991) by-product theory of political information points to a major source of the substantive content of political communication: popular culture. Lacking the resources necessary to process large amounts of political information, many citizens approach political decisions informed by their personal experiences. Popular culture permeates our personal spaces, and is increasingly the common tongue in which we converse. To better understand the stories about politics in our minds and on our television sets, we can turn to the stories of popular culture, the threads from which the tapestry of political communication is woven (see especially Nelson and Boynton 1997; G. Richardson 1995, 1998a).

POPULAR CULTURE AND POLITICAL ADVERTISING

Scholars have long recognized the importance of the audiovisual elements of campaign ads and have probed them in considerable analytical detail (see for example, Kaid and Davidson 1986; Kern 1989; Thorson, Christ, and Caywood 1991; Kepplinger 1991; Biocca 1991a, 1991b; Kaid and Bystrom 1999). While treating audio, video, and narrative elements separately has many virtues, such an approach overlooks how familiar packages of audio, video, and narrative elements combine to resonate widely throughout the culture. It is the holistic function of these elements, the way they work *together* as a whole, which has yet to be explored by students of political communication.

The resonance of recurring forms in popular culture is at the heart of what literary and film theorists refer to as "genre." Genres are essentially *categories* of texts, including the familiar horror stories, satires, romances, and biographies found in popular entertainment. By using the recognizable conventions of these classic forms, political communicators are able to place thirty-second spots in the context of a rich web of preexisting associations and emotions.

The notion of genre has figured prominently in communications research (see Campbell and Jamieson 1978), yet it is not the more formal genres of rhetoric but their kindred spirits in popular culture that have been neglected in the quest to unpack the meaning in campaign commercials. While taxonomic approaches have been used to classify different ads (see for example, Devlin 1986), genre has not been recognized as a source of the substantive meaning viewers derive from political advertising.[1]

In visual media, genres rely on the holistic synergy of several reinforcing stimuli. The music and sound effects matter, as do the rhythms and tones of the narrator's voice. More importantly, as Berger notes, "we quickly learn the conventions of a genre and expect to find them" (Berger 1995, 45). Viewers come to recognize what the pictures "should be" from their sense of how an announcer's voice sounds and how the music is played. Viewers of a horror story, for example, are aware of imminent danger as the musical score becomes tenser and as the scene darkens—even before the monster appears—because they know how the pieces fit together. Similarly, a sparse, high-tech soundtrack can combine with an appropriate narrative to evoke a sense of science fiction and the future. Words, sounds, and pictures work together in evoking a genre. These are the shared audiovisual conventions of popular culture in our times.[2]

The appeal of generic association was not lost on George H. W. Bush's advisors when they sought to wrap the vice president in the aura of Clint Eastwood's action hero, "Dirty Harry" Callahan. In August 1988, Bush's speechwriting team was sharply divided over whether to include in the vice president's acceptance speech at the Republican National Convention the now infamous line, "Read my lips: no new taxes!" "Stupid and irresponsible," argued Richard Darman, who had been designated editor-in-chief of the speech. Speechwriter Peggy Noonan admonished the informal speech committee: "whatever you guys do, don't screw with these lines." Darman claimed that huge budget deficits would be a drag on the economy and that the "no taxes" pledge would make governing very difficult. Ultimately, what media advisor Roger Ailes called the "Clint Eastwood factor" prevailed: politics for Ailes was theater, Bush needed to bury forever the "wimp factor," and mimicking Dirty Harry would do it (Woodward 1992).

Understanding how the conventions of popular genres of entertainment frame viewer response to political advertising can help us understand the narrative structuring of campaigns in two ways.[3] First, such conventions provide telling details that shape meaning, especially emotions. The crucial connective element that glues the components of compelling narratives together is often reinforced by generic evocations. Genres serve as emotional heuristics—self-teaching devices. The 1988 GOP attacks against Michael Dukakis, whose narrative structure is forcefully analyzed by Jamieson (1992a, 459–484), were easily absorbed by viewers more familiar with pop culture than criminal justice policy. The ads implied that Dukakis would turn every day into *Friday the 13th*. In addition, the evocation of genre can help viewers reconstruct a compelling narrative even *without* being exposed to detailed, highly elaborate verbal claims. That is, because viewers are familiar with generic forms, they can use those forums as shorthand ways of recouping the details they may have missed. Let us consider each of these themes in turn.

Genre and Thirty-Second Narratives

The broad narratives of American politics over the past decade can be discerned in rich detail in some of the shifting generic referents in campaign spots. In 1988, for example, the Bush–Quayle team used the popular genres of horror and dystopia through spots such as "Revolving Door," (Boston) "Harbor," and "New Jersey at Risk" to blast Michael Dukakis on crime and the environment, while also countering his claims to competence.[4] "Revolving Door" (the Bush campaign's prison furlough ad) evoked the genre of horror through stark black-and-white pictures of prison watchtowers matched to the soundtrack of a "slasher" film. "Harbor" also used the conventions of horror, including ominous and foreboding music, stark visual imagery, and a tone of narration and narrative strongly consistent with horror. (In 1992, the Bush team reprised many of these same themes in the dystopian "Arkansas," which featured a barren landscape and ominous storm clouds to signal the imminent danger of Clintonism.) In 1994, the genre of tabloid TV news, with its emphasis on the salacious and the scandalous, had become recognizable enough that evocation of its generic form powerfully communicated the charges of womanizing, fraternizing with drug dealers, and not telling the truth in Oliver North's attack on rival Charles Robb's character in the Virginia U.S. Senate race. In 1996, Richard A. Zimmer, Republican candidate for the U.S. Senate in New Jersey, aired an ad designed to look like a conventional television newscast. It featured a news anchor reading copy (including "Fox News reports that . . .") charging his opponent with corruption and mob association, grafting onto his ad the credibility of local news. Also during 1996, a Pat Buchanan ad used the "real-life" look and feel of the TV show *Cops* to evoke fear and urgency over the dark side of illegal immigration.

In the 1996 presidential campaign, the Clinton–Gore team's strategic focus on "soccer moms" and suburban voters found a powerful voice in the adoption of the generic form of family melodrama, which was used to portray "Dole–Gingrich" as the sinister threat to family life and Bill Clinton as the caring and benevolent father figure (conveniently countering charges of Clinton's own character flaws). The ad ("Protecting Our Values") shared generic conventions (including melancholy solo piano to underscore the threat and bright soft focus to underscore benevolence) with an actual melodrama on the Family and Medical Leave Act (in which the president made a cameo appearance) that aired during the winter following the campaign. By evoking the genre of family melodrama (tales of abused children, alcoholic parents, and so on), "Protecting Our Values" could combine both threat and response in a way that Bush's earlier "Grandchildren" ad (which combined a soundtrack of swelling strings with soft focus close-ups of a family picnic) could not.

An ad created for Reform Party candidate Jesse Ventura for the 1998 Minnesota gubernatorial contest is difficult to analyze save in terms of genre. It featured two children playing with action figures (Jesse "The Body" and "Special Interest Man"). An awareness of cartoon action dramas allows one to favorably fill in the details the ad seeks to convey: that Mr. Ventura will be a strong independent voice for Minnesota. If viewers were devoid of this pop culture background, simply seeing two children playing with dolls would probably fail to convey the intended political message.

In the 2000 campaigns, politicians sought to convey authenticity in their spots, and they did so by evoking the look and feel of home video or "real life" TV, not infrequently staging the candidate at the proverbial kitchen table or on the living room couch. Such audiovisual conventions can be readily distinguished from those that evoke integrity—a related yet distinguishable theme also prominent in Campaign 2000. Senator John McCain's heroic biography (emphasizing his five years as a prisoner of war in Vietnam) proved an appealing antidote at a time when politicians have proven all too mortal.

Genre and Information Processing

Genres do more than help flesh out the structure of narratives. They can actually allow viewers to reconstruct narrative details with which they haven't been formally presented. A brief digression into some recent work on political cognition and communication can help show how this is so.

An important thread of information processing research has emphasized schema theory.[5] Schemata can serve two important functions: first, they guide the processing and storage of information; second, they guide recall and interpretation of information in memory (Lau and Sears 1986b, 350–351). They operate in a top-down fashion, a point crucial in explaining how genres work in political advertising to affect meaning, memory, and recall. Lau and Sears describe the "reconstructive" nature of schemata this way:

> recall of some specific instance of a schema is often guided by the generic principles of the schema rather than by the particulars of that specific instance (Rothbart, Evans, and Fulero 1979; Snyder and Uranowitz 1978). For example, once a person has been categorized as having a particular trait or fitting into a particular category, people will falsely recognize that trait or category because schemata provide "default values" to fill in the blanks. (Minsky 1975)

Doris Graber (1997, 4) notes that "norms that are prevalent within cultural communities . . . provide a unifying mechanism" in cognitive processing, and that individuals describe their own thoughts "in terms of what they believe these shared norms to be rather than in terms of their own unique perceptions." She also notes that, "When people are asked to recall very specific situations, such as details from a news story, memory is apt to be weak or absent because details have not been stored in memory. Rather, people have stored general meanings as part of already existing schemata" (Graber 1997, 6).

Evoking popular genres provides the form that viewers use to reconstruct the details of content in political advertising, and is therefore crucial in shaping viewer "recall" of campaign spots.[6] Genres also provide substantial emotional content, thereby providing an additional indirect channel that further influences memory and evaluation.

The turn to genre is further reinforced by recognition of the important ways in which cognition is characterized by neuronal networks of association (Anderson 1983, 41–45, 126–131). Such networks provide linkages of spreading activation among associated concepts in memory. Graber points out that the "process of connecting neurons—the tiny chips of the mental mosaic—appropriately so they can form a recognizable mental schema is guided by mental maps or indexes that are developed by storing memories of past experiences" (Graber 1997, citing Hilts 1995).

Among political scientists, G. R. Boynton, Milton Lodge, and Kathleen Mc-Graw have been at the forefront of a movement to develop research techniques that measure such cognitive representational structures (see, for example, Boynton 1995, Lodge 1995a, McGraw and Steenbergen 1995, all collected in Lodge and McGraw 1995). If this work is on target, then genre analysis can contribute mightily to the phenomenology of ad experiences because genre conventions offer a social parallel to these associative operations of individual cognition (see also Biocca 1991b, 62, on the linkage between the semantic frames of political advertising and cognitive schemata). When viewers process an ad such as "Revolving Door" in terms of horror, they are literally activating a network of neuronal associations (some emotionally charged), prompted by the top-down recognition of a generic form. These associations, moreover, are likely to be similar across different viewers, each of whom is aware of the shared conventions of horror and its associated emotional response.

A genre approach integrates the various levels of meaning (narrative and audiovisual) within real forms of social experience and connects those forms with how individual viewers experience the ads. This enables the genre analyst to approximate the emotional experiences viewers have when watching the ads. In their analysis of focus groups exposed to a variety of campaign communication, for example, Just et al. (1996) found viewers who processed ad content in terms of genre (the Bush dystopian "Arkansas" about Bill Clinton's record as governor "frightened" one respondent [161]), but also found viewers who reacted to the ads by creating generic referents such as "Laurel and Hardy" and "Abbott and Costello" when describing the candidates (189–190). At the same time, the use of genre also enables the analyst to go beyond the culture's ordinary talk to engage the technical and political subtleties affecting campaign activities.

Genres draw upon the conventions, associations, and understandings that permeate our culture. In ads, they are the most notable manifestations of "the social construction of reality" (Berger and Luckmann 1966). As such, they provide the student of political advertising with an inherently powerful yet accessible tool for understanding the substantive meaning of campaign spots. Genres communicate to audiences precisely because audiences know what the package of conventional associations stands for. Unlike overt, verbal arguments, these packages span both logic and emotion. A genre approach to campaign spots invites us to explore how visual, audio, and narrative combine in culturally conventional fashion to convey substantive meaning, meaning that is often found beneath the surface. Such meaning must be at the core of what Trent and Friedenberg call the "only important reason to categorize types of political commercials: . . . to gain some understanding of their rhetorical purpose" (1991, 127).

ASSAULTS VERSUS COMPARISONS

How do viewers actually react to these genre-laden ads? I report here some exploratory data consisting of viewer responses to two political ads used in a small-group, quasi-experimental research project. The pair of spots allows us to contrast comparative and assaultive ads, as well as to explore generic evocations and various aspects of information processing. The response document included open-ended recall probes of viewers' recollections of the sights and sounds of the ads as well as explorations of the associations the ad triggered in their minds.

The two ads were produced for the 1990 Michigan U.S. Senate campaign of Republican Bill Scheutte. Both pointed out that opponent Carl Levin opposed the Maverick antitank missile and the battleship USS *Wisconsin*. One (titled "Never Again") featured Schuette in front of the Vietnam Memorial in Washington, D.C., and offered an explicitly comparative framework ("I voted for it, Carl Levin opposed it."). The other ("Levin of Arabia") featured a disheveled Levin, satirically ridiculed for his trip to the *Wisconsin* "for a photo shoot at taxpayers' expense." It attacks the opponent without even mentioning the sponsor's position. According to the Gronbeck trichotomy, the first of these ads is comparative, the second assaultive. (See ad scripts in appendix A.)

Detailed consideration of one respondent's reactions, however, illustrates the limits of comparison as a basis for describing viewer response to such ads. "Never Again" featured the candidate standing in front of the Vietnam Memorial in Washington, D.C., comparing his support for specific weapons with his opponent's opposition. When asked "how would you describe the ad to a friend," one respondent wrote: "He talked in short sentences w/regard to 2 or 3 weapons systems he supported that he said his opponent did not support."

This retelling casts the ad largely in comparative terms, yet this statement barely scratches the surface of how the respondent processed the ad. When asked to "describe your feelings" upon viewing the ad, the same respondent wrote: "I don't like to feel manipulated or be used, so my reaction was a feeling of disregard with a smile." Among the first five associations this viewer offered to the ad were, "He is using patriotism to his only personal advantage. . . . There are enough real issues that he should be debating w/o need to manipulate votes through fear."

In short, while this respondent fully and explicitly recognized the comparative structure of "Never Again," the respondent's *range* of reactions was much broader. Indeed, the generic evocation of patriotism seemed to generate the cynical attitude that some might see as one of the unsavory consequences of "negative" advertising, effectively overwhelming the ad's overt comparison.

In fact, most of the respondents who used the language of comparison did so in ways that offer little encouragement for those craving more enlightened political discourse. On the surface, viewer response to "Never Again" indicates that the comparison between the two candidates was something that many people picked up on. A majority of respondents made some reference to what can be at least loosely construed as comparison. This stands in stark contrast to the paucity of references to comparison offered by viewers of the satirical ad "Levin of Arabia," which included the same charge about Levin's opposition to two weapons but did not make the explicit comparison with candidate Schuette's position.

Those who did offer references to comparison did so in ways that often seemed almost ritualistic in nature. One respondent's initial association is illustrative. "He didn't, I did statement—stuck with me even after the commercial was over." In response to the probe seeking secondary associations, for "he didn't, I did," this viewer wrote, "Stuck w/me. Made other guy look bad. All politicians say it. Good way to attack." For this respondent, comparison was actually a technique of attack. Very little (if any) of this type of response can be categorized as a "healthy comparison of issue stands."

It is noteworthy that the assaultive "Levin of Arabia" ad actually generated *more* focus (both positive and negative) on the narrow policy issue at hand (support for specific weapons and the military in general) than the comparative ad "Never Again." One would be tempted to conclude that if the goal is to foster discussion of issues, one-sided assaultive ads can, at least on occasion, be even *more* effective than explicit comparisons.

THE COMPONENTS OF "NEGATIVITY"

How can we best "unpack" the meaning of negativity in viewers' minds? Four different uses or interpretations of negativity emerge from the exploratory response data: unbalanced, misleading, cutthroat, and emotional.

Taken as a whole, these four conceptualizations show that "negativity" is not a particularly coherent (or unidimensional) term, especially when coupled with the lack of connection between the content of ads and the reactions they generate. In other words, negativity is a far broader concept than has been acknowledged heretofore.

Negative Ads as Unbalanced

Perhaps the most pervasive sense of negativity among the respondents was that ads seemed one-sided, offering only an attack on the opponent with no statement of the ad sponsor's position. This reaction echoes Gronbeck's assaultive category, but it was also used to describe the explicitly comparative spot.

The ad "Never Again" was included in this study specifically because of its explicitly comparative nature—it named both candidates and stated both of their positions. Perhaps if that was all that was in the ad, viewer response would have been more benign, providing evidence for Gronbeck's contention that comparative ads need not wound the body politic. As with most ads, however, the visual, aural, and mythic aspects of "Never Again" went far beyond mere comparison.

Despite the fact that the ad says "I voted for it, Carl Levin opposed it," some viewers saw the ad as one-sided. One offered the following "retelling": "He was using the success of the war to play upon people's emotions of pride. It was one-sided, noninformative, slanted." This perception of the ad as being negative because it was one-sided suggests that for some viewers, a vague comparison is the same as no comparison.

Negative Ads as Misleading or Distorted

Another common way in which viewers saw the ads was by focusing on their alleged half-truths or distortion. One respondent provided this retelling of "Levin of Arabia": "It was a negative campaign ad, that probably lacked in complete accuracy and could very well be the beginning of a vicious round of mudslinging."

Although viewers often mentioned more than one reason why they considered the ad to be negative, the notion that the ad was negative because it tried (literally) to make Carl Levin "look bad" was particularly common. One respondent's initial associations included: "Looked negative toward the candidate—like someone else made it (opponent). Showed the politician w/his hair messed up and blowing. . . . Negative advertising—in a way cheating." This person elaborated with these secondary associations. "Showed bad and unpleasant pictures of him. All negative points. Hair blowing and messed up. . . . Very negative pictures."

Negative Ads as Evil Exemplars

A third reading of "negative" advertising was based on an assessment of campaign *tactics*. What these responses had in common was a profoundly loathsome view of the political process. If one looks beyond the immediate references to negative advertising in these responses, one finds a good deal of cynicism about politicians' mendacity. These viewers evidently perceive politicians and their modus operandi as despicable. One respondent offered a succinct response to the "feelings" probe: "I don't have too much emotion. I just felt like he was making a scam."

The assaultive "Levin of Arabia" ad prompted many viewers to describe the ad as "negative," yet in doing so, most respondents did not rely primarily on its assaultive, one-sided nature. Instead, viewers found the ad's visual depictions negative because it was yet another example of a debased political discourse, one characterized by falsehoods, half-truths, hypocrisy, and "bashing" one's opponents. These reactions were triggered, no doubt, by the ad's successful ridiculing of its target.

Negative Ads as Emotional

Finally, some viewers saw negativity in the ads' use of emotional appeals. Typically, it is the use of fear and graphic imagery that is seen by viewers and analysts alike as supplanting rational discussion of issues. Indeed, for some viewers, the comparative ad "Never Again" was seen as negative because it sought to play upon a combination of emotions, in this case fear and patriotism. One viewer responded to the feelings probe this way: "Disappointed that that ad was targeting people's fears in order to compel them to vote for someone who's pro-arms spending." They underscored this sentiment in retelling the story of the ad. "This candidate is pro-military and preys upon public's fears and hostility to try and get into office."

Of course, while an ad can be seen as "negative" because of the way it manipulates emotion, "positive" ads can be quite emotional too. In sum, upon unpacking, the attributes that lead viewers to describe ads as negative are untethered to attack per se. Distortion, emotional appeals, and one-sidedness rightly warrant academic attention and public condemnation, but they can easily be found in positive ads as well, and can be effectively cleaved from "negativity."

GENERIC EVOCATION

While "Never Again" and "Levin of Arabia" can be distinguished in terms of negativity, they can also be seen as generic examples. "Arabia," for example, can be seen loosely as a satire, somewhat akin to the infamous "Tank Ride" spot produced by the Bush campaign in 1988. "Never Again," while explicitly comparative, strongly evoked Vietnam, framing viewer response in terms of the conflicts and emotional scars of the war, vividly seared into popular culture through a series of feature films and television programs. This evocation effectively subverted the ad's presumptive focus on contemporary weapons issues.

Viewers of "Levin of Arabia" offered several responses consistent with the satirical nature of the ad. The most typical response was that Levin "looked stupid," a judgment fueled by the disheveled image of Levin onboard the *Wisconsin*, his hair blowing wildly in the wind, which the ad returned to time and again. A third of the respondents referred to Levin's appearance.

Others responded to the subtext of humorous ridicule, noting for instance the closing punch line, "if Carl Levin had his way, he wouldn't have a ship to stand on and neither would our troops." The ad also included a graphic targeting of the ship, which in the final frame disappears from the ocean, leaving only its wake visible on the water. That "Levin of Arabia" evoked satire for some viewers is particularly noteworthy because the ad itself is not particularly effective in doing so. Unlike "Tank Ride," which included rusty squeals and a rumbling, sputtering engine rising and falling in volume as aural punctuation of the ad's claims, "Levin" used no sound effects at all. Evidence of holistic, top-down processing by some viewers includes the fact that one respondent wrote of hearing "a bomb or a gun" going off before the ship disappeared. Another viewer suggested that the ad should have included patriotic music in its soundtrack. This almost certainly would have amplified the satirical evocation of the spot.

The generic evocation of Vietnam in "Never Again" actually served to subvert the ad's ostensible appeal—a call for a stronger military in the face of "another Hitler" in the Persian Gulf. Rather than focusing on that claim, many viewers revisited the ambivalence of Vietnam, specifically as seen through the lens of popular culture. These respondents referred to films such as *Full Metal Jacket, Platoon,* and *Born on the Fourth of July,* although they were not prompted to discuss movies. What did prompt them was the somber military drumroll featured in the ad and the emotional presence of the Vietnam Memorial, visible throughout the ad as the backdrop for the candidate's plea. Here, too, we find evidence of top-down processing. Many viewers described the patriotic scene unfolding in front of the memorial as a sunny setting in a park, and several indicated specifically that they recalled seeing flags. In fact, no flags actually appeared in the ad—although they are the kind of details that would fit the form.

Perhaps more importantly, many of the responses shared themes found in the narratives of Vietnam found in the cinema and on television. Communication scholar Pat Aufderheide suggests, for example, that beginning in the late 1980s, a subgenre of the war film centered on Vietnam emerged, featuring as its theme what she calls the "noble-grunt."

Films as different as *Platoon* (1986), *Full Metal Jacket* (1987), *Good Morning, Vietnam* (1987), *Hamburger Hill* (1987), *Gardens of Stone* (1987), *84 Charlie MoPic* (1989), *Off Limits* (1988), *Dear America* (1988), *Casualties of War* (1989), and TV series like *Tour of Duty* and *China Beach* have carried into film what author C. D. B. Bryan described for literature as "the Generic Vietnam War Narrative." This generic narrative features combat units in tales that chart "the gradual deterioration of order, the disintegration of idealism, the breakdown of character, the alienation from those at home, and finally, the loss of all sensibility save the will to survive." There is something terribly sad and embattled about these films and TV shows, even in their lighter and warmer moments. They celebrate survival as a form of heroism, and cynicism as a form of self-preservation. (Aufderheide 1990, 83–84)

These same themes appeared throughout viewer responses to "Never Again." Nearly two-thirds of the viewers of "Never Again" mentioned either the Vietnam War or the Vietnam Memorial in their responses, more than the number that mentioned "patriotism." Consistent with the "Generic Vietnam War Narrative," viewers' associations with Vietnam featured sadness, uncertainty, appreciation for the veterans, disillusionment, a sense of betrayal and anger (for fuller elaboration of this data, see G. Richardson 1995, 1998a).

In sum, exploratory data on viewer recall indicate that some viewers respond quite directly to the generic evocations found in political advertisements, and that these evocations can carry important emotional and political content. Indeed, in some cases, these generic evocations can overwhelm an ad's ostensible message, at least for some audiences. These evocations, moreover, emerge from the holistic functioning of audiovisual and narrative elements, often flying beneath the analytical radar screen. The exploratory data also suggest that extant conceptions of negativity fail to distinguish several very different senses of the term in viewers' minds.

FUTURE RESEARCH AND PRACTICE

The exploratory work presented here provides the foundation for a new agenda for political advertising research, taking seriously the audiovisual and narrative conventions of popular culture evoked in campaign spots, moving beyond negativity, and emphasizing emotional responses and associative networks. The quest to better understand how political advertising works can inform the new "adwatch" journalism that emerged in response to the perceived excesses of political advertising (Richardson 1998b).

Negativity emerges here as a multidimensional, contested concept. Several questions that can engage researchers remain. What exactly does negative mean when used by voters? I've identified four senses of negativity based on exploratory data. Are there still others? Which, if any, elements of negativity are truly injurious to the body politic? Is the political consultants' code of ethics a sufficient response to such concerns? Do citizens agree with the consultants? If a case can be made that certain negative appeals actually contribute to democratic civility, can voters be persuaded to avoid cynicism in response to "negative" ads? Perhaps most importantly, additional inquiry into how candidates can best respond to negative attacks may also help sustain forceful yet healthy debate. It is unlikely, after all, that candidates will stop criticizing their opponents. While the brunt of academic work to date has sought to document the effects of negative ads, political discourse may be well served by turning future efforts toward uncovering the rehabilitative potential of political advertising. Harnessing the power of the genres of popular culture may be a step in that direction.

This is not to discount political advertising's many critics. Indeed, reconciling our notions of democratic civility with our commitment to free, vigorous, and uninhibited debate remains an urgent theoretical task with substantial practical import. Diverse and varied research literatures can contribute to this effort, yet when studies indicate that highly informed voters are more resistant to attack ads and that those likely to be discouraged from voting are less informed, one can ask, "Is it so bad that only informed voters vote?" or "Is negative advertising actually a public service?"

Moving beyond negativity allows us to consider innovative alternative approaches to political discourse. Specifically, a more serious consideration of how popular culture permeates many aspects of communication and cognition is particularly promising. Political scientists have sought to discern the influences of ideological, partisan, and issue constraints on attitudes, but allowing respondents to speak in terms of popular culture may give voice to important aspects of political orientation. This is something that some pollsters and political consultants are already aware of. Veteran public opinion researcher Peter Hart, for example, has noted that otherwise reticent citizens offer rich and revealing responses to questions such as "What do you think it would be like to spend a weekend at George W. Bush's house?" Such techniques can be extended. The centrality of narratives in political discourse and political ads raises an obvious research probe: How would an ordinary voter tell the story of a particular candidate? A particular party? What pictures or images do they associate with them? What theme songs or styles of music might they choose for candidates or issues? We can do much to explore citizens' cultural literacy. Such data would challenge conventional methodological approaches to research but could be well worth the effort.

Additional work must address how well holistic and analytical models actually explain viewers' responses to political ads. What explains the effectiveness of competing narratives? To what degree is an ad's resonance with popular culture important? The work presented above suggests that addressing such questions will require data spanning the realms of cognitive processing, emotional imagination, and physiological response. Metaphorically if not literally, investigators may ultimately be able to say, "This is your brain. This is your brain on political advertising."

NOTES

Portions of this chapter have previously appeared in Richardson 1995, 1998a, 2000, 2001.

1. The idea of applying genres to the way viewers process political advertising was developed in my doctoral dissertation at the University of Iowa (Richardson 1995). That work owes much to G. R. Boynton and John S. Nelson, with whom these ideas were discussed at length.

2. The evocation of genre is not limited to politicians. A 1994 story in the *Washington Post* described the way Jeff Zucker, executive producer of NBC's *Now* newsmagazine, approached "Whitewater": "It's just so boring. . . . Is there anything to do on the Hillary thing? We should do the Rose Law Firm. This is 'The Firm' (a recent Hollywood film) and it should be played off the movie. They all have fancy houses and fancy cars. I want this to be 'The Firm.' Got it?" (Kurtz 1994).

3. Robert Entman notes that frames (often referred to as schemata) provide "thematically reinforcing clusters of facts or judgments," and that culture constitutes the "stock of commonly invoked frames" (Entman 1992). The genres of popular culture serve exactly this function, though their political significance may be more implicit than explicit.

4. It should be noted that it is not essential to the validity of a genre approach to political advertising to assume that ad producers consciously saw themselves as engaged in genre reproduction. It is merely enough that when they thought about how they could best convey the themes they wanted to communicate, their sense of what looked and sounded "right" would be shaped by the same pervasive cultural expectations (based on genre) that the viewing audience shared (see also Biocca 1991b, 84 for a similar argument).

5. Gina Garramone has applied schemata specifically to political advertising (Garramone 1984, 1986; Garramone, Steele, and Pinkleton 1991).

6. Some viewers of the 1988 Bush campaign's "Tank Ride" ad suggest that Michael Dukakis actually did not look that bad in the tank. They may be right, but the images of Dukakis are buttressed by richly satirical sound effects and the claim that Dukakis "opposed virtually every weapons system we've developed." A silly looking Dukakis fits the form, and that is what most people remember.

APPENDIX A

Script for "Levin of Arabia"

Carl Levin's antidefense record is so bad the *Detroit News* actually demanded he resign from the Armed Services Committee. As your senator, he opposed virtually every strategic defense system. Carl Levin opposed the Maverick antitank missile now on duty in the Arab desert. He voted against the battleship *Wisconsin*, now protecting our troops against Saddam Hussein. Yet Carl Levin flew to the *Wisconsin* at taxpayer's expense for a press release and TV cameras. If Levin had his way, he wouldn't have a ship to stand on and neither would our troops.

Script for "Never Again"

Americans differed over the Vietnam War, but we all agree never again will our soldiers fight without the support they deserve. In the Arab desert, our troops face another Hitler. Our soldiers are armed with the Maverick antitank missile. I voted for it, Carl Levin opposed it. They're protected by the battleship *Wisconsin*. I voted for it, Carl Levin opposed it. As a Republican congressman, I support a strong national defense. As your senator, I'll work with George Bush, so if we need to fight another war, we'll be ready.

References

Abelson, R. 1988. Conviction. *American Psychologist* 43:267–275.

Abelson, R. P., E. F. Loftus, and A.G. Greenwald. 1992. Attempts to Improve the Accuracy of Self-Reports of Voting. In *Questions about Questions: Inquiries into the Cognitive Bases of Surveys*, edited by J. M. Tanur. New York: Russell Sage Foundation.

Abramowitz, A. I. 1989. Viability, Electability, and Candidate Choice in a Presidential Primary Election: A Test of Competing Models. *Journal of Politics* 54:741–761.

———. 1995. It's Abortion, Stupid: Policy Voting in the 1992 Presidential Election. *Journal of Politics* 57:176–186.

Abramson, J. B., F. C. Arterton, and G. R. Orren. 1988. *The Electronic Commonwealth: The Impact of New Media Technologies on Democratic Politics*. New York: Basic.

Abramson, P., and R. Inglehart. 1995. *Value Change in Global Perspective*. Ann Arbor: University of Michigan Press.

Achen, C. 1975. Mass Political Attitudes and the Survey Response. *American Political Science Review* 69:1218–1231.

Aldrich, J. 1995. *Why Parties? The Origin and Transformation of Party Politics in America*. Chicago, Ill.: University of Chicago Press.

Aldrich, J. H., and D. W. Rohde. 1998. The Transition to Republican Rule in the House: Implications for Theories of Congressional Politics. *Political Science Quarterly* 112:541–567.

Almond, G. A. 1950. *The American People and Foreign Policy*. New York: Harcourt Brace.

Althaus, S. 1996a. Opinion Polls, Information Effects and Political Equality: Exploring Ideological Biases in Collective Opinion. *Political Communication* 13:3–21.

——. 1996b. Who Speaks for the People? Political Knowledge, Representation, and the Use of Opinion Surveys in Democratic Politics. Ph.D. diss., Northwestern University.

——. 1998. Information Effects in Collective Preferences. *American Political Science Review* 92:545–558.

Althaus, S. L., and D. Tewksbury. 2000. Patterns of Internet and Traditional News Media Use in a Networked Community. *Political Communication* 17:21–45.

Alvarez, M. 1997. *Issues and Information in Presidential Elections.* Ann Arbor: University of Michigan Press.

Alvarez, R. M., and C. H. Franklin. 1994. Uncertainty and Political Perceptions. *Journal of Politics* 56:671–688.

American Federation of Labor and Congress of Industrial Organizations. 1999. Social Security Campaign Update. Memorandum, 25 March.

Anderson, J. R. 1983/1990. *The Architecture of Cognition.* Cambridge, Mass.: Harvard University Press.

——. 1983/1990. *Cognitive Psychology and Its Implications.* New York: Freeman.

Ansolabehere, S., and S. Iyengar. 1995/1996. *Going Negative: How Political Advertisements Shrink and Polarize the Electorate.* New York: Free Press.

Ansolabehere, S., S. Iyengar, and A. Simon. 1999. Replicating Experiments Using Aggregate and Survey Data: The Case of Negative Advertising and Turnout. *American Political Science Review* 93:901–909.

Ansolabehere, S., S. Iyengar, A. Simon, and N. Valentino. 1994. Does Attack Advertising Demobilize the Electorate? *American Political Science Review* 88:829–838.

AP. 1998. China Solicits Comment via Internet. *The New York Times* [on the Web]. 9 December.

Atkin, C. K., and W. Gantz. 1978. Television News and Political Socialization. *Public Opinion Quarterly* 42:183–198.

Aufderheide, P. 1990. Vietnam: Good Soldiers. In *Seeing Through Movies,* edited by Mark Crispin Miller. New York: Pantheon.

Ball-Rokeach, S. J., and W. E. Loges. 1996. Making Choices: Media Roles in the Construction of Value-Choices. In *Values: The Ontario Symposium 8,* edited by C. Seligman, J. Olson, and M. Zanna. Hillsdale, N.J.: Erlbaum.

Ball-Rokeach, S. J., G. J. Power, K. K. Guthrie, and H. R. Waring. 1990. Value-Framing Abortion in the United States: An Application of Media System Dependency Theory. *International Journal of Public Opinion Research* 2:249–273.

Barber, B. 1999. Brave New World. *Review of The Information Age,* volumes 1–3, by Manuel Castells. *Los Angeles Times,* 23 May.

Barber, J. D. 1972. *The Presidential Character: Predicting Performance in the White House.* Englewood Cliffs, N.J.: Prentice Hall.

Barkham, P. 1999. Parliament Unplugged. *The Guardian,* 13 May.

Barnhurst, K. G., and D. C. Mutz. 1997. American Journalism and the Decline in Event-Centered Reporting. *Journal of Communication* 47:27–53.

Bartels, L. 1986. Issue Voting under Uncertainty: An Empirical Test. *American Journal of Political Science* 30:709–728.

——. 1988. *Presidential Primaries and the Dynamics of Public Choice.* Princeton, N.J.: Princeton University.

——. 1996. Uninformed Votes: Information Effects in Presidential Elections. *American Journal of Political Science* 40:194–230.

———. 2000a. Partisanship and Voting Behavior. *American Journal of Political Science* 44:35–50.

———. 2000b. *Voting Behavior.* Unpublished manuscript.

Beattie, J., and J. Baron. 1991. Investigating the Effect of Stimulus Range on Attribute Weight. *Journal of Experimental Psychology: Human Perception and Performance* 17:571–585.

Beckett, K. 1995. Media Depictions of Drug Abuse: The Impact of Official Source. *Research in Political Sociology,* vol. 7, edited by Philo C. Wasburn, 161–182. London: JAI Press, Inc.

Bellah, R., R. Madsen, W. M. Sullivan, A. Swidler, and S. M. Tipton. 1985. *Habits of the Heart.* Berkeley: University of California Press.

Bennett, W. L. 1993. Constructing Publics and Their Opinions. *Political Communication* 10:101–120.

———. 1996. *The Governing Crisis: Media, Money and Marketing in American Elections.* New York: St. Martin's.

Berelson, B. R., P. F. Lazarsfeld, and W. N. McPhee. 1954. *Voting: A Study of Opinion Formation in a Presidential Campaign.* Chicago: University of Chicago Press.

Berger, A. 1995. *Essentials of Mass Communication Theory.* Thousand Oaks, Calif.: Sage.

Berger, P. L., and T. Luckmann. 1966. *The Social Construction of Reality.* Garden City, N.Y.: Doubleday.

Bertot, J. C., and C. R. McClure. 1999. *The 1998 National Survey of U.S. Public Library Outlet Internet Connectivity: Final Report.* Washington, D.C.: NCLIS.

Bianco, W. T., and D. Lipinski. 1999. Reputation, Institutional Loyalty, and the 1994 Congressional Elections. Paper presented at the Midwest Political Science Association Annual Meeting in Chicago, Ill.

Billings, R. S., and S. A. Marcus. 1983. Measures of Compensatory and Noncompensatory Models of Decision Behavior: Process Tracing versus Policy Capturing. *Organizational Behavior and Human Performance* 31:331–352.

Biocca, F. 1991a. *Psychological Processes.* Vol. 1 of *Television and Political Advertising.* Hillsdale, N.J.: Erlbaum.

———. 1991b. *Signs, Codes and Images.* Vol. 2 of *Television and Political Advertising.* Hillsdale, N.J.: Erlbaum.

Blumer, H. 1958. Racial Prejudice as a Sense of Group Position. *Pacific Sociological Review* 1:1–7.

Bobo, L. 1991. Social Responsibility, Individualism, and Redistributive Policies. *Sociological Forum* 6:71–92.

Bobo, L., and V. L. Hutchings. 1996. Perceptions of Racial Group Competition: Extending Blumer's Theory of Group Position to a Multiracial Social Context. *American Sociological Review* 61:951–972.

Bobo, L., and J. R. Kluegel. 1991. Whites' Stereotypes, Social Distance, and Perceived Discrimination toward Blacks, Hispanics, and Asians: Toward a Multiethnic Framework. Paper presented at the annual meetings of the American Sociological Association, 23–27 Aug., Cincinnati, Ohio.

———. 1993. Opposition to Race-Targeting: Self-Interest, Stratification Ideology, or Racial Attitudes. *American Sociological Review* 58: 443–464.

Boorstin, D. 1990. Reprint. The Genius of American Politics. In *The American Polity Reader,* edited by A. G. Serow, W. W. Shannon, and E. C. Ladd, 19–23. New York: Norton. Original edition, Chicago, Ill.: University of Chicago Press, 1953.

Boynton, G. R. 1995. Computational Modeling: A Computational Model of a Survey Respondent. In *Political Judgment: Structure and Process,* edited by Milton Lodge and Kathleen M. McGraw. Ann Arbor: University of Michigan Press.

Brians, C., and M. P. Wattenberg. 1996. Campaign Issue Knowledge and Salience: Comparing Reception from TV Commercials, TV News and Newspapers. *American Journal of Political Science* 40:172–193.

Broder, D. 1972. *The Party's Over: The Failure of Politics in America.* New York: Harper and Row.

Brody, R. A. 1991. *Assessing the President: The Media, Elite Opinion, and Public Support.* Stanford, Calif.: Stanford University Press.

Brosius, H. B., and P. Eps. 1995. Prototyping through Key Events. *European Journal of Communication* 10:391–412.

Burke, K. 1966. *Language as Symbolic Action; Essays on Life, Literature, and Method.* Berkeley: University of California Press.

———. 1989. *On Symbols and Society.* Chicago, Ill.: University of Chicago Press.

Burnham, W. D. 1970. *Critical Elections and the Mainsprings of American Politics.* New York: Norton.

Burns, J. M., J. W. Peltason, and T. E. Cronin. 1981. *Government by the People.* 11th ed. Englewood, N.J.: Prentice Hall.

Bush, G. H. W. 1992. *President Bush's Acceptance Speech Delivered to the Republican National Convention,* Houston, Texas: 20 August.

Campaign Web Review. 1998. *A Kinder Gentler Medium?* [http://www.campaignwebreview.com/issues/10311998/index.html].

Campbell, A. 1960. Surge and Decline: A Study of Electoral Change. *Public Opinion Quarterly* 24:397–418.

Campbell, A., P. E. Converse, W. E. Miller, and D.E. Stokes. 1960. *The American Voter.* Chicago, Ill.: University of Chicago Press.

Campbell, D. T. 1969. Prospective: Artifact and Control. In *Artifact in Behavioral Research,* edited by Robert Rosenthal and Robert Rosnow. New York: Academic.

Campbell, K., and K. H. Jamieson. 1978. *Form and Genre: Shaping Rhetorical Action.* Falls Church, Va.: Speech Communication Association.

Capella, J., and K. H. Jamieson. 1997. *Spiral of Cynicism: The Press and the Public Good.* New York: Oxford University Press.

Carey, J. W. 1988. Media, Myths and Narratives: Television and the Press. *Sage Annual Reviews of Communication Research* 15. Newbury Park, Calif.: Sage.

Chaffee, S. H., and J. M. McLeod. 1972. Adolescent Television Use in the Family Context." In *Television and Social Behavior: Reports and Papers,* vol. 3, edited by G. A. Comstock and A. Rubinstein, 149–171. Rockville, Md.: National Institute of Mental Health.

Chaffee, S., and J. Schleuder. 1986. Measurement of Effects of Attention to Media News. *Human Communication Research* 13:76–107.

Chaiken, S. 1980. Heuristic versus Systematic Information Processing and the Use of Source versus Message Cues in Persuasion. *Journal of Personality and Social Psychology* 39:752–766.

Charters, W., and T. M. Newcomb. 1958. Some Attitudinal Effects of Experimentally Increased Salience of a Membership Group. In *Readings in Social Psychology*, edited by Eleanor Maccoby, Theodore Newcomb, and Eugene Hartley. New York: Holt and Co.

Citrin, J. 1974. Comment: The Political Relevance of Trust in Government. *American Political Science Review* 68:973–988.

Citrin, J., and D. P. Green. 1986. Presidential Leadership and the Resurgence of Trust in Government. *British Journal of Political Science* 16:431–453.

Clinger, J. H. 1987. The Clean Campaign Act of 1985: A Rational Solution to Negative Campaigning which the One Hundredth Congress Should Reconsider. *Journal of Law and Politics* 3:727–748.

CNN. 1999. Internet Helps Stem Human Rights Abuses, Group Says. *CNN Interactive*, 16 June.

Cohen, B. 1963. *The Press and Foreign Policy*. Princeton, N.J.: Princeton University Press.

Collins, A. M., and E. F. Loftus. 1975. A Spreading Activation Theory of Semantic Processing. *Psychological Review* 82:407–428.

Condit, C. M., and J. L. Lucaites. 1993. *Crafting Equality: America's Anglo-African World*. Chicago, Ill.: University of Chicago Press.

Connolly, C. 1997. Consultant Offers GOP a Language for the Future. *Washington Post*, 4 September.

Conover, P. J. 1984. The Influence of Group Identifications on Political Perception and Evaluation. *Journal of Politics* 46:760–785.

———. 1988. The Role of Social Groups in Political Thinking. *British Journal of Political Science* 18:51–76.

Converse, P. 1964. The Nature of Belief Systems in Mass Publics. In *Ideology and Discontent*, edited by D. Apter, 206–261. New York: Free Press.

———. 1970. Attitudes and Non-Attitudes: Continuation of a Dialogue. In *The Quantitative Analysis of Social Problems*, edited by E. Tufte, 168–189. Reading, Mass.: Addison Wesley.

———. 1990. Popular Representation and the Distribution of Information. In *Information and Democratic Processes*, edited by J. Ferejohn and J. Kuklinski, 369–388. Urbana: University of Illinois Press.

Converse, P., and A. Campbell. 1960. Political Standards in Secondary Groups. In *Group Dynamics* (2nd ed.), edited by Dorwin Cartwright and Alvin Zander. New York: Harper and Row.

Cook, T. E. 1989. *Making Laws and Making News*. Washington, D.C.: Brookings.

———. 1998/1999. *Governing with the News: The News Media as a Political Institution*. Chicago, Ill.: University of Chicago Press.

Cox, G., and M. McCubbins. 1993. *Legislative Leviathan: Party Government in the House*. Berkeley: University of California Press.

Cronin, T. J. 1974. The Textbook Presidency and Political Science. In *Perspectives on the Presidency*, edited by S. Bach and G. T. Sulzner, 54–74. Lexington, Mass.: D. C. Heath.

Dartmouth College/WMUR New Hampshire Primary Election Poll. 1996. Dartmouth College: Hanover, N.H.

Davidson, R., and W. Oleszek. 1998. *Congress and Its Members*. Washington, D.C.: Congressional Quarterly.

Dealey, S. 1999. Rep. J. C. Watts Threatens to Quit Leadership Post. *The Hill*, 4 August.

Dean, K. 1999. Let the Documents Go Free. *Wired*, 28 June [http://www.wired.com/news/news/politics/story/20461.html].

Delli Carpini, M. X., and S. Keeter. 1993. Measuring Political Knowledge: Putting First Things First. *American Journal of Political Science* 37:1179–1206.

———. 1996. *What Americans Know about Politics and Why It Matters*. New Haven, Conn.: Yale University Press.

Deming, C. 1889. Town Rule in Connecticut. *Political Science Quarterly* 4:408–432.

Democracy Online Project. 1999. Democracy online survey. [http://democracyonline.org/databank/dec6findings.html].

Dennis, E. E., and A. H. Ismach. 1981. *Reporting Processes and Practices*. Belmont, Calif.: Wadsworth.

Dennis, J. 1991. Theories of Turnout: An Empirical Comparison of Alienationist and Rationalist Perspectives. In *Political Participation and American Democracy*, edited by W. Crotty, 23–65. New York: Greenwood.

Denzin, N. K. 1989. *Interpretive Interactionism*. Newbury Park, Calif.: Sage.

Devlin, L. P. 1986. An Analysis of Presidential Television Commercials, 1952–1984. In *New Perspectives on Political Advertising*, edited by L. L. Kaid, D. Nimmo, and K. R. Sanders, 21–54. Carbondale: Southern Illinois University Press.

Diamond, E., and S. Bates. 1988. *The Spot: The Rise of Political Advertising on Television*. Cambridge, Mass.: MIT Press.

Dionne, E. J. 1991. *Why Americans Hate Politics*. New York: Simon & Schuster.

Dixon, T. L., and D. Linz. 2000. Overrepresentation and Underrepresentation of African Americans and Latinos as Lawbreakers on Television News. *Journal of Communication* 50:1–24.

Dominick, J. R., and M. C. Pearce. 1976. Trends in Network Prime-Time Programming, 1953–1974. *Journal of Communication* 26:70–80.

Domke, D., and D. V. Shah. 1995. Interpretation of Issues and Voter Decision-Making Strategies: A New Perspective on "Issue-Oriented" Election Coverage. *Journalism and Mass Communication Quarterly* 72:45–71.

Domke, D., D. V. Shah, and D. Wackman. 1998a. Media Priming Effects: Accessibility, Association, and Activation. *International Journal of Public Opinion Research* 1:51–74.

———. 1998b. Moral Referendums: Values, News Media, and the Process of Candidate Choice. *Political Communication* 15:301–321.

———. 2000. News Coverage of "Moral" Issues, Priming of Candidate Integrity, and the Vote Choice. *Political Psychology*.

Doob, L. 1935. *Propaganda, Its Psychology and Technique*. New York: Holt.

Downs, A. 1957. *An Economic Theory of Democracy*. New York: Harper and Row.

Drinkard, J. 2000. McCain Closing In on Bush on the Balance Sheet. *USA Today*, 17 February.

Dukakis, M. 1988. A Strong and Secure America. Campaign address at Georgetown University, Washington, D.C. 14 September.

Dulio, D. A., D. L. Goff, and J. A. Thurber. 1999. Untangled Web: Internet Use during the 1998 Election. *PS: Political Science and Politics* 32:53–59.

Edelman, M. 1964. *The Symbolic Uses of Politics.* Urbana: University of Illinois Press.

———. 1971. *Politics as Symbolic Action: Mass Arousal and Quiescence.* New York: Academic.

———. 1977. *Political Language.* New York: Academic.

———. 1993. Contestable Categories and Public Opinion. *Political Communication* 10:231–242.

Edsall, T. B., and M. D. Edsall. 1992. *Chain Reaction: The Impact of Race, Rights, and Taxes on American Politics.* New York: Norton.

Eldersveld, S. J. 1982. *Political Parties in American Society.* New York: Basic.

Eliasoph, N. 1998. *Avoiding Politics: How Americans Produce Apathy in Everyday Life.* New York: Cambridge University Press.

Enelow, J. M., and M. J. Hinich. 1981. A New Approach to Voter Uncertainty in the Downsian Spatial Model. *American Journal of Political Science* 25:483–493.

———. 1984. *The Spatial Theory of Voting.* New York: Cambridge University Press.

Entman, R. M. 1990. Modern Racism and the Images of Blacks in Local Television News. *Critical Studies in Mass Communications* 7:332–346.

———. 1992. Framing: Towards Clarification of a Fractured Paradigm. *Journal of Communication* 43:51–58.

———. 1995. Television, Democratic Theory and the Visual Construction of Poverty. *Research in Political Sociology* 7:139–159.

Erickson, R., and K. Tedin. 1995. *American Public Opinion.* Boston: Allyn and Bacon.

Ericsson, K. A., and H. Simon. 1984. *Protocol Analysis.* Cambridge, Mass.: MIT Press.

Erikson, R. S., G. C. Wright, and J. P. McIver. 1993. *Statehouse Democracy: Public Opinion and Policy in The American States.* New York: Cambridge University Press.

Evans, C., and W. J. Oleszek. 1999. The Procedural Context of Senate Deliberation. Paper presented at conference on civility and deliberation in the United States Senate, 16 July.

Eveland, W. P. Jr. 1997. The Process of Political Learning from News: The Roles of Motivation, Attention, and Elaboration. Ph.D. diss., University of Wisconsin–Madison.

Eveland, W. P. Jr., and D. A. Scheufele. Forthcoming. Political Communication Effects Gaps: Communication Channel and Criterion Measure Matter. *Political Communication.*

Fan, D. P. 1994. *Information Processing Analysis System for Sorting and Scoring Text.* U.S. Patent 5,371,673.

Fazio, R. H. 1989. On the Power and Functionality of Attitudes: The Role of Attitude Accessibility. In *Attitude Structure and Function,* edited by A. R. Pratkanis, S. J. Breckler, A. G. Greenwald, 153–179. Hillsdale, N.J.: Erlbaum.

Fenno, R. F. Jr. 1978. *Home Style: House Members in Their Districts.* Boston: Little, Brown.

Ferejohn, J., and J. Kuklinski, eds. 1990. *Information and Democratic Processes.* Urbana: University of Illinois Press.

Finer, S. E. 1980. *The Changing British Party System, 1945–1979.* Washington, D.C.: American Enterprise Institute.

Finkel, S. E. 1993. Re-Examining the "Minimal Effects" Model in Recent Presidential Campaigns. *Journal of Politics* 55:1–21.

Finkel, S. E., and J. G. Geer. 1998. A Spot Check: Casting Doubt on the Demobilizing Effect of Attack Advertising. *American Journal of Political Science* 42:573–595.

Fiorina, M. 1981. *Retrospective Voting in American National Elections.* New Haven, Conn.: Yale University Press.

———. 1991. Divided Government in the States. *PS: Political Science and Politics* 24:646–650.

Fischhoff, B., P. Slovic, and S. Lichtenstein. 1980. Knowing What You Want: Measuring Labile Values. In *Cognitive Processes in Choice and Decision Behavior,* edited by T. Wallsten. Hillsdale, N.J.: Erlbaum.

Fishkin, J. S. 1991. *Democracy and Deliberation: New Directions for Democratic Reform.* New Haven, Conn.: Yale University Press.

———. 1995. *The Voice of the People: Public Opinion and Democracy.* New Haven, Conn.: Yale University Press.

Fishkin, J. S., and R. C. Luskin. 1999. Bringing Deliberation to the Democratic Dialogue. In *The Poll with a Human Face: The National Issues Convention Experiment in Political Communication,* edited by M. McCombs and A. Reynolds, 3–38. Mahwah, N.J.: Erlbaum.

Fiske, A. P., and P. E. Tetlock. 1997. Taboo Trade-Offs: Reactions to Transactions That Transgress the Spheres of Justice. *Political Psychology* 18:255–297.

Fiske, S. F., R. R. Lau, and R. A. Smith. 1990. On the Varieties and Utilities of Political Expertise. *Social Cognition* 8:31–48.

Fiske, S. T., and S. E. Taylor 1991. *Social Cognition.* New York: McGraw-Hill.

Foucault, M. 1970. *The Order of Things: An Archeology of the Human Sciences.* New York: Pantheon.

Franklin, C. H. 1991. Eschewing Obfuscation? Campaigns and the Perceptions of U.S. Senate Incumbents," *American Political Science Review* 85:1193–1214.

Franklin, C. H., and J. E. Jackson. 1983. The Dynamics of Party Identification. *American Political Science Review* 77:957–973.

Free, L., and H. Cantril. 1968. *The Political Beliefs of Americans: A Study in Public Opinion.* New York: Simon & Schuster.

Freedman, P., and K. M. Goldstein. 1999. Measuring Media Exposure and the Effect of Negative Campaign Ads. *American Journal of Political Science* 43:1189–1208.

Fromkin, V., and R. Rodman. 1974. *An Introduction to Language.* New York: Holt, Rinehart and Winston.

Gaertner, S. L., and J. F. Dovidio. 1986. The Aversive Form of Racism. In *Prejudice, Discrimination, and Racism,* edited by J. F. Dovidio and S. L. Gaertner, 61–89. Orlando, Fla.: Academic.

Gaines, B. J., and D. Rivers. 1996. The Incumbency Advantage in the House and Senate: A Comparative Institutional Analysis. Unpublished manuscript.

Gamerman, E. 2000. McCain's Bus Gets Popular Vote. *The Baltimore Sun,* 18 February.

Gamson, W. A. 1992. *Talking Politics.* New York: Cambridge University Press.

Gamson, W. A., and A. Modigliani. 1987. The Changing Culture of Affirmative Action. In *Frontiers in Social Movement Theory,* edited by R. G. Braungart and M. M. Braungart, 53–76. New Haven, Conn.: Yale University Press.

———. 1989. Media Discourse and Public Opinion on Nuclear Power: A Constructionist Approach. *American Journal of Sociology* 95:1–37.

Gans, H. J. 1980. *Deciding What's News: A Study of CBS Evening News, NBC Nightly News, Newsweek, and Time.* New York: Vintage.

Garramone, G. M. 1984. Audience Motivation Effects: More Evidence. *Communication Research* 10:59–76.

———. 1986. Candidate Image Formation: The Role of Information Processing. In *New Perspectives on Political Advertising,* edited by Lynda Lee Kaid, Dan Nimmo, and Keith R. Sanders, 235–247. Carbondale: Southern Illinois University Press.

Garramone, G. M., C. K. Atkin, B. E. Pinkleton, and R. T. Cole. 1990. Effects of Political Advertising on the Political Process. *Journal of Broadcasting and Electronic Media* 34:299–311.

Garramone, G. M., E. Steele, and B. Pinkleton. 1991. The Role of Cognitive Schemata in Determining Candidate Characteristic Effects. In *Television and Political Advertising: Psychological Processes,* edited by Frank Biocca, 311–328. Hillsdale, N.J.: Erlbaum.

Geer, J. G. 1989. *Nominating Presidents.* New York: Greenwood.

———. 2000. Assessing Attack Advertising: A Silver Lining. In *Campaign Reform: Insights and Evidence,* edited by Larry M. Bartels and Lynn Vavreck. Ann Arbor: University of Michigan Press.

Geertz, C. 1973. Thick Description: Toward an Interpretive Theory of Culture. In *The Interpretation of Cultures: Selected Essays,* edited by Clifford Geertz, 3–30. New York: Basic.

Gelman, A., and G. King. 1993. Why Are American Presidential Election Campaign Polls So Variable When Votes Are So Predictable? *British Journal of Political Science* 23 (4): 409–452.

Gephardt, R. A. 1999. Gephardt Statement on the Republican Tax Cut. Press release, 20 July.

Gilens, M. 1999. *Why Americans Hate Welfare: Race, Media, and the Politics of Antipoverty Policy.* Chicago, Ill.: University of Chicago Press.

Gilliam, F. D., S. Iyengar, A. Simon, and O. Wright. 1996. Crime in Black and White: The Violent, Scary World of Local News. *Harvard International Journal of Press/Politics* 1 (6): 6–23.

Gitlin, T. 1980. *The Whole World Is Watching.* Berkeley: University of California Press.

Glendon, M. A. 1991. *Rights Talk: The Impoverishment of Political Discourse.* New York: Free Press

Globetti, S. 2000. Ideological Campaign Rhetoric and Its Effects. Ph.D. diss., University of Texas at Austin.

Globetti, S., and M. J. Hetherington. 2000. Anti-Government Campaign Rhetoric and Political Trust. Presented at the annual meeting of the Midwest Political Science Association, Chicago, Ill., 27–30 April.

Goffman, E. 1974. *Frame Analysis.* New York: Harper and Row.

Graber, D. 1980. *Crime News and the Public.* New York: Praeger.

———. 1997. Hardware and Software for Political Learning: New Discoveries about How Human Brains Process Audio-Visual Data. Paper presented at the annual meeting of the Midwest Political Science Association, Chicago, Ill.

Green, D. P., and I. V. Blair. 1995. Framing and the Price Elasticity of Private and Public Goods. *Journal of Consumer Psychology* 4:1–32.

Green, D. P., and I. Shapiro. 1994. *Pathologies of Rational Choice Theory: A Critique of Applications in Political Science.* New Haven, Conn.: Yale University Press.

Greenfield, M. 1995. It's Time for Some Civility: Good, Frontal, Rough Debate Is What We Should Be About. *Washington Post,* 29 May.

Greenwald, A. G., and S. J. Breckler. 1985. To Whom Is the Self Presented? In *The Self and Social Life,* edited by B. R. Schlenker, 126–145. New York: McGraw-Hill.

Greer, J., and M. LaPointe. 1999. Meaningful Discourse or Cyber-Fluff? An Analysis of Gubernatorial Campaign Web Sites throughout the 1998 Election Cycle. Paper presented at the annual meeting of the International Communication Association, 29 May, San Francisco, Calif.

Gronbeck, B. 1994. Negative Political Ads and American Self Images. In *Presidential Campaigns and American Self Images*, edited by Arthur H. Miller and Bruce Gronbeck. Boulder, Colo.: Westview.

Gross, R. E., and A. W. Seibel. 1979. *American Citizenship: The Way We Govern.* Englewood Cliffs, N.J.: Prentice Hall, Inc.

Grossman, M. B., and M. J. Kumar. 1981. *Portraying the President: The White House and the News Media.* Baltimore, Md.: Johns Hopkins University Press.

Grunwald, M., and H. Dewar. 1999. Strains Drive Hill toward Gridlock: Parties Stress Differences, Not Deals. *Washington Post,* 1 August.

Haider-Markel, D. P., and K. J. Meier. 1996. The Politics of Gay and Lesbian Rights: Expanding the Scope of the Conflict. *Journal of Politics* 58:332–349.

Handy, R. 1970. *The Measurement of Values: Behavioral Science and Philosophical Approaches.* St. Louis, Mo.: Warren H. Green.

Harpham, E. J. 1999. Going On-Line: The 1998 Congressional Campaign. Paper presented at the annual meeting of the American Political Science Association, 2–5 September, Atlanta.

Hart, R. P. 1994. *Seducing America: How Television Charms the Modern Voter.* New York: Oxford University Press.

———. 1999. *Seducing America: How Television Charms the American Voter* (2d ed.). Thousand Oaks, Calif.: Sage.

———. 2000. *Campaign Talk: Why Elections Are Good for Us.* Princeton, N.J.: Princeton University Press.

Hart, R. P., and S. Jarvis. 1997. Political Debate: Forms, Styles, and Media. *The American Behavioral Scientist* 40:1095–1122.

Hart, R. P., D. Smith-Howell, and J. Llewellyn. 1991. The Mindscape of the Presidency: Time Magazine, 1945–1985. *Journal of Communication* 41 (3): 6–25.

Herek, G.M. 1986. The Instrumentality of Attitudes: Towards a Neo-Functional Theory. *Journal of Social Issues* 42:99–114.

Herstein, J. A. 1981. Keeping the Voter's Limit in Mind: A Cognitive Processing Analysis of Decision Making in Voting. *Journal of Personality and Social Psychology* 40:843–861.

Hetherington, M. 1996. The Media's Role in Forming Voters' National Economic Evaluations in 1992. *American Journal of Political Science* 40:372.

———. 1998. The Political Relevance of Political Trust. *American Political Science Review,* 92:791–808.

———. 1999. The Effect of Political Trust on the Presidential Vote, 1968–96. *American Political Science Review* 93:311–326.

Hetherington, M. J., and S. Globetti. 1999. Political Trust and Whites' Racial Policy Preferences. Presented at the annual meeting of the Midwest Political Science Association, 15–17 April, Chicago.

Hetherington, M. J., and F. M. Hess. 1998. Decreasing Support for Government Spending in 1990s: A Story of Political Distrust, Not Conservatism. Presented at the annual meeting of the Midwest Political Science Association, 24–26 April, Chicago.

Hetherington, M. J., and J. D. Nugent. 2000. Explaining Support for Devolution: The Role of Political Trust. In *Public Orientations toward Government in the United States,* edited by John R. Hibbing and Elizabeth Theiss-Morse. New York: Cambridge University Press.

Higgins, E. T., and G. King. 1981. Accessibility of Social Constructs: Information-Processing Consequences of Individual and Contextual Variability. In *Personality, Cognition, and Social Interaction,* edited by N. Cantor and J. Kihlstrom, 69–121. Hillsdale, N.J.: Erlbaum.

Hill, K., and J. Leighley. 1992. The Policy Consequences of Class Bias in State Electorates. *American Journal of Political Science* 36:351–365.

Hilts, P. J. 1995. Brain's Memory System Comes into Focus. *New York Times,* 30 May.

Hinich, M. J., and W. Pollard. 1981. A New Approach to the Spatial Theory of Electoral Competition. *American Journal of Political Science* 25:323–333.

Hogarth, R. M. 1987. *Judgment and Choice.* New York: Wiley.

Holbrook, T. M. 1994. Campaigns, National Conditions, and U.S. Presidential Elections. *American Journal of Political Science* 38 (4): 25–46.

———. 1996. *Do Campaigns Matter?* Thousand Oaks, Calif.: Sage.

House Republican Conference. 1999a. *Talking Points,* 23 February. [http://hillsource.house.gov/IssueFocus/TalkingPoints].

———. 1999b. *Talking Points,* 2 July. [http://hillsource.house.gov/IssueFocus/TalkingPoints].

Hovland, C. 1959. Reconciling Conflicting Results from Survey and Experimental Studies of Attitude Change. *American Psychologist* 14:8–17.

Hovland, C., A. Lumsdaine, and F. Sheffield. 1949. *Experiments on Mass Communication.* Princeton, N.J.: Princeton University Press.

Huckfeldt, R., and J. Sprague. 1987. Networks in Context: The Social Flow of Information. *American Political Science Review* 81:1197–1216.

———. 1995. *Citizens, Politics, and Social Communication: Information and Influence in an Election Campaign.* New York: Cambridge University Press.

Huntington, S. 1968. *Political Order in Changing Societies.* New Haven, Conn.: Yale University Press.

Hurwitz, J., and Peffley, M. 1987. How Are Foreign Policy Attitudes Structured? A Hierarchical Model. *American Political Science Review* 81:1099–1130.

Iyengar, S. 1991. *Is Anyone Responsible? How Television Frames Political Issues.* Chicago, Ill.: University of Chicago Press.

Iyengar, S., and D. R. Kinder. 1987. *News That Matters.* Chicago, Ill.: University of Chicago Press.

Jacobson, G. 1990. *The Electoral Origins of Divided Government.* Boulder, Colo.: Westview.

Jacoby, W. G. 1994. Public Attitudes toward Government Spending. *American Journal of Political Science* 38:336–361.

Jamieson, K. H. 1988. *Eloquence in an Electronic Age.* Oxford: Oxford University Press.

———. 1992a. *Dirty Politics: Deception, Distraction and Democracy.* New York: Oxford University Press.

———. 1992b. *Packaging the Presidency: A History of Criticism of Presidential Campaign Advertising.* New York: Oxford University Press.

Jasperson, A. E., D. V. Shah, M. D. Watts, R. J. Faber, and D. P. Fan. 1998. Framing and the Public Agenda: Media Effects on the Importance of the Budget Deficit. *Political Communication* 15:205–224.

Jessor, T. 1988. Personal Interest, Group Conflict, and Symbolic Group Affect: Explanations for White's Opposition to Racial Equality. Ph.D. diss., UCLA Department of Psychology.

Johnson, T., C. Hays, and S. Hays (eds.). 1998. *Engaging the Public: How Government and the Media Can Reinvigorate American Democracy.* Lanham, Md.: Rowman & Littlefield.

Johnson-Cartee, K. S., and G. A. Copeland. 1991. *Negative Political Advertising: Coming of Age.* Hillsdale, N.J.: Erlbaum.

Jones, N. 1997. *Campaign 1997: How the General Election Was Won and Lost.* London: Indigo.

Joslyn, R. A. 1986. Political Advertising and the Meaning of Elections. In *New Perspectives on Political Advertising,* edited by Lynda Lee Kaid, Dan Nimmo, and Keith R. Sanders. Carbondale: Southern Illinois University Press.

Just, M., A. Crigler, D. Alger, T. Cook, M. Kern, and D. West. 1996. *Crosstalk: Citizens, Candidates and the Media in a Presidential Campaign.* Chicago, Ill.: University of Chicago Press.

Kahn, K. F., and P. Kenney. 1999a. Do Negative Campaigns Mobilize or Suppress Turnout? Clarifying the Relationship between Negativity and Participation. *American Political Science Review* 93:877–890.

———. 1999b. *The Spectacle of U.S. Senate Campaigns.* Princeton, N.J.: Princeton University Press.

Kahneman, D., and A. Tversky. 1979. Prospect Theory. *Econometrica* 47:263–291

———. 1984. Choice, Values, and Frames. *American Psychologist* 39:341–350.

Kaid, L., and D. Bystrom, eds. 1999. *The Electronic Election: Perspectives on the 1996 Campaign Communication.* Mahwah, N.J.: Erlbaum.

Kaid, L., and D. Davidson. 1986. Elements of Videostyle: Candidate Presentation through Television Advertising. In *New Perspectives on Political Advertising,* edited by Lynda Lee Kaid, Dan Nimmo, and Keith R. Sanders, 184–209. Carbondale: Southern Illinois University Press.

KAKM. 1998. *Alaska Senate Debate,* 29 October.

Kedrowski, K. M. 1996. *Media Entrepreneurs and the Media Enterprise in the U.S. Congress.* Cresskill, N.J.: Hampton.

Kelley, H. H. 1955. Salience of Membership and Resistance to Change of Group-Anchored Attitudes. *Human Relations* 3:275–289.

Kelley, H., and E. Volkart. 1952. The Resistance to Change of Group-Anchored Attitudes. *American Sociological Review* 17:453-465.

Kelley, T. 1999. Candidate on the Stump Is Surely on the Web. *New York Times,* 19 October.

Kepplinger, H. 1991. The Impact of Presentation Techniques: Theoretical Aspects and Empirical Findings. In *Television and Political Advertising, vol. 1: Psychological Processes,* edited by Frank Biocca, 173–194. Hillsdale, N.J.: Erlbaum.

Kerbel, M. 1995. *Remote and Controlled.* Boulder, Colo.: Westview.

Kern, M. 1989. *30-Second Politics: Political Advertising in the Eighties*. New York: Praeger.

———. 1997. Social Capital and Citizen Interpretation of Political Ads, News, and Web Site Information in the 1996 Presidential Election. *American Behavioral Scientist* 40:1238–1249.

Kernell, S. 1997. *Going Public: New Strategies of Presidential Leadership*, 3rd ed. Washington, D.C.: Congressional Quarterly.

Key, V. O. 1949. *Southern Politics in State and Nation*. New York: Vintage.

———. 1964. *Politics, Parties and Pressure Groups*, 5th ed. New York: Crowell.

———. 1966. *The Responsible Electorate*. New York: Cambridge University Press.

Kinder, D., and T. Palfrey. 1993. On Behalf of an Experimental Political Science. In *Experimental Foundations of Political Science*, edited by Donald R. Kinder and Thomas R. Palfrey. Ann Arbor: University of Michigan Press.

Kinder, D., and L. Sanders. 1990. Mimicking Political Debate with Survey Questions: The Case of White Opinion on Affirmative Action for Blacks. *Social Cognition* 8:73–103.

———. 1996. *Divided by Color: Racial Politics and Democratic Ideals*. Chicago, Ill.: University of Chicago Press.

Kinder, D., and D. Sears. 1981. Prejudice and Politics: Symbolic Racism versus Racial Threats to the Good Life. *Journal of Personality and Social Psychology* 40 (3): 414–431.

———. 1985. Public Opinion and Political Action. In *Handbook of Social Psychology*, 4th ed., edited by G. Lindzey, and E. Aronson, New York: Random House

Kingdon, J. W. 1966. *Candidates for Office: Beliefs and Strategies*. New York: Random House.

Klapper, J. 1960. *The Effects of Mass Communications*. Glencoe, Ill.: Free Press.

Klein, E. 1984. *Gender Politics*. Cambridge, Mass.: Harvard University Press.

Kluegel, J. R., and E. R. Smith. 1986. *Beliefs about Inequality: Americans Views of What Is and What Ought to Be*. New York: Aldine de Gruyter.

Knoke, D. 1990. *Political Networks: The Structural Perspective*. Cambridge: Cambridge University Press.

Koch, J. W. 1994. Group Identification in Political Context. *Political Psychology* 15 (4): 687–698.

Kosicki, G. M., and J. M. McLeod. 1990. Learning from Political News: Effects of Media Images and Information-Processing Strategies. In *Mass Communication and Political Information Processing*, edited by S. Kraus. Hillsdale, N.J.: Erlbaum.

Kramer, R. M. 1999. Trust and Distrust in Organizations: Emerging Perspectives, Enduring Questions. *Annual Review of Psychology* 1:569–598.

Kranish, M. 1999. Narrowing Field Speeds GOP Race. *Boston Globe*, 28 September.

Kraut, R., M. Patterson, V. Lundmark, S. Kiesler, T. Mukopadhyay, and W. Scherlis. 1998. Internet Paradox: A Social Technology That Reduces Social Involvement and Psychological Well-Being? *American Psychologist* 53:1017–1031.

Krehbiel, K. 1991. *Information and Legislative Organization*. Ann Arbor: University of Michigan Press.

———. 1998. *Pivotal Politics*. Chicago, Ill.: University of Chicago Press.

Kress, G., and R. Hodge. 1981. *Language as Ideology*. London: Routledge & Kegan Paul.

Kriesberg, M. 1949. Cross-Pressures and Attitudes. *Public Opinion Quarterly* 13:5–16.

Krosnick, J. A. 1988. The Role of Attitude Importance in Social Evaluation: A Study of Policy Preferences, Presidential Candidate Evaluations, and Voting Behavior. *Journal of Personality and Social Psychology* 55:196–210.

———. 1990. Expertise and Political Psychology. *Social Cognition* 8:1–8.

———. 1991a. Response Strategies for Coping with the Cognitive Demands of Attitude Measures in Surveys. *Applied Cognitive Psychology* 5:231–236.

———. 1991b. The Stability of Political Preferences: Comparisons of Symbolic and Nonsymbolic Attitudes. *American Journal of Political Science* 35:547–576.

Krosnick, J. A., and L. A. Brannon. 1993. The Impact of the Gulf War on the Ingredients of Presidential Evaluations: Multidimensional Effects of Political Involvement. *American Political Science Review* 87:963–975.

Krosnick, J. A., and D. R. Kinder. 1990. Altering the Foundations of Support for the President through Priming. *American Political Science Review* 84:497–512.

Krosnick, J. A., and M. A. Milburn. 1990. Psychological Determinants of Political Opinionation. *Social Cognition* 8 (1): 49–72.

Kuklinski, J. H., P. J. Quirk, D. W. Schwieder, and R. F. Rich. 1998. Just the Facts, Ma'am: Political Facts and Public Opinion. *Annals of the American Academy of Political and Social Science* 560:143–154.

Kurtz, H. 1994. Sex! Mayhem! 'Now'! In the Newsmagazine Derby, NBC's Star-Drive Vehicle Puts a Sheen on Sensationalism. *Washington Post,* 14 March.

Ladd, C. E. 1985. *The American Polity: The People and Their Government,* 3rd ed. New York: Norton.

Lang, A. 1991. Emotion, Formal Features, and Memory for Televised Political Advertisements. In *Television and Political Advertising, vol. 1: Psychological Processes,* edited by Frank Biocca. Hillsdale, N.J.: Erlbaum.

Lau, R. 1982. Negativity in Political Perception. *Political Behavior* 4:353–377.

———. 1985. Two Explanations for Negativity Effects in Political Behavior. *American Journal of Political Science* 29:119–138.

———. 1989. Individual and Contextual Influences on Group Identification. *Social Psychology Quarterly* 52 (3): 220–231.

Lau, R., and D. O. Sears. 1986b. Social and Political Cognition: The Past, the Present and the Future. In *Political Cognition: The 19th Annual Carnegie Symposium on Cognition,* edited by Richard R. Lau and David O. Sears. Hillsdale, N.J.: Erlbaum.

Lau, R., L. Sigelman, C. Heldman, and P. Babbitt. 1999. The Effects of Negative Political Advertisements: A Meta-Analytic Assessment. *American Political Science Review* 93:851–876.

Lau, R., R. A. Smith, and S. T. Fiske. 1991. Political Beliefs, Policy Interpretations, and Political Persuasion. *Journal of Politics* 53:644–675.

Lazarsfeld, P. F., B. Berelson, and H. Gaudet. 1944/1948. *The People's Choice: How the Voter Makes Up His Mind in a Presidential Election.* New York: Columbia University Press.

Lemert, J. B. 1981. *Does Mass Communication Change Public Opinion after All? A New Approach to Effects Analysis.* Chicago, Ill.: Nelson Hall.

Lewinski, M. 1987. *Consent of the Governed: A Study of American Government.* Glenview, Ill.: Scott Foresman.

Lichter, R. S., and R. Noyes. 1995. *Good Intentions Make Bad News.* Lanham, Md.: Rowman & Littlefield.

Lichter, R., S. Rothman, and L. Richter. 1986. *The Media Elite.* Washington, D.C.: Adler and Adler.

Lipinski, D. Forthcoming. Shaping Public Perceptions of Congress: An Examination of the Communication Strategies Used by Members of the U.S. House of Representatives. Ann Arbor: University of Michigan Press.

———. 2000. Communication Strategies Exercised by Parties in Congress. Paper presented at the Midwest Political Science Association Annual Meeting in Chicago, Ill.

Littlejohn, S. W. 1989. *Theories of Human Communication,* 3rd ed. Belmont, Calif.: Wadsworth.

Lodge, M. 1995a. The Responsive Voter: Campaign Information and the Dynamics of Candidate Evaluation. *American Political Science Review* 89(2): 309–327.

———. 1995b. Toward a Procedural Model of Candidate Evaluation. In *Political Judgment: Structure and Process,* edited by Milton Lodge and Kathleen M. McGraw. Ann Arbor: University of Michigan Press.

Lodge, M., and R. Hamill. 1986. A Partisan Schema for Political Information Processing. *American Political Science Review* 80:505–519.

Lodge, M., and K. M. McGraw. 1995. *Political Judgment: Structure and Process.* Ann Arbor: University of Michigan Press.

Lodge, M., and B. Tursky. 1979. Comparisons between Category and Magnitude Scaling of Public Opinion Employing SRC/CPS Items. *American Political Science Review* 73:50–66.

Lowi, T. 1979. *The End of Liberalism,* 2nd ed. New York: Norton.

Luntz, F. 1997. *The Language of the 21st Century.* Arlington, Va.: Luntz Research Companies.

Lupia, A. 1994. Shortcuts versus Encyclopedias: Information and Voting Behavior in California Insurance Reform Elections. *American Political Science Review* 88:63–76.

Luskin, R. C. 1990. Explaining Political Sophistication. *Political Behavior* 12:331–361.

Luskin, R. C., and J. S. Fishkin. 1998. Deliberative Polling, Public Opinion and Democracy: The Case of the National Issues Convention. Working paper.

MacFarquhar, N. 1999. For First Time in War, E-Mail Plays a Vital Role. *New York Times,* 29 March.

Manheim, J. B. 1991. *All of the People, All the Time: Strategic Communication and American Politics.* Armonk, N.Y.: M. E. Sharpe.

Marcus, G. E., and M. B. MacKuen. 1993. Anxiety, Enthusiasm, and the Vote: The Emotional Underpinnings of Learning and Involvement during Presidential Campaigns. *American Political Science Review* 87:672–685.

Markus, G. B. 1979. The Political Environment and the Dynamics of Public Attitudes: A Panel Study. *American Journal of Political Science* 23:338–359.

———. 1988. The Impact of Personal and National Economic Conditions on the Presidential Vote: A Pooled Cross-Sectional Analysis. *American Journal of Political Science* 32 (1): 137–154.

Marsh, C. 1982. *The Survey Method: The Contribution of Surveys to Sociological Explanation.* London: Allen and Unwin.

Mayer, W. G. 1992. *The Changing American Mind: How and Why American Public Opinion Changed between 1960 and 1988.* Ann Arbor: University of Michigan Press.

Mayhew, D. 1974. *Congress: The Electoral Connection.* New Haven, Conn.: Yale University Press.

McCombs, M. 1998. Two Levels of Agenda Setting among Advertising and News in the 1995 Spanish Elections. *Political Communication* 15(2): 225–249.

McCombs, M., J. P. Llamas, E. Lopez-Escobar, and F. Rey. 1997. Candidate Images in Spanish Elections. *Journalism and Mass Communication Quarterly* 74:703–717.

McCombs, M., and D. Shaw. 1972. The Agenda-Setting Function of the Media. *Public Opinion Quarterly* 36:176–187.

McConahay, J. B. 1986. Modern Racism, Ambivalence, and the Modern Racism Scale. In *Prejudice, Discrimination and Racism,* edited by J. F. Dovidio and S. L. Gaertner. Orlando, Fla.: Academic.

McGraw, K. M., and N. Pinney 1990. The Effects of General and Domain-Specific Expertise on Political Memory and Judgment. *Social Cognition* 8(1): 9–30.

McGraw, K. M., and M. Steenbergen. 1995. Pictures in the Head: Memory Representations of Political Candidates. In *Political Judgment: Structure and Process,* edited by Milton Lodge and Kathleen M. McGraw. Ann Arbor: University of Michigan Press.

McGuire, W. 1985. Attitudes and Attitude Change. In *Handbook of Social Psychology,* vol. 2, 3rd ed., edited by G. Lindzey and E. Aronson. New York: Random House.

McLeod, J. M., D. A. Scheufele, and P. Moy. 1999. Community, Communication, and Participation: The Role of Mass Media and Interpersonal Discussion in Local Political Participation. *Political Communication* 16:315–336.

Mendelberg, T. 1997. Executing Hortons: Racial Crime in the 1988 Presidential Campaign. *Public Opinion Quarterly* 61:134–157.

Merkle, D. M. 1996. The National Issues Convention Deliberative Poll. *Public Opinion Quarterly* 60:588–619.

Merritt, R. L. 1966. *Symbols of American Community.* New Haven, Conn.: Yale University Press.

Milbank, D. 2000. W Is for Warm and Fuzzy: George Bush Injects His Conservatism with a Liberal Dose of Compassion. *Washington Post,* 20 March.

Miller, A. 1974. Political Issues and Trust in Government, 1964–70. *American Political Science Review* 68:951–972.

Miller, A., E. Goldenberg, and L. Erbring. 1979. Type-Set Politics: Impact of Newspapers on Public Confidence. *American Political Science Review* 73:67–84.

Miller, A. H., C. Wlezien, and A. Hildreth. 1991. A Reference Group Theory of Partisan Coalitions. *The Journal of Politics* 53:1134–1149.

Miller, G. 1999. A Safe Bet: There'll Be More Legislation. *Los Angeles Times,* 27 December.

Miller, S., and D. O. Sears. 1986. Stability and Change in Social Tolerance: A Test of the Persistence Hypothesis. *American Journal of Political Science* 30(1): 214–236.

Minsky, M. 1975. A Framework for Representing Knowledge. In *The Psychology of Computer Vision,* edited by P. H. Winston. New York: McGraw-Hill.

Mondak, J. J. 1994. Question Wording and Mass Policy Preferences: The Comparative Impact of Substantive Information and Peripheral Cues. *Political Communication* 11(2): 165–183.

Morris, D. 1999. *Vote.com: How Big-Money Lobbyists and the Media Are Losing Their Influence, and the Internet Is Giving Power to the People*. Los Angeles: Renaissance Books.

Morris, Jon D., M. S. Roberts, and G. F. Baker. 1999. Emotional Responses of African American Voters to Ad Messages. In *The Electronic Election: Perspectives on the 1996 Campaign Communication*, edited by Lynda Lee Kaid and Diane Bystrom. Mahwah, N.J.: Erlbaum.

Moy, P., and M. W. Pfau. 2000. *With Malice toward All: The Media and Public Confidence in Democratic Institutions*. Westport, Conn.: Praeger.

Moy, P., D. A. Scheufele, and R. L. Holbert. 1999. Television Use and Social Capital: Testing Putnam's Time Displacement Hypothesis. *Mass Communication and Society* 2:27–45.

Muller, E., and T. O. Jukam. 1977. On the Meaning of Political Support. *American Political Science Review* 71:1561–1595.

Myrdal, G. 1944. *An American Dilemma: The Negro Problem and Modern Democracy*. New York: Harper.

Napoli, P. M. 1998. The Internet and the Forces of "Massification." *Electronic Journal of Communication* 8(2).

National Committee to Preserve Social Security and Medicare. 1999. Seniors Group Unveils Ads Critical of Congressional Tax Cut Bill. Press release, 8 September.

NBC. 2000. *NBC Nightly News*, 9 January.

Nelson, J. S., and G. R. Boynton. 1997. *Video Rhetorics: Televised Advertising in American Politics*. Urbana: University of Illinois Press.

Nelson, M. 1995. Why Americans Hate Politics and Politicians. *PS: Political Science and Politics* 28(1): 72–78.

Nelson, T. E., R. A. Clawson, and Z. M. Oxley. 1997a. Media Framing of a Civil Liberties Conflict and Its Effect on Tolerance. *American Political Science Review* 91:567–583.

Nelson, T. E., and D. R. Kinder. 1996. Issue Framing and Group-Centrism in American Public Opinion. *Journal of Politics* 58:1055–1078.

Nelson, T. E., Z. M. Oxley, and R. A. Clawson. 1997b. Toward a Psychology of Framing Effects. *Political Behavior* 19:221–245.

Neuman, R. W., M. R. Just, and A. N. Crigler. 1992. *Common Knowledge*. Chicago, Ill.: University of Chicago Press.

Neumann, M. 1998. Neumann for Senate. [http://www.neumannforsenate.com/new.html]

Neustadt, R. 1960. *Presidential Power*. New York: Macmillan.

Newhagen, J., and B. Reeves. 1991. Emotion and Memory Responses for Negative Political Advertising: A Study of Television Commercials Used in the 1988 Presidential Election. In *Television and Political Advertising, vol. 1: Psychological Processes*, edited by Frank Biocca. Hillsdale, N.J.: Erlbaum.

Nie, N. H., and Lutz Erbring. 2000. *Internet and Society: A Preliminary Report*. Stanford, Calif.: Stanford Institute for the Quantitative Study of Society.

Nie, N. H., J. Junn, and K. Stehlik-Barry. 1996. *Education and Democratic Citizenship in America*. Chicago, Ill.: University of Chicago Press.

Nie, N. H., S. Verba, and J. R. Petrocik. 1976. *The Changing American Voter*. Cambridge, Mass.: Harvard University Press.

Nielsen, J. 1996. A Web Site Design Expert Reviews Candidates' Sites. *New York Times* [on the Web], 20 September.

Noelle-Neumann, E. 1999. *Wegweiser: Wie Jugendliche zur Zeitung finden (Directions: How Teenagers Find Their Way to Reading Newspapers)*. Bonn, Germany: ZV Zeitungs-Verlag Service.

Norrander, B. 1988. *Super Tuesday: Regional Politics and Presidential Primaries*. Lexington: University Press of Kentucky.

———. 1993. Nomination Choices: Caucus and Primary Outcomes, 1976–1988. *American Journal of Political Science* 37:343–364.

Ogburn, W. F., and N. S. Talbot. 1930. A Measurement of the Factors in the Presidential Election of 1928. *Social Forces* 8:175–183.

Olson, D. V. A., and J. W. Carroll. 1992. Religiously Based Politics: Religious Elites and the Public. *Social Forces* 70:765–786.

Onken, J., R. Hastie, and W. Revelle. 1985. Individual Differences in the Use of Simplification Strategies in a Complex Decision-Making Task. *Journal of Experimental Psychology: Human Perception and Performance* 11:14–27.

Orren, G. 1997. Fall from Grace: The Public's Loss of Faith in Government. In *Why People Don't Trust Government*, edited by Joseph S. Nye Jr., Philip D. Zelikow, and David C. King. Cambridge, Mass.: Harvard University Press.

Ostrogorski, M. 1902/1964. *Democracy and the Organization of Political Parties*. New York: Doubleday Anchor.

Ostrom, C. W., and D. M. Simon. 1985. Promise and Performance: A Dynamic Model of Presidential Popularity. *American Political Science Review* 79:334–358.

Page, B. I. 1996. *Who Deliberates? Mass Media in Modern Democracy*. Chicago, Ill.: University of Chicago Press.

Page, B. I., and R. Shapiro. 1992. *The Rational Public: Fifty Years of Trends in Americans' Policy Preferences*. Chicago, Ill.: University of Chicago Press.

Paletz, D. L. 1999. *The Media in American Politics: Contents and Consequences*. New York: Longmans.

Pan, Z., and G. M. Kosicki. 1993. Framing Analysis: An Approach to News Discourse. *Political Communication* 10:55–75.

Paolino, P. 1995. Group-Salient Issues and Group Representation: Support for Women Candidates in the 1992 Senate Elections. *American Journal of Political Science* 39(2): 294–313.

Patterson, T. E. 1980. *The Mass Media Election: How Americans Choose Their President*. New York: Praeger.

———. 1982. Television and Election Strategy. In *The Communications Revolution in Politics*, edited by Gerald Benjamin. New York: Academy of Political Science.

———. 1993. *Out of Order*. New York: Knopf.

Payne, J. W., J. R. Bettman, and E. J. Johnson. 1992. Behavioral Decision Research. *Annual Review of Psychology* 43:87–131.

Peffley, M., T. Shields, and B. Williams. 1996. The Intersection of Race and Crime in Television News Stories: An Experimental Study. *Political Communication* 13:309–327.

Petrocik, J. 1996. Issue Ownership in Presidential Elections, with a 1980 Case Study. *American Journal of Political Science* 40:825–850.

Petty, R. E., and J. T. Cacioppo. 1986. *Communication and Persuasion*. New York: Springer-Verlag.

Pew Foundation. 2000. *Audiences Fragmented and Skeptical: The Tough Job of Communicating with Voters*. 5 February.

Pew Research Center. 1998. *Deconstructing Distrust: How Americans View Government*. Washington, D.C.: The Pew Research Center for the People and the Press.

Pew Research Center for the People and the Press. 1999. *Online Newcomers More Middle-Brow, Less Work-Oriented*. [http://www.people-press.org/tech98que.htm]

Pinker, S. 1999. *How the Mind Works*. New York: Norton.

Plott, C. 1967. A Notion of Equilibrium and Its Possibility under Majority Rule. *The American Economic Review* 57:787–806.

Polsby, N. 1983. *Consequences of Party Reform*. Oxford: Oxford University Press.

Pomper, G. M. 1992. *Passions and Interests: Political Party Concepts of American Democracy*. Lawrence: University of Kansas Press.

Popkin, S. 1991/1994. *The Reasoning Voter*. Chicago, Ill.: University of Chicago Press.

Presser, S., and M. Traugott. 1992. Little White Lies and Social Science Models: Correlated Response Errors in a Panel Study of Voting. *Public Opinion Quarterly* 56:77–86.

Price, D. 1999. Dole's Star Dims in Presidential Campaign. *Detroit News*, 12 October.

Price, V. 1989. Social Identification and Public Opinion: Effects of Communicating Group Conflict. *Public Opinion Quarterly* 53:197–224.

Price, V., and D. Tewksbury. 1996. News Values and Public Opinion: A Ttheoretical Account of Media Priming and Framing. In *Progress in Communication Sciences*, edited by G. Barnett and F. Boster. Norwood, N.J.: Ablex Pub. Corp.

Price, V., D. Tewksbury, and E. Powers. 1997. Switching Trains of Thought: The Impact of News Frames on Readers Cognitive Rresponses. *Communication Research* 24:481–506.

Putnam, R. 1995. Bowling Alone: America's Declining Social Capital. *Journal of Democracy* 6:65–78.

———. 1996. The Strange Disappearance of Civic America. *The American Prospect* 7:24 (1 December).

———. 2000. *Bowling Alone*. New York: Simon & Schuster.

Rabinowitz, G., and S. E. Macdonald. 1989. A Directional Theory of Issue Voting. *American Political Science Review* 83:93–121.

Raney, R. F. 2000. Study Finds Internet of Social Benefit to Users. *New York Times*, 11 May.

Reagan, R. 1980. *Speech to the Republican National Convention*. Detroit, Mich., 17 July.

Reeves, J., and R. Campbell. 1994. *Cracked Coverage: Television News, the Anti-Cocaine Crusade, and the Reagan Legacy*. Durham, N.C.: Duke University Press.

Reno v. ACLU. 1997. 117 S CT 2329. [http://www.aclu.org/issues/cyber/trial/sctran.html].

Richardson, B. 1995. Debate on the Personal Responsibility and Right to Work Act. *Congressional Record*, 21 March.

Richardson, G. 1995. Genre and Political Information Processing: How Political Advertising Works. Ph.D. diss., University of Iowa.

———. 1998a. The Popular Culture Context of Political Advertising: Linkages and Meanings in Political Information Processing. *Political Communication* 15 (special electronic volume on CD-ROM).

——. 1998b. Building a Better Adwatch: Talking Patterns to the American Voter. *Harvard International Journal of Press/Politics* 3:76–95.

——. 2000. Pulp Politics: The Genres of Popular Culture in Political Advertising. *Rhetoric and Public Affairs* 3:603–626.

——. 2001. Looking for Meaning in All the Wrong Places: Why "Negative" Advertising Is a Suspect Category. *Journal of Communication* 51.

Robinson, M. 1976. Public Affairs Television and the Growth of Political Malaise. *American Political Science Review* 70:409–432.

Robinson, M., and M. Sheehan. 1983. *Over the Wire and on TV*. New York: Russell Sage Foundation.

Rodgers, D. T. 1987. *Contested Truths: Keywords in American Politics since Independence*. Cambridge, Mass.: Harvard University Press.

Rogers, E. M., J. W. Dearing, and D. Bregman. 1993. The Anatomy of Agenda-Setting Research. *Journal of Communication* 43:68–84.

Rohde, D. 1991. *Parties and Leaders in the Post-Reform House*. Chicago, Ill.: University of Chicago Press.

Rokeach, M. 1973. *The Nature of Human Values*. New York: Free Press.

Roper, J. 1997. Political Campaigns in Cyberspace: An Expansion of the Public Sphere? New Zealand Political Parties on Line: The World Wide Web As a Political Marketing Tool. Paper presented at the annual meeting of the New Zealand Political Studies Association, 6–8 June, Hamilton, New Zealand.

Roper Organization Report. 1991. *America's Watching: Public Attitudes toward Television*. New York: Network Television Association and the Roper Organization.

Rothbart, M., M. Evans, and S. Fulero. 1979. Recall for Confirming Events: Memory Processes and the Maintenance of Social Stereotyping. *Journal of Experimental Social Psychology* 15:343–355.

Sabato, L. 1991. *Feeding Frenzy*. New York: Free Press.

Sadow, J., and K. James. 1999. Virtual Billboards? Candidate Web Sites and Campaigning in 1998. Paper presented at the annual meeting of the American Political Science Association, 2–5, September, Atlanta.

Sanders, M. S. 1996. Beneath Stormy Waters: The Evolution of Individual Decision Making in the 1984 and 1988 Presidential Elections. Ph.D. diss., University of Rochester.

Schattschneider, E. E. 1942. *Party Government*. New York: Rinehart.

——. 1960. *The Semisovereign People: A Realist's View of Democracy in America*. New York: Holt.

Scheufele, D. A. 1999a. Framing as a Theory of Media Effects. *Journal of Communication* 49:103–119.

——. 1999b. Examining Differential Gains from Mass Media and Their Implications for Participatory Behavior. Paper presented to the annual convention of the Midwest Association for Public Opinion Research, Chicago, Ill.

Scheufele, D. A., P. Moy, and L. Friedland. 1999. Deliberation and Democracy: Toward an Understanding of Deliberative Processes. Paper presented to the annual convention of the Association for Education in Journalism and Mass Communication, New Orleans, La.

Schlesinger, J. A. 1985. The New American Political Party. *American Political Science Review* 79:1152–1169.

Schudson, M. 1998. *The Good Citizen: A History of American Civic Life.* New York: Free Press.

Sears, D. O. 1983. The Persistence of Early Political Predispositions: The Roles of Attitude Object and Life Stage. In *Review of Personality and Social Psychology,* vol. 4, edited by Ladd Wheeler. Beverly Hills, Calif.: Sage Publications.

———. 1988. Symbolic Racism. In *Eliminating Racism,* edited by Phyllis A. Katz and Dalmas A. Taylor. New York: Plenum Press.

Sears, D. O., and C. L. Funk. 1991. The Role of Self-Interest in Social and Political Attitudes. *Advances in Experimental Social Psychology* 24:1–91.

Sears, D. O., C. P. Hensler, and L. K. Speer. 1979. Whites' Opposition to "Busing": Self-Interest or Symbolic Politics? *American Political Science Review* 73:369–384.

Sears, D. O., and Leonie Huddy. 1990. On the Origins of Political Disunity among Women. In *Women in Twentieth Century American Politics,* edited by Patricia Gurin and L. Tilly. New York: Russell Sage Foundation.

Sears, D. O., R. Lau, T. Tyler, and H. Allen Jr. 1980. Self Interest vs. Symbolic Politics in Policy Attitudes and Presidential Voting. *American Political Science Review* 74:670–684.

Sears, D. O., C. van Laar, M. Carrillo, and R. Kosterman. 1997. Is It Really Racism? The Origins of White Americans' Opposition to Race-Targeted Policies. *Public Opinion Quarterly* 61(1): 16–53.

Sellers, P. 1999. Promoting the Party Message in the U.S. Senate. Paper presented at the Midwest Political Science Association Annual Meeting, Chicago, Ill., 15–17 April.

Shah, D. V. 1999. Value Judgments: News Framing and Individual Processing of Political Issues. Ph.D. diss., University of Minnesota.

Shah, D. V., D. Domke, and D. B. Wackman. 1996. To Thine Own Self Be True: Values, Framing, and Voter Decision-Making Strategies. *Communication Research* 23:509–561.

———. 1997. Values and the Vote: Linking Issue Interpretations to the Process of Candidate Choice. *Journalism and Mass Communication Quarterly* 74:357–387.

———. Forthcoming. The Effects of Value-Framing on Political Judgment and Reasoning. In *Framing in the New Media Landscape,* edited by S. D. Reese, O. H. Gandy Jr., and A. Grant. Mahwah, N.J.: Erlbaum.

Shah, D. V., M. D. Watts, D. Domke, D. P. Fan, and M. Fibison. 1999. News Coverage, Economic Cues, and the Public's Presidential Preferences: 1984–1996. *Journal of Politics* 61:914–943.

Shapiro, V. 1993. The Political Uses of Symbolic Women: An Essay in Honor of Murray Edelman. *Political Communication* 10:141–154.

Shaw, D. R. 1999. The Effect of TV Ads and Candidate Appearances on Statewide Presidential Votes. *American Political Science Review* 93:345–361.

———. 2000. Is Reform Really Necessary? A Closer Look at Media Coverage, Candidate Events, and Presidential Votes. In *Campaign Reform: Insights and Evidence,* edited by Larry M. Bartels and Lynn Vavreck. Ann Arbor: University of Michigan Press.

Shepsle, K. A. 1972. The Strategy of Ambiguity: Uncertainty and Electoral Competition. *American Political Science Review* 66:555–568.

Shoemaker, P., and S. Reese. 1996. *Mediating the Message: Theories of Influence on Mass Media Content.* White Plains, N.Y.: Longmans.

Silver, B. D., B. A. Anderson, and P. R. Abramson. 1986. Who Overreports Voting? *American Political Science Review* 80:613–624.

Simon, A. F., and M. Xenos. 2000. Media Framing and Effective Public Deliberation. *Political Communication* 17:363–376.

Simon, H. 1979. *Models of Thought.* New Haven, Conn.: Yale University Press.

Simon, H. A. 1985. Human Nature in Politics: The Dialogue of Psychology with Political Science. *American Political Science Review* 79:293–304.

Sinclair, B. 1995. *Legislators, Leaders, and Lawmaking: The U.S. House of Representatives in the Post-Reform Era.* Baltimore, Md.: Johns Hopkins University Press.

———. 1999. Transformation Leader of Faithful Agent? Principal–Agent Theory and House Majority Party Leadership. *Legislative Studies Quarterly* 24:421–449.

Smith, E., and P. Squire. 1990. The Effects of Prestige Names in Question Wording. *Public Opinion Quarterly* 54:97–116.

Sniderman, P., R. Brody, and P. Tetlock. 1991. *Reasoning and Choice: Explorations in Political Psychology.* New York: Cambridge University Press.

Snyder, M., and K. G. DeBono. 1987. A Functional Approach to Attitudes and Persuasion. In *Social Influence: The Ontario Symposium,* vol. 5, edited by M. P. Zanna, J. M. Olson, and C. P. Herman. Hillsdale, N.J.: Erlbaum.

———. 1989. Understanding the Function of Attitudes: Lessons for Personality and Social Behavior. In *Attitude Structure and Function,* edited by A. R. Pratkanis, S. J. Breckler, and A. G. Greenwald. Hillsdale, N.J.: Erlbaum.

Snyder, M., and S. W. Uranowitz. 1978. Reconstructing the Past. *Journal of Personality and Social Psychology* 36:941–950.

Sorauf, F., and P. A. Beck. 1988. *Party Politics in America,* 6th ed. Glenview, Ill.: Scott Foresman.

Sparrow, B. H. 1999. *Uncertain Guardians: The News Media as a Political Institution.* Baltimore, Md.: Johns Hopkins University Press.

Spiliotes, C. J., and L. Vavreck. 2000. Campaigning and Governing: The Invisible Link between Candidate Discourse and Legislative Performance. Paper delivered at the annual meeting of the Midwest Political Science Association.

Srull, T. K., and R. S. Wyer Jr. 1978. Category Accessibility and Social Perception: Some Implications for the Study of Person Memory and Interpersonal Judgments. *Journal of Personality and Social Psychology* 37:841–856.

Steele, C. M. 1988. The Psychology of Self-Affirmation: Sustaining the Integrity of the Self. In *Advances in Experimental Psychology,* edited by L. Berkowitz. New York: Academic.

Stevenson, R. T., and L. Vavreck. 2000. Does Campaign Length Matter? Testing for Cross-National Effects. *British Journal of Political Science* 30:217–235.

Stimson, J. 1990. A Macro Theory of Information Flow. In *Information and Democratic Processes,* edited by J. Ferejohn and J. Kuklinski. Urbana: University of Illinois Press.

———. 1999. *Public Opinion in America: Moods, Cycles, and Swings,* 2nd ed. Boulder, Colo.: Westview.

Strategis Group. 1999. U.S. Internet Breaks the 100-Million Mark. [http://www.strategisgroup.com/press/pubs/iut99.html].

Tacitus. 1830. *The Works of Cornelius Tacitus,* translated by Arthur Murphy. London: Jones and Co.

Tajfel, H. 1981. *Human Groups and Social Categories*. Cambridge: Cambridge University Press.

Taylor, C. 1985. *Human Agency and Language*. Cambridge: Cambridge University Press.

———. 1989. *Sources of the Self: The Making of the Modern Identity*. Cambridge, Mass.: Harvard University Press.

Tetlock, P. E. 1986. A Value Pluralism Model of Ideological Reasoning. *Journal of Personality and Social Psychology* 50:819–827.

———. 1989. Structure and Function in Political Belief Systems. In *Attitude Structure and Function*, edited by A. R. Pratkanis, S. J. Breckler, and A. G. Greenwald. Hillsdale, N.J.: Erlbaum.

Thomas, C. W. 1998. Maintaining and Restoring Public Trust in Government Agencies and Their Employees. *Administration and Society* 30:166–193.

Thorson, E., W. Christ, and C. Caywood. 1991. Effects of Issue-Image Strategies, Attack and Support Appeals, Music and Visual Content in Political Commercials. *Journal of Broadcasting and Electronic Media* 35:465–486.

Thurber, J. A., C. J. Nelson, and D. A. Dulio, eds. 2000. *Crowded Airwaves: Campaign Advertising in Elections*. Washington, D.C.: Brookings.

Tocqueville, A. 1835/1984. *Democracy in America*. New York: Penguin.

Tourangeau, R., and K. Rasinski. 1988. Cognitive Processes Underlying Context Effects in Attitude Measurement. *Psychological Bulletin* 103:299–314.

Trent, J., and R. Friedenberg. 1991. *Political Campaign Communication: Principles and Practices*, 2nd ed. New York: Praeger.

Tuchman, G. 1978. *Making News*. Glencoe, Ill.: Free Press.

Turner, J. 1984. Social Identification and Psychological Group Formation. In *The Social Dimension: European Development in Social Psychology*, edited by H. Tajfel. Cambridge: Cambridge University Press.

———. 1987. *Rediscovering the Social Group: A Self-Categorization Theory*. New York: Basil Blackwell.

Tversky, A., and D. Kahneman. 1981. The Framing of Decisions and the Psychology of Choice. *Science* 211:453–458.

———. 1986. Rational Choice and the Framing of Decisions. *Journal of Business* 59:251–278.

U.S. House Democratic Policy Committee. 1999. The Republicans Confess . . . Their Tax Scheme Is a Shameless Fundraising Gimmick. 9 September. [http://www.house.gov/democrats/outrage].

Uzzi, B. 1997. Social Structure and Competition in Interfirm Networks. *Administrative Science Quarterly* 42:35–67.

Valentino, N. A. 1999. Crime News and the Priming of Racial Attitudes during Evaluations of the President. *Public Opinion Quarterly* 63:293–320.

VandeHei, J., and J. Bresnahan. 1999. Watts Threatened to Quit GOP Leadership. *Roll Call*, 5 August. Washington, D.C.: The Economist Group.

van Dijk, T. A. 1988. *News as Discourse*. Hillsdale, N.J.: Erlbaum.

Vavreck, L. 1997. More Than Minimal Effects: Explaining Differences between Clarifying and Insurgent Campaigns in Strategy and Effect. Ph.D. diss., University of Rochester.

———. 2000. The Reasoning Voter Meets the Strategic Candidate: The Lack of Direct and Veiled Party Cues in Candidate Advertising. Paper delivered at Midwest Political Science Association meeting, Chicago, 15–17 April 1999.

Vavreck, L., C. J. Spiliotes, and L. L. Fowler. 1999. First in the Nation: Voter Learning in the New Hampshire Primary. Paper delivered at Dartmouth College Conference on Presidential Primaries, Hanover, N.H., July 1999.

Verba, S., K. L. Schlozman, H. E. Brady, and N. Nie. 1995. *American Citizen Participation Study, 1990.* Ann Arbor, Mich.: Inter-University Consortium for Political and Social Research.

Ward, L. 1998. Blair's Cyber Glitches Frustrate Net Surfers. *The Guardian,* 30 April.

Wattenberg, M. 1990. *The Decline of American Political Parties.* Cambridge, Mass.: Harvard University Press.

———. 1991. *The Rise of Candidate-Centered Politics.* Cambridge, Mass.: Harvard University Press.

Wattenberg, M., and C. Brians. 1999. Negative Campaign Aadvertising: Mobilizer or Demobilizer? *American Political Science Review* 93:891–900.

Weaver, R. 1953. *The Ethics of Rhetoric.* New York: Regnery.

West, D. M. 1992. Reforming Campaign Ads. *PS: Political Science and Politics* 25:74–77.

———. 1997. *Air Wars: Television Advertising in Election Campaigns.* Washington, D.C.: Congressional Quarterly.

West, D. M., and B. A. Loomis. 1998. *The Sound of Money: How Political Interests Get What They Want.* Washington, D.C.: Congressional Quarterly.

Whitten, J. 1964. Debate on the Civil Rights Act of 1964. *Congressional Record,* 3 February.

Whorf, B. 1956. *Language, Thought, and Reality.* New York: Wiley.

Williams, R. 1976. *Keywords: A Vocabulary of Culture and Society.* New York: Oxford.

Woodward, B. 1992. The Anatomy of a Decision: Six Words That Shaped—and May Sink—the Bush Presidency. *Washington Post* (National Weekly Edition), 12–18 October.

Woody, C. H. 1930. *The Case of Frank L. Smith.* Chicago: Chicago University.

Wright, P. 1975. Consumer Choice Strategies: Simplifying vs. Optimizing. *Journal of Marketing Research* 12:60–66.

Wright, P., and F. Barbour. 1975. The Relevance of Decision Process Models in Structuring Persuasive Messages. *Communication Research* 2:246–259.

Zaller, J. 1992. *The Nature and Origin of Mass Opinion.* New York: Cambridge University Press.

Zaller, J., and S. Feldman. 1992. A Simple Theory of the Survey Response: Answering Questions versus Revealing Preferences. *American Journal of Political Science* 36:579–616.

Index

McCain, John, 91, 95–96, 101, 106, 199;
advertising and, 204, 210
McGovern, George, 93, 130
media, 6, 13; agenda setting and, 75–76;
Congressional communication and,
171, 173–75; content of coverage, 16,
23, 28; hard-news use, 26; Internet
and, 188–90; media effects, 75–76,
81; nature of coverage, 23, 28; new
long journalism, 23, 28, 30;
participation and, 21–23; priming,
75–76; professional dynamics, 6–7;
racialized issues and, 149–50, 152;
rights talk and, 56–58; strategy-
oriented coverage, 105–6; topics
covered, 137; trust and, 23, 105–6,
118–19. *See also* advertising; crime
news; framing; Internet; negativity;
television
memory, 7–8, 78, 149, 210–11; applied
to framing, 81–83; associative
network model, 75, 81–86, 211
Message Group, 173–74
message politics, 181
Michigan school, 4–6
minimal effects, 75, 92, 93
minority leaders, 176
mixed condition, 136–37
mobilizing condition, 136–37
mob psychology, 146
momentum candidate, 8
Morris, Dick, 110
motivation, 58–60
Murkowski, Frank, 189

narratives, 206–7
National Committee to Preserve Social
Security and Medicare, 172–73
National Election Survey, 23, 32(n2), 33,
35, 39, 44, 51, 110–12
National Opinion Research Center, 25
National Republican Campaign
Committee, 182
"Nature of Belief Systems in Mass
Publics, The" (Converse), 5
negativity, 130–31, 179, 193–94, 203–4;
components, 213–15; incivility and,

204–6; policy *vs.* personal attacks,
205–6; types, 205, 214–15. *See also*
advertising; media
Nelson, Michael, 136
net metaphor, 81–82
Neumann, Mark, 197
"Never Again," 212–20
New Agendas in Political
Communication conference, vii–viii,
2, 3, 15
New Hampshire primary, 13, 91, 95–97,
101, 106, 199
news framing, 57–58, 60, 62–63, 67, 80
newspapers, 26, 30
New Zealand First, 196
noncompensatory models, 60, 62, 63,
66, 68
Noonan, Peggy, 208
North, Oliver, 209

object, 82–83
one-minute speeches, 173, 174,
183–84(n8)
on-line processing, 7–8
optimizers, 62
out-groups, 151–53
outlets, 9–10
Out of Order (Patterson), 105

participation. *See* political participation
parties. *See* political parties
past, 135–36, 138
persuasion, 85–86
Pew Foundation, 10, 106, 109
Pew Internet and American Life Project,
200
policy agenda, 154; political trust and,
109–14; sacrifices and, 115–17
policymaking: Congressional
communication and, 181–82;
framing and, 88–89. *See also*
decisionmaking
political communication, 2–3, 49,
123–24, 189; changes in, 9–12;
framing and, 67–71; group priming
and, 164–65. *See also* Congressional
communication

About the Contributors

Scott L. Althaus is an assistant professor of speech communication and political science at the University of Illinois at Urbana-Champaign.

Roderick P. Hart holds the Shivers Chair in Communication & Government and is director of the Annette Strauss Institute for Civic Participation at the University of Texas at Austin.

Marc J. Hetherington is an assistant professor of government at Bowdoin College.

Sharon E. Jarvis is an assistant professor of communication studies at the University of Texas at Austin.

Robert Klotz is an assistant professor of political science at the University of Southern Maine.

Daniel Lipinski is an assistant professor of political science at the University of Tennessee.

Glenn W. Richardson Jr. is an assistant professor of political science at Kutztown University.

Dietram A. Scheufele is an assistant professor of communication at Cornell University.

Dhavan V. Shah is an assistant professor of journalism and mass communication at the University of Wisconsin at Madison.

Daron R. Shaw is an associate professor of government at the University of Texas at Austin.

Adam F. Simon is an assistant professor of political science at the University of Washington.

Nicholas A. Valentino is an assistant professor of communication studies at the University of Michigan.

Lynn Vavreck is an assistant professor of government at Dartmouth College.